D0445439

THE
MomShift

ALSO BY REVA SETH

First Comes Marriage:
Modern Relationship Advice from the
Wisdom of Arranged Marriages

THE
MomShift

WOMEN SHARE THEIR STORIES OF

CAREER SUCCESS

AFTER HAVING CHILDREN

REVA SETH

RANDOM HOUSE CANADA

PUBLISHED BY RANDOM HOUSE CANADA

Copyright © 2014 Reva Seth

All rights reserved under International and Pan-American Copyright
Conventions. No part of this book may be reproduced in any form or by any
electronic or mechanical means, including information storage and retrieval
systems, without permission in writing from the publisher, except by a reviewer,
who may quote brief passages in a review. Published in 2014 by Random House
Canada, a division of Random House of Canada Limited, Toronto.
Distributed in Canada by Random House of Canada Limited.

www.randomhouse.ca

Random House Canada and colophon are registered trademarks.

Library and Archives Canada Cataloguing in Publication

Seth, Reva, author
The momshift : women share their stories of career success
after having children / Reva Seth.

Issued in print and electronic formats.

ISBN 978-0-345-81264-3

1. Working mothers—Anecdotes. 2. Motherhood—Anecdotes.
3. Mother and child—Anecdotes. 4. Work and family—Anecdotes.
5. Work-life balance—Anecdotes. I. Title.

HQ759.48.S48 2013   306.874'3   C2013-905438-3

Text design by Rachel Cooper

Cover design by Terri Nimmo

Printed and bound in the United States of America

2 4 6 8 9 7 5 3 1

For my boys, Seth, Avery and Devan

&

For my mother, Manju—thank you

CONTENTS

"Having it all is a myth, girls, so just make sure your daughters marry rich men."   INDIA KNIGHT, *The Sunday Times,* May 17, 2009

"It's time to stop fooling ourselves . . . the women who have managed to be both mothers and top professionals are superhuman, rich, or self-employed."   ANNE-MARIE SLAUGHTER, *The Atlantic,* June 13, 2012

"Several factors hold women back at work. Too few study science, engineering, computing or math. Too few push hard for promotion. Some old-fashioned sexism persists, even in hip, liberal industries. But the biggest obstacle (at least in most rich countries) is children."
                    The Economist, August 25, 2012

Welcome to the MomShift

What Is the MomShift?

I grew up with the very clear message that children were, quite simply, a career obstacle.

Ironically, the people giving me this message were my own parents and our family friends, people who were and are some of the most devoted parents I've ever met. But for them, parenthood—well, motherhood—was a burden that required continual personal sacrifice.

My mother never worked outside the home, but very early in my life I understood that she had wanted a career in medicine. However, right out of university, she'd gotten married, immigrated to Canada and within a year, given birth to me—all by the age of twenty-three.

Could my mom have had a career? Of course—and many women in situations like hers did. But for my mother, the obstacles were overwhelming.

I won't lie; as a child I loved having a stay-at-home mother. Although it wasn't her first choice to be there, my mother is a naturally optimistic and happy person to be around and she created an incredibly warm and loving home for me and my brother. But as I got older, I felt a certain confusion about her early decisions. My father, usually in an effort to persuade us to do something, frequently reminded us to "... be grateful that your mother gave up everything for you."

As a teenager, I didn't want to be told to be "grateful"—I hadn't asked for this sacrifice and I didn't want the accompanying guilt. I would have preferred to know that my mother was happy and fulfilled by her choices and life—knowing instead that she had wanted one path and had gone down the other, I wasn't sure.

I'm still not.

But I am convinced that it might have been easier or different for her if it hadn't seemed like the two paths were quite so separate.

Why Are We Still Here?

Astonishingly, almost forty years later the tension between career and family not only continues, but has intensified, as a generation of women raised with different expectations than those of my mother feel that they face similarly stark life choices.

Culturally, two competing narratives continue to dominate. The first is that of the successful career woman; the second is that of the "happy housewife." These two archetypes run on parallel streams and rarely do we see them meeting—at least publicly.

In 2003, *The New York Times* published "The Opt Out Revolution" (which became the most e-mailed article of the year), firmly cementing the "either/or" framework of work or family for another generation of women.

The article looked at a number of highly qualified professional women who were also mothers. Feeling that they were doing neither their paying job nor their parenting job well, they were instead opting to drop out of the workforce to stay home with their kids.

Fast-forward nine years to Anne-Marie Slaughter's cover story in *The Atlantic,* "Why Women Still Can't Have It All," about work/life balance for women in high-ranking government and professional jobs. The article broke readership records on the magazine's website and generated reams of columns, responses, blogs and discussion.

Both of these articles, and the public and media buzz they created, are examples of what novelist Chimamanda Adichie described in a TED talk as the dangers of a "single story" in a culture. This refers to the phenomenon where a dominant narrative emerges and then self-perpetuates, becoming self-fulfilling and obscuring alternatives or nuances. And in our current culture there is a powerful single story about women and work: that (barring having superstar status and income) having children hinders a woman's career and is an obstacle to her ambition.

Accepting this single story means overlooking or ignoring many of the "ordinary" post-baby career success stories all around us—most of which are far more relevant and applicable to the lives of more working mothers today than the ones that the media continues to focus on. This became starkly clear to me seven years ago when I became unexpectedly pregnant with my eldest son, and was completely frustrated by the lack of working-mom role models that I felt I could relate to.

It seemed that the only success stories I read or heard about were either celebrities with their "best post-baby body ever!" or female CEOs whose lives and achievements, although inspirational—even aspirational—were not relevant to the immediate choices and struggles I was facing.

The Story in Numbers

For the first time in history, women are the majority in the workforce—but the story in numbers shows that there is still a long way to go. Women remain grossly underrepresented at the top of almost every profession. At the time of writing:

> Of 199 heads of state in the world, only seventeen are women.[1]
> Of all the people who are in parliaments around the world, only 13 percent are women.
> In the corporate sector, women in the top C-level jobs (CEO, COO, etc.) and on corporate boards top out at 15 to 16 percent.
> In the nonprofit world, often considered a female stronghold, only 20 percent of the top jobs are held by women.
> More than two-thirds of married male senior managers have children, but only one-third of their married female counterparts do.
> According to the National Center for Education Statistics (NCES), between 1999 and 2009 female college enrollment climbed by 40 percent. By 2013, women will comprise 57 percent of university undergraduates, and yet the statistics on women in senior leadership roles have barely moved since 2002. And, in 2010, the U.S. Department of Labor reported that women still earn only 79 cents for every dollar earned by a man.

Of course, what's measured is what matters—at least on the surface. And so we carefully track how many women have become CEOs, how many are making partner and how many are holding public office.

As we should.

However, *their* successes, struggles and issues have come to both define and dominate the working mother discussion. As we watch and analyze what is and isn't working for this handful of women, we simultaneously have come to ignore both the challenges and the successes of the majority of working mothers—to both our collective and individual detriment.

Take Marissa Mayer's appointment as the CEO of Yahoo. In addition to being six months pregnant at the time of her appointment, she was also nearly twenty years younger than the average CEO for a Standard & Poor company. Mayer also joined a very exclusive group, as only 4 percent of Fortune 500 CEOs are female, and most of those became so after their childbearing years were over.

However, the idea that Marissa Mayer's appointment to Yahoo while pregnant should help end the debate about whether women can handle senior roles along with pregnancy, childbirth or child rearing is incredibly naive given the elite world that Mayer already inhabits (including her existing net worth of $350 million). (As Anne-Marie Slaughter noted in a tweet about Ms. Mayer's appointment: ". . . But she makes my point. She's superhuman, rich, and in charge . . . !")

Mayer's subsequent decision to eliminate telecommuting for Yahoo employees and the resultant backlash by critics who felt she was being unsympathetic to and letting down other mothers at Yahoo (particularly given that she had a nursery built in her office for her own child) also illustrates the danger of placing so much emphasis on what is happening at the top: it is unfair to the individual, and unrealistic to think that simply having a woman in an elite position will benefit other women.

It might, but there's certainly no guarantee.

What we need to do instead is shift our collective cultural focus away from the corporate elites and 1 percent supermoms (even though their stories are admittedly often pretty compelling in a "Lifestyles of the Rich and Famous" sort of way), and instead turn our attention to the thousands of working mothers, from a diverse range of professional and personal backgrounds, who are successfully navigating career and family in a variety of different ways.

In her 2005 book, *Perfect Madness*, author Judith Warner examined the American style of hyper-parenting (particularly among upper-middle-class professional women) and the detrimental impact it is having on their career trajectories and choices. She concludes that ". . . . what happens when you focus constantly on how the ambitions of the so called best and brightest are incompatible with mother-hood is that you end up with the conclusion that *ambition* is incompat-ible with motherhood. When you explore time and time again how hotshot careers can't be balanced with family life, you end up with the conclusion that *work* can't be balanced with family life. And you end up with the overall impression that the problems of motherhood today are simply intractable. . . .

"And yet you *can* accommodate the demands of a more average kind of ambition with motherhood. The kind of ambition that *most* women and men have: to work a sufficient number of hours, at work they find interesting, meaningful or enjoyable and to earn enough money to buy their families a sufficiently good standard of living."[2]

When I first read this, I instinctively reacted against the words "average kind of ambition" since I believed we should be encourag-ing women (and men) to go fully for their career (and family goals)—to, in the words of Sheryl Sandberg, "lean in."

On consideration, however, I realized that she is completely right. It's time we recognized and provided practical ideas and templates for the different forms that our individual ambition takes, particularly as it may grow or change over the course of our life. I admire Sheryl Sandberg and Marissa Mayer greatly but I don't actually aspire to the day-to-day that either of their careers would involve (which is just as well, since it's not actually an option for me!) Instead, I think it's time for a deeper and more positive look at all of the options that fall in the middle of the spectrum—between the extreme of career success out-liers and a complete and permanent opt out from the work world.

It's also time to look at career models and success stories that go beyond what works in a corporate setting or for a traditional institu-tional career.

Successful and fulfilling work no longer has to follow that model, but as yet we rarely hear about how working mothers are finding other ways of structuring their lives and careers. What might we decide to change or do from hearing about the other forms or patterns that career success and family life can take? And what lessons can we learn from these other, often overlooked models of work and family?

A Vicious Cycle: Perception Matters

The danger of the current single story on career success and ambition is not just that it discourages and limits individual women, but that it influences how colleagues, employers and society at large view the impact of children on professional and career success—all with very real results for a large group of women.

Currently, some 71 percent of women in the U.S. with children under the age of 18 either work or are looking for work, according to the U.S. Bureau of Labor Statistics (2011). In the U.K., 66 percent of mothers are now in some paid work, and in Canada, 79.3 percent of mothers are in the workforce.

So although the majority of mothers in our society are working outside the home, the myth that motherhood is incompatible with career success continues to create very real barriers, with resulting financial implications.

As an example, consider the award-winning 2008 Cornell study, *Getting a Job: Is There a Motherhood Penalty?* in which researchers sent out fake résumés for both a childless woman and a mom; both were equally qualified. The only difference was that the mom's résumé listed "Parent-Teacher Association Coordinator" under the heading of "Other Relevant Activities" as a discreet way of informing employers that it was a parent's résumé. The researchers quickly discovered that the moms were viewed less favorably than the non-moms and were less likely to be hired. Even more disturbing, mothers were offered an average of $11,000 a year less in compensation than the childless job candidate with the same qualifications.

In contrast, the men in the research sample were not penalized for being fathers and actually benefited from their parenthood status by being considered *more* committed to their jobs. As a result, fathers on average were offered $6,000 more than non-fathers. Jane Waldfogel, a Columbia professor who studies families and work, sums it up as: "Women today do almost as well (in opportunity and earnings) as men, as long as they don't have children."

A recent study conducted by Marianne Bertrand, Claudia Goldin and Lawrence Katz tracked business school graduates from the University of Chicago and found that in the early years after graduating, men and women had "nearly identical labor incomes and weekly hours worked." Men and women also paid a similar career price for taking time off or working part time. Women, however, were vastly more likely to do so. The result was that fifteen years after graduation, the men were making about 75 percent more than the women. The study did find one subgroup whose careers resembled those of men: women who had no children and never took time off.

The fact remains that as long as children are portrayed as an obstacle to career success, all working mothers will continue to pay the price.

In the face of these stark statistics, it's hardly surprising that women in greater numbers are deliberately delaying or forgoing children.

Fertility rates in the U.S., for instance, are now at the lowest level since reliable numbers were first kept in 1920 and it's a trend that appears here to stay.[3]

A recent study by the Center for Work-Life Policy found that nearly half (43 percent) of college-educated, working Generation X women (those between the ages of 33 and 46) are childless, even though three-quarters of these women are in established relationships.

My Story

After growing up with the message that I could have either kids *or* a career, to say that I panicked when I found out I was pregnant (three days after my wedding!) would be an incredible understatement. I hyperventilated in the shower and then alternated between crying and escaping into sleep for the next few weeks.

It wasn't quite the honeymoon that my husband and I had been hoping for.

Hormones were certainly part of it. But in large part I was simply terrified that my career was now over—even before it had really begun.

Even as I mentally adjusted to the idea of a baby and started tentatively looking forward to motherhood (I still remember when I first caught myself happily browsing newborn onesies at Target), I couldn't shake the feeling that this baby's arrival would mean that despite all of my education, planning and work, I'd now forever lost my chance at a successful and fulfilling career.

A big part of the problem was that at that point in my life, I wasn't entirely sure what career path I actually wanted to pursue. And if I was still struggling to articulate what my career would be, what chance did I have of doing it with a child?

At university, I'd studied international relations and then gone on to law school. Since all my classmates wanted a job at one of the big national law firms, I decided I did also—and then succeeded in getting one. Unfortunately, after just three months at my prestigious law firm job, I could tell it wasn't for me. Not ready to give up, I tried different practice areas within the firm. I told myself it was worth it for the money and that it would get better as I got used to it.

And yet, a year in, I dreaded going to work each day. My stomach hurt all the time and my doctor sent me for X-rays. I drank too much, distracted myself with high drama relationships and then finally just admitted to myself that after all that work, all those years—and all that tuition money—I just wasn't made to be a lawyer.

It was a terrifying time and I felt completely lost. If not law, then what?

I took a policy and communications job for a year, both to pay my bills and to have some semblance of a plan. Meanwhile, I daydreamed about fantasy careers that were increasingly impractical (dress designing? cookbook writing?).

A year later, I met my husband, Rana, at a friend's party in Toronto. He was visiting from the U.K. We talked about careers (mostly my angst) and exchanged e-mails. I ran into him again at a political fundraiser later that week. Five dates later, we got engaged and I started planning my move to the U.K. After doing a couple of interviews at law firms in London, I decided to start an entirely new career in public relations and corporate communications. Since my legal experience didn't count for much in the PR world, I had to start at the bottom. As a result, I was years older than the other people at my level, vastly overeducated for the role and being paid much less than I'd made at my summer jobs while in law school. But I was determined to make this new career work, no matter how junior I was or behind my peers both in law and now in PR.

And that's where I was in my "career" when I found out I was pregnant—with only six months to go.

I decided that to prevent myself from going crazy, what I needed were role models: real women (not celebrities with oodles of money and multiple nannies) who had made their professional mark *after* children. I would find women whose stories spoke to me, and their experiences would be a source of ideas, lessons and templates for creating my own version of success in my quickly approaching new life stage. If nothing else, it would distract me from all my anxiety around my pregnancy.

The Birth of The MomShift

It was after my second pregnancy that I began formally interviewing women I called "MomShifters": women I defined as those who, in the years after starting their families, had achieved greater professional success than before they had children.

By this time, Rana and I had left London and were living in Toronto; my eldest son was two. At the time I was working full time as a communications consultant between three different social enterprises (a fantastic setup in terms of my interest but an arrangement that I soon found out would not allow me to qualify for any paid maternity leave).

In all three of these organizations, I regularly worked with interns who were graduate students: educated, intelligent and privileged women on the cusp of starting their careers. My pregnancy was a popular point of discussion, and the conversation regularly turned to the issue of careers and children. I was surprised at the frequency with which I heard these women say that they felt that they would soon have to choose between a career or a family life, since they hadn't seen anyone who was really happy doing both.

I couldn't believe that the story was repeating itself like this with another generation. And so that's when I decided to do something with my idea on the need to hear more from accessible and relatable women about their stories of post-baby career success and the myriad ways they had achieved it. It had been inspiring for me to hear how women I knew and could identify with had managed families and fulfilling careers, and I was sure it would be useful for other women as well.

To help source the initial interviews, I enlisted the help of organizations such as Deloitte, Scotiabank, KPMG, Edelman, MarketStart, Ryerson University, Dentons and Unilever. Their support also enabled me to conduct focus groups from within their networks and better tap into what issues working and professional women were struggling with.

Through word of mouth, a dedicated website and the help of social media, I soon had a regular stream of women interested in sharing their experiences.

Like almost all of my interviewees, who tended to hesitate to call their own lives "success stories" (since too many of us seem to think that if we aren't a household name, we somehow aren't a success), I was caught by surprise at the idea that I had actually become a MomShifter myself.

In those messy early days of new motherhood, when I was living in London and trying to find my way forward, I had heard stories about other women's post-baby career success, and their experience had provided me with numerous practical ideas on how to nudge my own career and family life in the direction I wanted: from child-care options to work-from-home arrangements and ways to manage my time and my goals.

Along the way, Rana and I had our children in day care, invested in nannies (part-time, live-out and live-in), carved out early-morning work times, enlisted the help of extended family, and most important, learned to take a flexible but focused approach to both career and family life.

Most of all, the stories I heard gave me the confidence to keep going with the belief that professional fulfillment and family can coexist. I learned that there are no "right" ways to go about it and that it's an ongoing journey. Like most of the women I spoke with, I certainly don't *feel* successful on a day-to-day basis—because I'm tired, usually behind on something and just focused on what needs to get done.

Now, three kids and two books later, I've learned a lot. I took on freelance work to more rapidly advance my professional experience (by taking on more challenging projects than I might have had access to if I weren't self-employed), contract work to move into new fields such as social-enterprise start-ups, and in-house communications roles for periods of greater financial stability. I'm currently in the midst of bringing together these experiences in an entrepreneurial venture. Of course, none of this belongs in the category of extreme, overnight success that tends to dominate the working mother discussion, but for that very reason I think my experience, just like the stories I share in this book, might actually be more helpful than tales of exceptional achievement.

Personally, I remain delighted but also pretty shocked by my post-baby career experiences. Not once had anyone ever indicated to me that having a family might *jump-start* my career rather than stall it indefinitely. Motherhood actually ended up giving me an increased sense of focus and an added level of maturity that my professional life, in all honesty, had lacked until then. My children also provided me with a new and surprisingly unexpected source of constant joy, because despite all the discussions on the challenges of working mothers that I had read and absorbed, I had somehow missed—until I experienced it!—that ultimately, having children, being a parent, is an endless source of life-affirming fun.

"But I Don't Feel Successful"

Success through the eyes of others does not equal satisfaction and fulfillment through the eyes in the mirror.[4]

What does being "more successful" after children actually mean?

This was and is the hardest part of the MomShift project, since ultimately "success" is an individual assessment: a complex and nuanced mix of personal and professional goals and expectations.

Success is also not a place or static mode of being.

From my interviews, I discovered that very few of us have a defined sense of what it means to have "made it" or "have it all."

So, for the purposes of the MomShift book and project, "success" is defined as the achievements of women who have not found their children to be an impediment or handicap to professional success or career fulfillment. Their post-baby careers may have included a higher income, promotions or more professional recognition; some took a career or professional leap that brought them closer to a bigger career milestone or target (going back to school, starting a business or a social enterprise). Although the nature of their achievements and paths to success vary, all of the women's stories disprove the discouraging cultural belief that children are a hurdle to achievement or personal/professional ambition.

This doesn't mean that they won't be doing even more, but that they have already defied the "single story" of what children can mean for a woman's career.

And So, The MomShift Project Was Born

I began this project four and a half years ago, and over that time I interviewed more than five hundred women from a variety of personal and professional backgrounds.

I approached these interviews not as a career expert (which I'm not) but as a writer, a journalist and an invested, interested party, wanting and hoping to learn as much as possible about how women defy conventional wisdom and achieve greater career success once they become mothers.

I also had countless more conversations, group discussions and exchanges with other women in the midst of their own MomShift journeys.

How to Use this Book

Amanda Lang, the mother of an eight-year-old son, a best-selling author and the senior business correspondent for CBC News, succinctly summarized the discussion of working mothers to me as "A situation of universal angst but with no universal answer."

I couldn't agree more.

The MomShift website (which features additional profiles, advice and updates on the stories shared here) and the book both contain a range of suggestions, advice and tips. However, this is not a standard career advice book, because the overarching lesson that I've learned from my interviews and research is that *there is no one template for post-baby professional success.*

Just as the needs of each child are unique, so are our personal and family situations. What I have found is that no matter where you are in your life or career when you become a parent, your career dreams are all still possible and achievable. Your success might emerge from an alternative path or in a different form than you first thought, but you can still get to wherever you want to be.

The success stories and solutions that I share in these pages and on the website are all deliberately very different. The goal is to showcase that we have many more choices and options than most of us realize, and that rather than trying to follow one path to success, we should instead look to confidently carve out and adapt our own individual solutions and approach towards our careers, lives and families—even in the face of the systemic obstacles and hurdles that continue to exist.

In the book *Women's Reality*, Anne Wilson Schaef discusses how, without realizing it, women often circumscribe their own choices, self-limiting their beliefs of what is possible for them.

Lois Frankel, author of the international best-seller *Nice Girls Don't Get the Corner Office*, makes the analogy that the traditional norms for careers, work and professional success and the ways that they negatively impact working mothers are like pollution: if you live and breathe it long enough, you come to believe that's just how it's supposed to be. It's not until you see the blue skies of some unspoiled territory that you realize other options are possible and out there.

My hope is that these personal positive stories are like those blue skies. That they can help guide and inspire you and give you new ways of thinking about your own career and life. The stories that speak to you now may not be the same ones that resonate six months or a year from now—as your personal and professional journey changes, so will the challenges, goals, tools and ideas needed to address them.

I deeply believe that the more women have access to real stories such as these, the more options we will become aware of and the more informed our choices can be. My hope is that MomShift—website, book and idea—will be the start of a new and more positive conversation that shifts the discussion away from the current zero-sum approach: that a woman must choose between career success (defined in one very limited way) and children.

Getting the word out won't be easy. And even to come close to achieving it, the MomShift Project will require your support.

The current frameworks of careers, family life and success are deeply entrenched in our culture, and those who accept them are very influential; being heard among these dominant voices is a challenge. And while I believe the strength of the MomShift is in showcasing and sharing the overlooked stories of a diversity of working moms, I'm also conscious that it lacks the easy sell of having a celebrity name attached to the project.

But I believe that together, if we share these stories and the positive messages they contain, we can make a difference. And so I want to ask you to please consider:

> **Buying an extra copy of this book.** Give it to a friend or recommend it to other women in your life.

> **Sharing your story and experiences.** Go to the website at www.themomshift.com.

> **Talking about the book** and project on Facebook and on Twitter using #themomshift.

> **Planning an online or live event.** It could be at your office, school or organization.

Thank you in advance for your support and I sincerely hope that the stories you are about to read will inspire and spark your own continued MomShift journey.

Reva

ONE

Is There a Right Time or
a Best Time to Have a Baby?

Throughout the research and writing of the book, I spoke to many women in their mid- to late twenties about the project and my research. Most were in the very early stages of their careers and had no kids yet, but they were keenly aware, almost hyper-conscious, of this issue. Consistently, the question they asked most often was, "Based on your interviews and research, when is the 'right' time to have a baby?"

My answer was always disappointing to them.

"There is no 'right' or 'best' time," I would inevitably respond, ". . . since like everything to do with careers, ambition, children and family, it's a very personal and individual choice. And either way, any choice you make comes with its own challenges—but nothing that you can't work with, or work around, to achieve what you want, both personally and professionally."

I could tell they hated my answer.

But I see this as a good-news situation, since no matter when or how you start your family, you can still fulfill your personal and professional goals. Almost anything you want to do really does remain possible post-children—even if, as so many of the women I spoke with reiterated, "It didn't happen the way I thought it would or had planned." Admittedly, certain stages or points in your life can make having children financially and organizationally easier to combine with professional goals and career plans.

Conventional wisdom tends to follow a standard path: first, finish college or university; next, complete any graduate or professional schooling; then start your career. Later, when you are financially secure and have at least the semblance of professional establishment, it will be time to tackle the question of motherhood. Of course, when you add in some travel and personal enjoyment, not to mention the continued ideal of meeting someone and forming a stable relationship, it's not surprising that an increasing number of women are in their thirties before the idea of having children even seems remotely viable. The average age of first-time mothers in Canada is now 28 years old,[5] in the U.S. it's 25 years old,[6] and in the U.K. the average first-time mother is 29 years old.

The challenge with this approach is that for women in the corporate sector the typical time frame for getting pregnant and navigating new motherhood is generally in direct conflict with the professional time frame for taking on increased levels of work responsibility, in competition with male colleagues who (if they are childless or have a supportive primary care partner) are working much longer and harder than before.

For many of the women I spoke with, achieving a level of professional success, a solid set of skills and an established reputation before they had their children was a secure path to continuing on after they became mothers. It can be a smart strategy, particularly since according to a 2011 McKinsey report, men are promoted based on potential, while women are promoted based on accomplishments.[7]

Caroline,* a vice president of retirement and financial planning, was weeks away from having her first child at 41 when we spoke about this topic: "I never planned on having kids this late, but when I was younger, I didn't want to jump off the career bandwagon and then, I never thought that the decision about when you get pregnant can be made for you [it took her and her husband several years to achieve a successful pregnancy]. That said, I feel like I'm in a good place career-wise since I have the seniority to control my schedule, an established reputation, and we are in a stronger financial place to give my son a better life and for me to get the help I'll need to transition back to work."

---

* Indicates name changed by request

Suzanne,* a senior vice president in a private investment firm in New York, and mother of two girls who are now 24 and 26, reflected that, "For women in my generation, having kids before you were somewhat senior in an organization just didn't seem like an option if you wanted a serious and successful career. We were still too new in the corridors of power to take the risk of reminding everyone that hey, we are women! And women have kids. I see my daughters and their friends and the changes in the work culture and I just don't think that applies anymore. You can have kids and carve out a career far more on your own terms now."

Deciding Not to Decide

As in Caroline's case, having children once your career is more "established" comes with several advantages: increased financial security, a developed professional reputation and the flexibility and the increased schedule control that often accompanies increased seniority.

However, the career (and personal) advantages of having children younger is increasingly part of the larger cultural discussion on this issue—particularly given issues around infertility. For every star we see having a baby at 45 or 46, we also see a media story warning about the fertility decline that women face after 35, and the potential health and financial implications of addressing that decline down the road.

Journalist and columnist Judith Timson wrote about facing this issue when it came to her own daughter, her fertility and her career in the face of these biological concerns. "I not only had my children successfully in my mid-thirties after my career was well established, but I have proselytized since my daughter was young that getting a career well under way before you have babies is paramount. Now that she is 25, I am wondering if I should keep my mouth shut. Giving in to biology," she acknowledges, "feels like a retreat from everything women have fought for . . ."[8]

In the same piece she quotes Anne Richard Ford, executive director of the Canadian Women's Health Network, who suggests that this new pressure to have babies while they are younger puts women "in a damned-if-you-do, damned-if-you-don't situation that is deeply unfair."

Some research is suggesting that this conflicting message on careers and motherhood is creating an unexpected backlash among groups of younger women, who are more and more undecided and ambivalent about pregnancy. Research from the National Campaign to Prevent Teen and Unplanned Pregnancy found that nearly 50 percent of American pregnancies are unplanned, and three-quarters of those are in women 29 and younger.[9] And it is women with a college degree who are more likely to experience an unintended pregnancy than those who haven't attended college. The report found that while 86 percent of unmarried young women feel that pregnancy should be planned (and 88 percent said it's important that they not get pregnant right now), only about half were using birth control consistently. "I'd guess many women are more faithful to their diet than to their birth control," says Kelleen Kaye, senior director of research for the National Campaign to Prevent Teen and Unplanned Pregnancy.

The speculation is that the pressure to find the perfect time to insert having a baby into their career plans is instead leading women to

---

IVF

A new study appearing in the U.K. *Journal of Human Reproduction* says that university-aged young adults who plan to have children don't know the facts about how fertility declines with age, and overestimate the success rates of assisted-reproductive technologies they may be counting on as a backup plan.

Fifty-two percent of women and 64 percent of men also overestimated the chances that a couple undergoing one treatment of in vitro fertilization (IVF) would be successful (the actual success rate is 30 percent). After age 44, the success rate is 3 percent.

A 2010 study found similar patterns among Canadian women, who overestimated women's fertility at age 35 and older.

Many of the women I interviewed had had their children through IVF or were undergoing IVF for a second or third child and they raised the observation that while we regularly hear about the costs of IVF (a round can cost between $10,000 and $15,000) as well as the challenges it can pose emotionally and health-wise, very little is still openly discussed about the challenges that IVF can bring to the office.

"... just deciding not to decide. I expected a lot of women would say, 'I don't want to get pregnant,'" says Kaye. "And I expected that others would say, 'I do want to have a baby.' I *didn't* expect that the same people would say both. There's this push-pull going on."[10]

Name: Christine*
Role: Lawyer, sole practitioner
Children: David, 4; Simone, 2

Christine recently opened her own patent law practice: "Running my own business was never part of my plan. I had been fairly contented in my previous job as a senior associate at a large global law firm."

However, IVF changed her career path.

"IVF is an emotional and hormonal roller coaster. Although I worked in a fairly forgiving and flexible environment for a law firm (due to the nature of my practice), during the years of various treatments, I missed out on a lot of opportunities, and also made some career-altering mistakes. Part of this was due to sheer exhaustion and, at times, a lack of focus. In essence, going through IVF is like being pregnant for a very extended period of time—but without being able to tell your co-workers or clients what's going on. There are lots of doctor appointments, some bed rest, hormonal changes, etc. If you have to go through the process numerous times (she underwent three rounds with her first and two with her second), over an extended period of time, small things can add up to leave lasting impressions on co-workers and 'superiors.'

"When I say this, I am not talking about the mental capability it takes to actually perform the legal work; I am talking about the 'politics' of surviving and moving up the ladder in a legal/corporate environment, particularly towards partner track."

For Christine, this translated into missed speaking and travel opportunities, and, in one case, accepting a ruling that normally she would have challenged. "But at the time, I was mid-treatment although no one at work knew this and I just felt that I did not have the time or energy to take on extra battles. It was a poor decision though and one that subsequently impacted my professional reputation.

"I do think it has all worked out—I now love having my own business, and I wouldn't have changed any of the decisions that I made—but I do wish I'd known more about the toll it would take on my career life so that I could have planned for it, and it would be great to feel as though it was actually permissible to share what was happening with me."

Relationships

Until very recently, the topics of motherhood, careers, work and relationships tended to be discussed separately, segregated into neat but artificial silos—as though what was happening in one had no impact on the other. Of course, the reality is that they all crash up together and spill over into each other.

My last book, *First Comes Marriage: Modern Relationship Advice from the Wisdom of Arranged Marriages*, was based on interviews with more than three hundred women who decided to have an arranged marriage—many of the women I spoke with came to this decision after first dating and living with potential partners. The goal of my interviews was to see what I could take from the arranged marriage approach to relationships and instead apply them to the dating lives of women like myself.

One observation was that the practical focus of arranged marriages meant that from the start, potential marriage candidates were assessed from the perspective of what kind of career they had, how it would develop, how it would combine with the other person's career and what their joint synergy would mean for their future family life. Since many of the women I spoke with were highly educated and ambitious professional women (most of whom were born and raised in North America) this ability to have an open discussion on how their careers would merge was often a real focus point.

And yet, for those of us raised in the culture of rom-coms and the ideal that "love can conquer all," assessing a potential partner in this practical (and admittedly unromantic) way can be very difficult.

For instance, Sheryl Sandberg, the COO of Facebook, caused a flurry of excitement when she stated, "The most important career choice you'll make is who you marry." She explains that there's a "stalled revolution for women" right now, and that "having a support-ive spouse—a real partner—will play a huge part in your success."[11]

In *Lean In* she expands her dating advice, counseling, "When look-ing for a life partner, my advice to women is date all of them: the bad boys, the cool boys, the commitmentphobic boys, the crazy boys. But do not marry them. The things that make the bad boys sexy do not make them good husbands. When it comes time to settle down, find someone who wants an equal partner." She also suggests that ". . . at the start of a romance, even though it may be tempting for you to show a more classic girlfriend-y side by cooking meals and taking care of errands, hold yourself back from doing this too much. If a rela-tionship begins in an unequal place, it is likely to get more unbal-anced if and when children are added to the equation."[12]

It's good advice but, more importantly, it represents a shift: a recog-nition that an individual's career evolution and success don't happen in isolation from personal decisions and choices.

Name: Rena Heer
Role: On-air anchor/reporter, CP 24
Children: Arjun, 7; Rassna, 2

"My husband—despite his traditional South Asian back-ground—is a true believer in equality. He may not do his share of the housework consistently, but he does fundamen-tally believe that men and women should have an equal opportunity to pursue our goals and fulfill our potential. He wants a strong role model for his daughter. He was always very clear—when we were dating and much younger—that one of the things he loved about me was my independence and my willingness to take chances. And when he sees me slipping, whether it's in my professional life or my personal life, he is always quick to remind me of what I can do.

"When my son was born, we were living in Vancouver and I had just been hired by CTV, from Global, for the *Canada AM* western edition broadcast. Four months after launching the show, CTV pulled the plug. At that point, I was told I could find some work at CTV BC to keep me busy, or I could take a leap and head to a newly acquired station that they were in the process of rebranding in Toronto. I spoke to my husband about it and he asked me fairly bluntly, 'Is this something you want to do?' I told him the opportunity seemed exciting and I guess I would always wonder if I should have taken it. I think that's all he needed. He started the process of looking for a buyer for his business and within a few weeks we were on our way. He also went on to say that I supported him fully when he was launching his business and he wanted to support me back. He did not hesitate for a second.

"The toughest challenge, I think, was the fact that he was staying at home when we first moved to Toronto. It was hard for him not to be going to work every day and making money. I also expected him to do more housework than before because he was staying home.

"The change meant I also had to work on my expectations. I had to be OK with my husband as the primary caregiver to our son. I had to step back, let them eat at Subway more than I would like, but I also got a chance to appreciate the fact that my husband and son had/have a pretty amazing bond. That bond became much stronger during that period of time. After two years, he was able to open his own business and we were able to hire a caregiver.

"Looking back, it was great to have our family work together as a unit during that time. We have seen families split for short periods to accommodate a work opportunity, but that was never a choice for us. A friend of mine moved here from Philadelphia with her daughter, and her husband comes down on weekends. Our decision early on was that we do everything we can as a family. We all have a voice, we all have a say (including the kids) and at the end of the day if we do everything together, we are happier and healthier as a unit.

"Now that my daughter is almost three, I am conscious of being a good role model for her. I don't want to pass on the guilt, the hesitation, the second thoughts. I want to pass on the fact that THEY (my children) matter more than anything in the world, but I also want them to know that they can set goals, have dreams, do work they love and improve the world in some small way. I also want my daughter to know that she needs to be independent and self-sufficient for herself and her family. I also want my son to know he can find a partner that he can lean on emotionally and, if he needs to, financially, without any shame . . ."

Kids First, Career Second?

Best-selling author and career blogger Penelope Trunk is part of the growing trend of thought leaders advising women to reconsider their sequencing of career and kids. Specifically, she advises that they reverse their thinking and have children early.

Trunk advises Gen Z women to learn from the "mistakes" of Gen X and Y. Instead of following the path of career building until they are in their thirties and then having kids and trying to combine family with professional advancement, they should have their kids by 25 so that by 45 they can focus on "having a huge career" if that's what they want. To make this work she suggests that between the ages of 20 and 25, women focus on dating and marrying older men interested in settling down, and then build their career slowly in the interim years; for instance, by doing advanced degrees to stay relevant for future career options.[13]

Retrograde as this advice might sound (particularly since it's based on the assumption that a woman wants to be primarily at home with her kids, doesn't have a supportive spouse and can't or won't handle a more engaged career), advocates argue that it has its place in the discussion on career and family. In her much discussed article in *The Atlantic*, Anne-Marie Slaughter also muses on the benefits of having children younger:

"Many of the top women leaders of the generation just ahead of me—Madeleine Albright, Hillary Clinton, Ruth Bader Ginsburg, Sandra Day O'Connor, Patricia Wald, Nannerl Keohane—had their children in their twenties and early thirties, as was the norm in the 1950s through the 1970s. A child born when his mother is 25 will finish high school when his mother is 43, an age at which, with full-time immersion in a career, she still has plenty of time and energy for advancement.

"Yet this sequence has fallen out of favor with many high-potential women, and understandably so. People tend to marry later now, and anyway, if you have children earlier, you may have difficulty getting a graduate degree, a good first job or opportunities for advancement in the crucial early years of your career. Making matters worse, you will also have less income while raising your children, and hence less ability to hire the help that can be indispensable to your juggling act."[14]

In retrospect, maybe part of the reason that I felt so pressured and stressed during my first pregnancy was that I had always unconditionally accepted that the formula for career success was *first* you establish yourself and *then* you have children, most likely because I had never encountered role models that presented me with an alternative to this scenario.

Name: Sharon Edmondson
Role: Vice President, Human Resources, the Americas,
            Regus
Children: Christian, 15; Holden, 13; Sarah, 9; Kaitlyn, 7

Sharon Edmondson was 18 when she got married and had her first son. "I was just starting married life, working in retail and muddling through it all. Early on though, I did realize that I was a much better mother when I was working. Work made me much more intentional with my time and my focus."

This was a surprising revelation for Sharon, since both her mother and mother-in-law had been stay-at-home moms and she hadn't expected that she would either enjoy work so much or have the opportunity and ability to pursue her career to the levels she has.

Sharon had reached the position of the Global Vice President of Human Resources at Regus, a supplier of flexible and temporary office space in more than ninety-five countries—a job that required managing a staff of 5,500-plus personnel. About two years ago, when the company asked her to relocate, she instead chose to return to a prior role, in which she had focused on the more than three thousand Regus employees in the Americas, rather than uproot her family.

"There is a season for everything. Having children early in my life allows me the opportunity to experience seasons multiple times during my professional career. Another opportunity to take on a role with global breadth will present itself again at a time where it's right for me professionally and for my family."

It was after her second child was born that Sharon began down her current career path. "I started with a temp job in the recruiting division with IBM and I loved it. It felt like a perfect fit." Two years later, after expanding her skill set within the recruiting division, she was offered a permanent job in the human resources department of HQ Global Workplaces (which was later bought by Regus).

"It was absolutely an entry-level job, but I was eager to learn everything I could and I had a great mentor, whom I worked with very closely. I used to sit in on strategic planning meetings and was able to learn a great deal, just by being a part of things and finding ways to help where I could and absorbing the knowledge in the room.

"Looking back, there's a real naïveté to having kids so young. You're trying to figure out children, life, work, your relationship and even who you are. But I really believe being a mother helped me professionally. I brought a different level of responsibility to all my roles, even the most entry-level jobs, because having children changes you like that—I did take things more seriously and I think it showed."

Sharon loved her job, but she was initially hesitant about taking on any expanded responsibilities. She was ambitious but worried about how to manage both a job that was fast becoming a career and her growing family.

"It was a challenge. I loved the HR world, but I never saw myself as an 'executive' and from what I saw of the lives of male executives, I thought it would be impossible for me to balance work and family. I saw all these men having their assistants doing stuff for their kids, stuff that I wanted to be the one doing for my family. It was really important for me not to delegate my home life. But we're lucky since we have lots of family around us and so I rarely had to have anyone other than family to help us out."

While initially her career advances were the result of learning on the job, working hard and then taking on more when and how she could, this also changed over time.

"When I started, I didn't have an intentional plan or goal in mind, but then on my third pregnancy, I realized that if I created a plan and became more strategic professionally (with the projects I worked on and the targets I set) I could control my career more, and that if I became more senior within the organization, it would mean I would also have greater control over my life."

Right before the birth of her fourth child, Sharon was asked to temporarily step in on an interim basis as the Global VP of HR. "It was a temporary role, but when I came back from my maternity leave a few months later, I decided to put my name forward for the position. It felt like a huge jump in some ways, but I decided to go for it since I had already been doing some of the work involved—and to be honest, I really wanted it."

She got it and soon became the only woman at Regus at the executive level.

"Being a young mother was a definite asset as I started to become more senior in my career—there was no worry about how I would manage if and when I had kids. No one had ever known me professionally *without* children and so they all knew that it wasn't going to be a problem. Luckily my line manager and COO also had four children each, but they also had stay-at-home wives. I had to help them realize that my schedule wouldn't always reflect theirs, but that it was about productivity, not about when I worked."

She's taken this same focused, intentional approach with managing her family life and marriage, particularly since marrying and having children young also means growing up together—with changing roles and expectations. "Today my husband works in Web development and radio and I'm the solid career person in the family. But in the beginning of our relationship, both of us expected that we would have a more traditional arrangement to our marriage. And it took several years for us to be comfortable with the shift. It was also a sense of discovery for myself, the personal excitement I felt as I was exposed to the more strategic side of the business and realized that I can do this, I'm good at it and I love it.

"I'm also extremely intentional in terms of scheduling time

with each of the kids. I take each of them on an individual overnight trip every summer, and when I travel, especially globally, I try and share the experience with them as much as I can—through text, e-mails and Skype.

"From what I've seen, corporate America still, unfortunately, sees children and family as a weakness. But from what I've observed, many women really come into their own, discovering talents, when they become mothers. The majority of the driven leaders with a great ability to multitask, stay organized and delegate that I have had the opportunity to work with are mothers."

Seniority and Control

The relationship between increased seniority and having more options was a theme I regularly heard throughout my interviews with women in corporate or institutional roles. Barbara,* a mother of three and SVP at one of the large retail brands, put it to me this way: "Sheryl Sandberg highlights the issue of how women make a series of small decisions and accommodations that they believe are necessary to have a family and career, but that ultimately leads to them stepping out of the workforce—it's what she calls 'leaving before you leave.' What the discussion glosses over is that as you become more senior, yes, you have additional responsibilities, but you also have a completely different set of tools and options (in part from an increased salary) and none of this is fully apparent until you actually arrive in that senior role."

There's Young, and There's Super Young

While the "right" age to have a baby may be debatable, there is a general cultural consensus that teen pregnancy usually means the end of opportunity, and instead, life as a "statistic." If you've ever watched MTV's hit show *Teen Mom*, it will unfortunately (and probably unfairly) confirm virtually every stereotype you've had about teen mothers.

In an interview, Lauren Dolgen, senior vice president of the MTV's Series Development (who created and developed the hit shows *Teen Mom, Teen Mom 2* and *16 and Pregnant*) said the concept was in reaction to reading that 750,000 teen girls get pregnant each year in the U.S. Her goal with the show(s) was to share the realities of what life is actually like for teen moms, married or unmarried.

Whether MTV's show succeeds is debatable. Yes, the girls are on the covers of tabloids, but the show does also show the grim sides of teen pregnancy—the stress, the financial struggle, the frustrations and the often incredibly immature fathers.

Redefining Motherhood?

Andrea O'Reilly, a women's studies professor at York University and director of the Association for Research on Mothering, believes that just as older women are gaining acceptance as new mothers, adolescent girls are claiming their maternal rights too. "There's a redefining of motherhood. Teen moms are saying, 'Why can't I be a mother now?'[5] Before, the time of motherhood was so restricted. Now it's OK at 48. So why not at 18?"

The feminist motherhood movement, as O'Reilly refers to it, is based on the growing support for moms of all ages and has people questioning societal expectations about when is the right time to have children. "It's part of a larger re-envisioning of motherhood: queer mothers, old mothers, young mothers. That wasn't possible twenty years ago."

Even if motherhood is being gradually redefined, the media and cultural discussion remains very much focused on and driven by a certain type of mother: a woman who was in her late twenties to mid- to late thirties when she had kids, with a university degree and usually married. It's a focus that perpetuates the idea that there is one path or route to successful motherhood and work.

"Most of the parenting blogs seemed based on some 'white picket fence' view of the world that I didn't relate to . . . the community and audience seemed older, more affluent and never seemed to mention the issues I was seeing around me," says Carolina Pichardo, the founder of the website and community Young Urban Moms (YUM).

Ten years after finding out she was pregnant in her freshman year at NYU, Carolina graduated with a bachelor's degree in communications with her ten-year-old daughter proudly looking on. "Being a young mom means having your life and your choices portrayed extremely negatively, but I don't think we're different than any other groups of working mothers in terms of what we are trying to achieve for ourselves and our families."

Statistically, the odds for teen mothers remain grim. They are more likely to drop out of high school, they are less likely to go to college, their siblings and children are more likely to be teen parents, and they are more likely to live in poverty. And so, if there was ever a group that needed to define their own framework in order to succeed, it's teen mothers, who generally have both genuine obstacles against them as well as a cultural framework that tells them that they have already "failed."

Name: Gloria Malone
Role: Student, Baruch College (studying public affairs);
                founder, www.teenmomnyc.com.
Children: Leilani, 7

I first came across Gloria from a guest post that she had written on the Young Urban Moms website, called "Balancing Tips from a Teen Mom."

In the course of my research, I felt like I had seen every sort of advice for mothers—but never *from* teen mothers.

And yet, a successful teen mother has overcome an amplified version of all the issues that working mothers face: societal judgment, endless advice from teachers, parents and friends, financial struggles, uncertainty about how to be a good mother, relationship strains, identity loss, redefining who they are in the context of family, friends and peer groups.

The teen mothers I spoke with were some of my favorite interviews. I was in awe of what they had accomplished despite significant hurdles.

Gloria grew up in a small town in Florida. A good student involved in many extracurricular activities, she surprised her family, teachers and friends when she got pregnant at 15. The father was her boyfriend, who was literally the boy next door.

Gloria managed to graduate from high school with a 4.0 GPA, while at the same time holding down a full-time job and juggling her roles and responsibilities as a mother, fiancée and housekeeper. She then enrolled at a local community college and obtained an associate degree in economics. Upon graduation, she made a series of brave moves: she left a good job at a prestigious Florida law firm, ended her six-year relationship with the father of her child and moved to New

York City. "I had to leave. I felt like I was living the life that I had been told as a teen mother I should want and was what I deserved. But it wasn't the one I wanted."

To reach this point, Gloria overcame a broken relationship and people who told her that she should just do a "practical" degree like becoming a dental assistant versus following her long-held dreams of policy and politics. There were friends who didn't stand by her, severe financial issues and a period of depression when financial difficulties forced her to miss a semester.

Yet Gloria says her biggest challenge was to ". . . overcome the voice in my head that said I didn't belong at this college, that I couldn't do it and that I wasn't like the other students and that I didn't deserve to be here. I had to learn to just ignore it and keep going."

Consider:

› **What do you really want?** When it comes to combining career and family, everyone will have (usually well-intentioned) advice on what you should or shouldn't do, how, when and where. Throughout my interviews, I consistently heard that the best way to handle these conflicting pressures is to become very clear on what your own true priorities are, both at work and at home. "When I finally actually wrote down my own list of what I wanted for myself professionally and for my family, I felt much less vulnerable to trying to compete or keep up with what my sister-in-law or my colleagues were doing," shared Susan,* a mother of two and marketing executive.

› **Be mindful of self-sabotage.** Managing the "internal voice" is an ongoing process. "It doesn't go away, it just changes how it's limiting you," said Cindy,* who recently retired from a senior role at a global marketing company and is a mother of three boys. "I just learned to work around it and to rationally challenge myself: Was I not taking on something because I really didn't want to do it, or because I thought I couldn't?"

› **You are on your own path.** Finally, consider the advice of Mozilla co-founder and chairwoman Mitchell Baker, 55 (she founded the initial iteration of the browser in 1998): "Some people have kids early in life, others late. Commit to your path. Don't second-guess yourself constantly."

How Many?

How does the number of kids you have also affect your professional life?

In 1959, in Canada the average number of children per family was 3.94. In 2008, it was 1.68. Similarly, in the U.S. approximately two kids remains the average. From one to two or more, how does each additional child affect a woman's career? After all, it seems logical to think that if one child involves a certain number of doctor visits, sick days and school functions, then all of these demands and pull factors would be multiplied by the number of kids you have—not to mention the financial impact of each additional pregnancy and maternity leave (economist Ann Crittenden estimates that a college-educated woman loses about $1 million in lifetime earnings after having just *one* child).[16]

A recent study in Australia, called *Fertility and Labour Market Participation*, found that women with three or more children are significantly less likely to be in the workforce than those with two or just one child.

"Early on, I recognized that it would be difficult to manage a career in the corporate world with a large family of small children, and since I wanted a large family, I'd always planned on an entrepreneurial career in order to create the flexibility I knew I would need," says Victoria Sopik, the president and CEO of Kids & Company, a provider of child-care services for corporate clients. The company was named the fastest-growing business in Canada in 2008 by *Profit* magazine and now operates in over twenty cities. She is also the mother of eight children between the ages of 15 and 28 years.

"From an advice perspective, I would say that you cannot underestimate the value of reliable and trustworthy domestic assistance. When my children were young, my first job was to be their mother, and the second job was to run my business. I hired wonderful people to take care of the many other important jobs around the house. Delegating domestic work and paying for it was worth every penny! It allowed me to focus either on the children or on my growing business."

Name: Janet*
Role: Senior Vice President, Global Financial Services
Children: Adam, 7

"I deliberately made the decision that, strictly for career reasons, I'll only be having one child. I've always set high goals for myself and I would say I'm pretty competitive, so the idea of either slowing down or pausing my career was never something I considered. I knew I wouldn't be happy on that route."

Carol's company is known for their in-house training and management track—a path she was selected for when she had been there for six years. "It was something that I was working towards since the day I applied, so it was a huge deal for me."

At around the same time, her partner started more seriously raising the issue of kids. "He was keen to have two or maybe three children, and was getting concerned that time was passing and we were getting older."

Carol was ambivalent. "I come from a family of three and I'm very close with both my older brothers, but I didn't want to pause on my career and, to be honest, just never felt a huge maternal instinct. I always said I'm perfect favorite aunt material!"

Her compromise was Adam. "I worked until my last week of pregnancy and then was back in eight weeks. He's a great kid; he's funny and smart and I have to say I enjoy motherhood more than I ever expected, and of course Adam is now the center of our family and lives—but still there's no question about us having another one. I just don't think it would be fair to myself or my family to be torn between things. I'm looking to put myself forward for a significantly more senior role in the coming couple of years, and yes, it could still happen with another baby, and yes, we could get more help, but I don't want additional conflicts or distractions right now. I think it's important to be honest about what works for you and your family, and even though our extended family keeps pushing us to think about a sibling for Adam, I also have to think about what works for me, and I think doing it all again with a newborn is more than I can or want to take on."

Name: Carrie Denton
Role: Managing Director, Global Banking and Markets,
        Scotiabank
Kids: Mark, 19; Emma, 14; Sean, 12; Tessa, 9

"I always liked the idea of a big family, and while I was realistic about the work and logistics it brings with it, I never thought of it as a career obstacle or challenge. Banking was something I progressed into following summer jobs at financial institutions. I graduated in a recession and there were no jobs in what I had studied (environmental studies–urban planning) so I accepted an offer into a management training program at TD Bank."

As she worked her way up, she got married and then went to New Zealand, where she started another training program at an Australian bank and got training in and exposure to the capital markets side of the business. "Since it was a smaller trade floor, I was able to get a great deal of experience and exposure that would have taken me much longer elsewhere.

"I knew that I would always go back to work. My mother had worked when I was younger. I also had friends who were older, with kids, and so I learned a great deal from their experience, especially not to sweat the small stuff. After the birth of our first child, I took a six-month maternity leave, which was the standard at that time. In terms of child care, it was important for me to set myself up for success. Hiring a nanny allowed me to resume my career in the capital markets sector—which regularly involves long hours. In fact our nanny has been with us since our first child was born, and he is now 19!

"As a result of being able to find someone I could really trust, I was able to be completely committed at work, while at the same time I had confidence in our child-care arrangements and didn't worry about what was happening at home. While I had been on leave, several structural changes occurred that resulted in the formation of what is now known as the Global Banking and Markets division at the bank. With these changes came new opportunities, and shortly after returning from my first leave, I assumed additional responsibilities by managing a foreign exchange sales team. Since the birth of our first child, progressive opportunities were presented to me at work. I took on larger sales mandates, launched an online trading platform and became more involved in the strategic initiatives of the foreign exchange business. I am now a senior member of the management team in foreign exchange.

"There are a number of reasons why we decided to adopt. For a start, my husband and I are both from large families and we wanted more than one child. Following several years of unsuccessful fertility treatment we knew that being parents and having a family was more important to us than how the child was delivered to us.

"With the premature deaths of my mother at 65 of cancer and my brother at 42 from a brain tumor, I quickly learned that I wanted to live life to the fullest and not have any regrets, so we went for it! We felt that we had a lot to offer and wanted to share what we had. This was especially so for our second and third adoptions after seeing the children in the orphanages and knowing that many would never experience family life but grow up in an institution with a very limited future ahead of them.

"Once we decided on adoption we started the process immediately by finding an agency and having our home study done. We received our letter of approval from the Province of Ontario in December 1999, and in January 2000 we were presented with a dossier for our eldest daughter. My husband, son and I went to Russia in March 2000 for two weeks to finalize our daughter's adoption (which is a court process in Russia). All in all, it took eight months from the time we started our home study to bring our daughter home.

"All of our children were adopted from Russia. However, the process did change over the years, becoming increasingly arduous and very complicated. Our eldest daughter, Emma, was adopted when she was ten months old in 2000. Our third child (and second adoption), Sean, came home in May 2003 when he was seventeen months old. This adoption was very drawn-out since the region in Siberia, Russia, that we adopted from was considering closing its doors to international adoption. None of the previous paperwork (home studies, references, police checks, immigration, etc.) for the first adoption could be reused and we had to completely restart all that paperwork as well as the new requirements!

"My husband and I made two trips to Russia, one in February 2003 and a final one in May 2003 to bring Sean home. Our youngest, Tessa, came home in February 2006 at sixteen months of age. This was the most complicated adoption. On Labour Day weekend, September 2005, we traveled to Russia for our first trip to meet her and have a Canadian medical doctor examine her. We were told to come back to Russia for the court appearance prior to Thanksgiving. However, at this point the Russian government closed their doors to international adoption and we were caught in the middle of it. We did not know if we would get our daughter home or not. Eventually, they opened their doors and we were the first family to travel in February 2006 to bring Tessa home.

"Overall, we went back to Russia five separate times as part of the adoption processes for our children. After each adoption, I usually took about six weeks of parental leave to settle the family in. We were fortunate in that our children were healthy, they adapted very well to family life in Canada and we had the consistency of the same nanny over the years. In some ways it was easier than pregnancy and childbirth, because I didn't have the physical recovery, and to be honest, taking such a short time probably made it easier for me to keep the pace versus if I had taken a full year out [for maternity leave].

"I was lucky that all four of our kids were healthy and adjusted well. For us, creating a reliable support system has been essential. My husband also has a very busy career and we didn't have family close by to help us. With the age range of my children, juggling all their activities is difficult, so in addition to the nanny I've hired someone to help with all the driving to the different activities. It's a lot of logistics and organization with four active kids.

"Building this kind of support system is critical, but I think you need to take a longer-term perspective on careers—you need to make it easier on yourself to get ahead and reduce stress where possible. With four kids, I have to be very proactive about planning ahead, anticipating when the busy and stress triggers are so I can plan support both in the office and at home around it. I love what I do. I find the capital markets very interesting and dynamic, the clients are great to work with and the products and solutions are innovative, all of which keeps me very focused and engaged. It's also very important for me to be a strong role model for my daughters and sons. I want my girls to see that it's possible to successfully combine a career and family. Equally important is that my sons see this too, as one day they may be in relationships where both partners are focusing on careers and raising families.

"Combining a busy career and a bigger family does mean that the early years can be a bit frustrating and tiring and it can be easy to self-select out, but it's important to think longer term—one day it's going to be you and your career and so it's essential to keep investing in that side of yourself.

"It's not perfect but we seem to be making it work!"

TWO

Maternity Leave:
The Big Jump

For many women, maternity leave is the first time that they've had the chance to pause in some way from the entrenched routines of their work lives.

Obviously, being at home with a newborn (and possibly with other children as well) is not exactly a restful pause, but it nevertheless involves stepping away to some degree from their work and professional identities.

And with the first child, it can feel a bit like stepping into the unknown.

Plus, there is often an element of the wild card to maternity leave planning. There's uncertainty about how you'll really feel (both physically and mentally), how the baby will be and what you'll really do. And if *you* feel confident about what your post-baby plans are, those around you (as I experienced), whether colleagues or family, may remain skeptical about the accuracy of your intentions.

"Even though it was my first, I knew I was going to be back at work after four months. Not only had I already invested ten years into my career but I was also the primary breadwinner in our family, so I *had* to be back. But since I didn't want to share the financial requirements of my situation, I faced a lot of patronizing comments about how I might change my mind or reconsider once I met the baby," said Alicia,* a mother of two, who works as an IT security consultant in Santa Fe.

What's Maternity Leave For?

Should women who adopt get the same paid maternity leave as women who become pregnant? And what about paternity leave? Or same-sex couples?

The purpose of maternity leave is the core question of a lawsuit that was filed by a Long Island, N.Y., woman against her employer, a pharmaceutical company based in Lexington, Mass.

Kara Krill, a clinical business manager, sued Cubist Pharmaceuticals for not extending maternity leave benefits to her after the birth of her twins by a surrogate. Specifically, her employer only wanted to give her the five-day leave that adoptive mothers and all fathers are entitled to, as opposed to the twelve weeks that birth mothers receive. Krill argues that she is not adopting her twins; she has a legal document stating that she and her husband are the biological parents to these children, so she should be given the full maternity leave.

The real issue is not the details of the contracts but the question of what the underlying purpose of maternity leave is. Specifically: "If maternity leave is offered so that women can recover from what is, at best, the incredibly messy and strenuous business of giving birth, then new mothers like Krill who use surrogates would not really deserve paid leave, since they are not doing the hard yards of labor and delivery.

"But paid maternity leave could also be regarded the same way as paid leave for jury duty—something a company does out of civic responsibility. Supporting new mothers as they bond with their children, learn to care for them and give them a good start is beneficial for society and for the survival of the species."[17]

Employers haven't had to face many of these kinds of issues before, since surrogacy is still relatively uncommon in the U.S. (figures are fuzzy, but the Society for Assisted Reproductive Technology put the number of surrogate births at fewer than three hundred a year in 2006).

Ultimately, Krill's case will probably be decided on a fine reading of the company's medical leave policies, but the good news is that these questions may help increase the case for paternity leave. The state of Massachusetts does not mandate paid maternity leave, only unpaid. And in most workplaces in the U.S., maternity leave is granted as part of a company's provision for disability leave.

June Carbone, a law professor at the University of Missouri–Kansas City School of Law, told ABC News that she thinks the case is a tough one. "I can't see that an employer would be able to provide women with maternity leave for the purpose of bonding with a child, where the woman has not given birth, and not be obligated to provide men with the same benefit."

The Maternity Spectrum

Discussing maternity leave and parental benefits is challenging in that what is legally offered differs widely by nation and by company.

For instance, the U.S. (along with Papua New Guinea, Swaziland, Liberia and Lesotho) is one of the few countries that do not mandate some type of paid maternity leave. In contrast, the Canadian system provides at least a partial ongoing income for almost a year (provided that the criteria have been met).

In 2001, when the Canadian government increased parental leave from ten to thirty-five weeks, employers across the country panicked. In a survey conducted in Alberta at the time, anxious employers predicted heightened workplace tensions and potential discrimination against young job seekers. "People in childbearing years will be at a disadvantage when it comes to new positions opening up," warned one, while another admitted, "We have learned to avoid hiring people we feel will be having families."[18]

Ellen,* now a senior executive at Canada's largest telecom company and mother of two, was pregnant just when the new maternity leave benefits came into effect. "I certainly had no intention of being the first in our company to use the benefits and, to be honest, I didn't actually want to. I couldn't imagine leaving for a year and successfully returning to the fast-paced career track I was on. Yes, under the new law I would still have a job, but I was pretty sure it wasn't going to be one I wanted."

A decade in, the Canadian women I interviewed who had the option of the full year remained mixed on whether or not to take it. As Alex,* a social worker and Toronto mother of a six-year-old and a ten-month-old, told me, "I know that many of my friends feel like I do: that there's this unspoken pressure to take a full year of maternity leave. Since we can in Canada, people wonder what's wrong with you if you don't."

Legal entitlements are of course the framework for the maternity-leave discussion, but they are only part of the equation. Numerous other factors influence an individual's maternity-leave decision, including employer expectations, professional norms, personal (and partner) preferences, the needs of your individual child and, of course, what is and is not affordable for your family.

As many of the women I interviewed told me, if you've spent around a decade climbing up the ladder, forging a career, juggling important projects, managing staff and loving it, then the prospect of months in work wilderness can be a bleak thought.

For others, a period away from work was a hugely positive experience, both personally with their families but also in terms of their professional development. Termed "power maternity leave," it refers to women taking time off to have a child and then learning new skills, starting businesses or tackling other ventures, and signifies a shift in the perception of how maternity leave should work.

Maternity Leave:
Three Countries, Three Approaches

Canada

The Canadian government offers both a leave and a benefits component (with the latter being administered by provincial employment insurance plans). Depending on the length of employment history and the hours worked, new mothers can take between seventeen and fifty-two weeks of leave from their jobs. Their employers are required to accept the employees back into their jobs, or an equivalent job, at the end of the mandated leave at the same rate of pay with the same employment benefits.

In addition, the government offers paid leave for one or both parents through Canada's employment insurance plan. A pregnant employee or new mother can take a paid maternity leave of up to fifteen weeks. Either the mother or father can take thirty-five weeks of parental leave after the baby is born or adopted. The parents can share the leave however they choose. If eligible for the program, the benefits equal 55 percent of the parent's average weekly insurable wage, up to a maximum of $485 per week. For low-income families, the rate of benefits can increase to up to 80 percent, with the same maximum of $485 per week.

Statistics Canada said most mothers—83 percent—took paid leave. Around one in five mothers took unpaid leave. The average length of paid leave was forty weeks, while the average for unpaid leave was 4.5 weeks.

The United States

The U.S. (along with Papua New Guinea, Swaziland, Liberia and Lesotho) is one of the few countries in the world that doesn't mandate some type of paid maternity leave for new mothers. The federal Family and Medical Leave Act (FMLA) signed into law in 1993 requires employers to provide up to twelve weeks of unpaid leave for several medical conditions— one of which is the birth of a baby. If the mother has pre-birth complications, she may be able to take part of the leave under the medical component. Before the law was enacted, the U.S. had no laws requiring that employers provide any leave. There are still gaping holes in the FMLA, however. It exempts small employers, defined as those having fewer than fifty employees. Some states have their own version of the FMLA and have an even lower threshold for employer exemption.

Although the FMLA allows at least a brief window for mothers to recuperate and care for a child after birth or an adoption, there is no federal or state law mandating maternity benefits.

A few states, including California and New Jersey, include maternity benefits as part of the state's disability insurance plan, which provides at least a partial offset of lost income.

In 2011, only 11 percent of private sector workers and 17 percent of public workers reported that they had access to paid maternity leave through their employer. And for first-time mothers, only about half can take paid leave when they give birth.

(From: http://thinkprogress.org/health/2012/05/24/489973/paid-maternity-leave-us/?mobile=nc)

The United Kingdom

In the U.K., women are entitled to fifty-two weeks, known as Statutory Maternity Leave. A recent amendment makes it mandatory for women to take a minimum of two weeks' maternity leave immediately after childbirth (four weeks' minimum for factory workers). Pregnant employees may also be eligible for a Sure Start Maternity Grant, a one-time, tax-free payment that does not have to be paid back, offered to low-income mothers to buy supplies for the baby.

The Pressure: How Long Is the Right Time?

Much like pregnancy (and child-raising in general), women from all professional and personal backgrounds are subject to fairly relentless criticism for their choices and decisions on maternity leave (and let's not forget the troublesome inner critic).

When I held group discussions with MomShifters across Canada and the U.S., the issue of maternity leave was one that created an incredible amount of debate: How long to take? How to best transition back? Should you check in with work during the time off or is it a sacred "do not disturb" period?

When Yahoo CEO Marissa Mayer was quoted in *Fortune* magazine saying that her maternity leave would just be a few weeks long and that she would be working throughout, columnists, bloggers and commentators attacked. Was she setting unrealistic expectations for other women? Was she failing to sufficiently recognize the value of maternity leave? What message was she sending to corporate employers? To other working mothers?

Many of Mayer's critics appeared to overlook that, as a CEO with a net worth of $350 million, Mayer could afford a good deal more paid help than the average working mother and has many more choices. And that outside of that rarefied compensation realm, it is in fact quite common for working women to take only a few weeks for maternity leave.

Women in the service and retail sectors frequently have few if any benefits and are required to be physically present to work. And for many women entrepreneurs, freelancers and consultants, even when they do qualify for leave time, they feel a certain responsibility to keep up with their clients or company during their short leaves. Women entrepreneurs, freelancers, consultants and part-timers (who may not qualify for any leave) often work through their few weeks of short maternity leave.

Katherine Reynolds Lewis, founder of the blog CurrentMom, wrote a post on her site called "I'm a Freelancer. Where's My Maternity Leave?" "The thing is, I really didn't know if I was on maternity leave or not. I'm an independent contractor. I work from home and am accountable to myself. There's no chance of taking any family medical leave, no paperwork to fill out, making it official, and unless I sent a mass e-mail announcing a leave, it wasn't clear that I was taking one."

In my own case, my first son was born in the U.K., where, based on the time I had been with my employer, I had six weeks of paid leave. I then took three months' unpaid before starting to freelance from home. By the time he was seven months old, I had returned to full-time work.

With my second son, I was living in Canada but didn't qualify for any maternity benefits since, although I worked full time, I was dividing my time as a consultant among three different organizations. As a result, I returned to work two days a week after two weeks and then was back full time by the third month. My mom came to help for the first two months (and my eldest was in day care) and then we hired a live-out nanny. I was lucky that I felt physically fine, and since I really enjoyed my job I was actually quite happy to be back—even though I'll admit I never enjoyed telling people how short a time I had taken, since I continually felt they disapproved.

With my third, the division between work and home is once again blurred (my two-week-old son is asleep next to me as I write), but since I work from home, have a full-time nanny and am able to control my client schedule, it feels manageable.

Do I feel like I missed out? Yes and no. The nature of my career is completely self-driven, so consciously stopping it for a year would be difficult. I could have planned ahead and taken an organizational or corporate role that would have allowed me the security of maternity leave with benefits and a role to return to (an approach that many mothers I spoke with deliberately took), but to be honest, that level of foresight and sheer practicality would have required me to be a completely different person.

Like many other women I spoke with who were also in similar self-employed arrangements, going back to work sooner, even if it was only part-time, was easier than the stress (both emotional and financial) of staying fully away.

In October 2010, a U.S. Department of Commerce report found that the number of women-owned businesses in the U.S. is growing twice as fast as businesses owned by men. However, how female entrepreneurs manage their time after they give birth does not appear to have been studied comprehensively as yet.[19]

For its part, Statistics Canada has found that "Both mothers and fathers who were self-employed took shorter leaves, even after considering factors such as whether the child was first-born, the mother's age, parental education and income."[20]

Name: Katie Hellmuth Martin
Role: Co-founder, Tin Shingle (among other
             entrepreneurial ventures)
Children: Ruby, 3; Cole, 1

Katie is a co-founder of Tin Shingle, a brand-building platform and consultancy for small businesses.

As an entrepreneur, she didn't have an official maternity leave, and since she owns and runs a service business, she had clients to attend to, projects to finish and new projects to start—regardless of maternity leave.

In Martin's blog entry on the next page, she captures the

tension and pressures that entrepreneurs and other working mothers face when it comes to what is "right" for their post-baby maternity plan.

"Ignore Them and Carry On"

"'How long are you taking maternity leave?' is the question I am asked most often now. Friends and family see me hustling my bustle before the birth of my second child comes, and this is their question, and their concern.

"The question of 'work' has always been a sensitive topic for me. When I give friends and family the honest answer of 'I don't know . . . maybe two weeks,' I get exasperated when they gasp in horror, and I can see their wheels spinning of how they are going to talk me off the ledge and into 'enjoying this time' and relaxing.

"That is a fair statement and wish, and let me tell you—I do. I enjoy most of my life because of the way I have struc-tured it. That may be hard for people who have full-time jobs to understand. The life and drive of an entrepreneur, be that a service-preneur or product-preneur (I happen to be both), are vastly different from those who do not live this path. An entrepreneur lives with uncertainty from risks taken to make a living. But within that uncertainty, other life goals can be fulfilled, including paying bills and saving for the future.

"I am now finding logic in fibbing about my maternity leave, or just dodging the question by moving to another issue. It's easier than explaining where my approach to work is coming from.

"Professionally, my business partners know that I am available for anything (and that's the benefit of having busi-ness partners who you trust completely). My clients know that their needs will be met, as it's my job to set up a system before my 'maternity leave' that takes care of them even if I'm not able to check e-mail for several hours.

"But my friends and family . . . sigh. Hence the title of this post: 'Ignore Them and Carry On.' Kind of like 'keep calm and carry on' . . . remember, folks, not all 'preneurs have paid maternity leaves, certainly not in the ways that employees do with paid leaves and forced returns back into an office at a certain time each day."[21]

Planning for the Perfect Maternity Leave

Regardless of the form it takes, most women will take some form of maternity leave, so whether it's a full year or just a few months, what can you do to make sure it supports your personal and career goals?

Over the course of my interviews and research, I heard the full range of maternity success stories, many of which completely contradicted each other—proving that you don't have to follow the path of your colleagues or anyone else in order to transition or go back successfully after any amount of maternity leave.

Staying in Touch

Among the questions that raised a great deal of discussion was whether the better strategy was to take a complete break from the office during maternity leave (if that was even an option) or to stay up to date on what was happening by checking in regularly. Of course, many women have no choice but to quickly return to work because they need the paycheck or can't risk losing their job. And waitresses, nannies and teachers, for instance, can't send e-mails from their iPhones and call it "working."

For women who work in an office environment, however, the question of whether to check in during maternity leave, and if so how often and to what extent, can rouse conflicting emotions. When high-profile women willingly forgo their right to a "secluded" maternity leave (being fully left alone during their time away), does it send the message that taking any significant time off is only for the uncommitted? Or is it just that maternity leave is yet another victim of our always-on culture?

Just as the professional woman's vacation time is punctuated with work e-mails, maternity leave is increasingly not lived 100 percent disconnected, either. Some parents resent having to accept this half-on, half-off state.

"There's something so special about those first few weeks at home with an infant—I did check my e-mails daily since I felt it was expected of me, and let's be honest, sitting on the sofa sending a few e-mails with my baby in my lap wasn't a huge deal, but I still resented the invasion of my work life into my post-baby bubble," said New York financial analyst Serena,* mom to a sixteen-month-old.

In certain work environments, a complete maternity leave is an outdated notion, and those in client- and project-related roles pointed out that fully leaving for a long stretch of time opens you to the risk of being overlooked for advancement and losing what you've built.

Name: Carolyn Lawrence
Role: President and CEO, Women of Influence
Children: Jack, 17 months

"I am a planner. In fact, I was in the process of having my eggs frozen, to delay this important decision until the time was right to start a family—and it was right before my hormone injections were to start—when I found out, to my complete surprise, that I was actually pregnant.

"Our mission at Women of Influence (a North America–wide event, media, coaching and consulting company) is to connect women and provide access to female role models in order to help advance women in business. So even as the news about my pregnancy was still sinking in, my mind immediately started thinking, 'I have no idea how I'm going to do this given how hard I work.' But I also knew that I'm in contact daily with successful women who are also mothers and I kept reminding myself that I'm not the first person to do this.

"I started booking lunches almost immediately with other successful entrepreneurs with kids in order to get their advice on what I needed to do to get ready. I lined up child care. I lined up emergency child care. My partner is also an entrepreneur, so we both have a degree of flexibility but we also have all-consuming jobs where very often a decision or response can't wait till later, something I was very conscious of trying to plan for.

"At work, I started to strategically consider how the team could manage without me on a day-to-day basis, reassigning responsibilities and staffing up in certain areas. I wasn't planning on being gone completely or for very long, but I did want to feel like it was all in order. I worked in the office until the last Friday of my pregnancy and then had a C-section that

Monday. I then had one week without my laptop. My plan had been to stay out of the office for a month but to be online and do weekly calls with my managers and then begin coming in once a week. Jack was born in March, and by August, I was back in the office full time.

"The truth is that even with all my planning on the home and business fronts, it wasn't as seamless or as smooth as I'd hoped. Our numbers had slipped without me there day to day and when I returned I had to work really aggressively to get them back to where we needed to be.

"But what I'd never realized or anticipated was how grounded I would feel when I became a mother, and how that would translate to every other part of my life. I feel as ambitious for my business as I ever did—that hasn't changed for me—but what has is that I've expanded the ways in which I'll be able to achieve my goals."

Consider:
› **Consult your network.** When planning your maternity leave, look to speak with role models, colleagues and friends about their experiences with maternity leave (what worked, what didn't, what do they wish they had done and what would they do next time?) Start with women in your organization and industry and then branch out. "My company assigned me a formal mentor to help me plan my maternity leave, which was great, but really the best advice I got was from women in other, competitor organizations, since it gave me some new ideas about how to manage my time away and my return," shared Jenni,* a tax accountant at a global full services firm and mother of six-year-old twins.

Preparing for Maternity Leave: Which Way Are You Leaning?

In the book *Lean In*, Sheryl Sandberg, Facebook's COO, expands on a point she first made in her viral TED talk, "Why We Have Too Few Women Leaders." Specifically, she describes a current cultural phenomenon: as soon as a woman starts thinking about a child, she starts wondering how she will make room for that child, asking herself, "How am I going to fit this into everything else I am doing?"

The result, according to Sandberg, is that she starts "leaning back" in her career before the child is born, or even before she becomes pregnant. "Leaning back" means she stops looking for the next career move, stops raising her hand for new projects, stops putting herself forward for new opportunities.

By subconsciously stepping back in preparation for a baby, Sandberg believes women often undermine themselves early on and simultaneously remove the passion from their careers, making it even harder when the baby is born to go back or continue on.

Of course the "choosing" not to come back to a career that you're not passionate about is a fairly limited option (since it means having the financial ability to completely opt out of paid work).

Perhaps it is not surprising, then, that the women who told me they *had* to work were often the ones to achieve significant post-baby success. They never mentally opted out because they couldn't afford to do so.

Name: Rakhi Henderson
Role: Senior Manager, ING Direct
Children: Zak, 12; Sammi, 10

"I've always worked, part time while I was in school and then, days after my university graduation, I started working full time and just continued on. Maternity leave was the first time that I was actually able to pause and consider what would be the right next step for my career. But staying home was not an option."

Today, Rakhi is Senior Manager of Human Resources for ING Direct, and she was recently selected for their elite two-year rotational program that allows senior managers to learn all aspects of the business from marketing to strategy.

"After Zak was born, I went back to work at Bank of Montreal [her previous employer] after ten months. I was anxious to get back, I was worried about my client portfolio and frankly wanted a full salary again. At the time, I was working downtown but living in the suburbs, so I requested and was approved for a schedule where I would be in the office three days a week and work from home the other two.

"Coming back, I was given a new portfolio, but I found that I was able to learn it quite quickly since my work style had also changed: I was more driven and more focused. I had to be since I had to get home for Zak. I was also more assertive. I started saying no to additional activities in the office that in the past I would have said yes to, everything from planning someone's birthday lunch to supporting projects that didn't really relate to my remit, or where my support would never be noticed or acknowledged. In the past, I would have done the work regardless, just to help out, but now my time was more precious, so I became more strategic with my choices."

Rakhi's first post-baby promotion came about when she heard that several recent hires who were much less experienced were actually being paid more than she was. "I actually found this out very innocently. I was sitting with a group at lunch who were all talking about their 'levels' and I noticed that they were in a higher level grade than me. I was very shocked and upset to hear it, especially since I had the same credentials, was experienced and had been told many times I was rising to better things. I immediately went to my manager, who was quite nervous and just avoided the discussion. I then went to the VP and asked why there was a discrepancy in levels when the job was the same.

"I was angry and upset. Before Zak was born, though, I probably would have left the matter alone until it was time for my annual review, but now the unfairness of it made me feel less afraid about doing something about it."

She built her case, documenting her skills and her successes both before and after her maternity leave. It worked. Five months after she'd returned to work, Rakhi was promoted to another audit area in the bank. Her new role had greater seniority and, with it, more responsibility and freedom. "I loved it and I was able to implement several new processes that led to greater department efficiencies. Then, just as I was feeling like I was on the way up again (fourteen months after Zak was born) I found out I was pregnant again."

During her second maternity leave, which lasted a full year, Rakhi decided to begin looking at and interviewing for "reach positions," roles that were significantly more senior than what she'd been doing.

Her rationale?

"It's much easier to be confident about a job interview when you already have a job lined up to go back to. My job search at that time wasn't about the money but the reality of my situation. With two kids under two, a downtown commute was going to be too difficult to manage, especially in the winter." Rakhi's husband, Mike, couldn't help; his work commute was almost an hour and a half each way in the opposite direction. "One of us had to find work that was closer to the kids." Initially she started looking for another role internally. "But I was also putting the word out to my [external] networks, telling them I was interested in other opportunities."

An old colleague called to tell her about the role at ING. "It was more senior than my previous role, but I quickly applied. When the offer came, it was more money, but most importantly, it was only two kilometers from home." What surprised Rakhi was the discouragement from family and friends when they heard about her taking on a new and more challenging role, right after her second baby.

"People kept reminding me that I had it good with Bank of Montreal and that I would never find such a cushy job now that I had kids. I was shocked at how scared people were at the notion of women finding good jobs after kids and surprised that no one seemed to believe that I *didn't* want to 'coast along.' I really did want interesting work that kept me engaged and learning."

Rakhi admits that a new job with two babies under two was still a big adjustment.

"Life wasn't easy then. I had to do drop-off and pickup at two separate day cares since I couldn't get [my kids] into the same one. I nursed Sammi until she was 18 months old, so I would feed her at 7:30 and then drive over to her day care at my lunch hour and then make sure I was there at six for the next feeding. I was still getting up twice a night with her, so it was exhausting.

"The worst was that during the first presentation I did in my new role, my milk let down just as I started speaking, and I could feel wet patches soaking through my blouse. I spent the next twenty minutes talking with my arms folded across my chest, hoping no one would notice. I'm sure they all wondered why my body language was so standoffish!

"What really helped was that for the first time I had a boss who was also a mother of two little kids. I'd always worked for men with wives who stayed home or single women so it was a relief to have someone who understood what I was going through and where I felt I could be a bit more honest than in the past about challenges I was facing on the home or kid front."

Consider:

> **Find your support network.** In an ideal world, the people closest to us would also be our career champions and provide us with a community of support. But if for whatever reason they can't or won't, then it's time to create your own support network. "Last year I decided to go back to school and do my MBA. It's not that my husband isn't supportive but, like my close friends and family, he doesn't quite understand, I think, why I'm doing this right now," said Erin,* a Michigan-area nurse and mother of three. "At first, I was really uncomfortable at school, and none of the nurses I worked with wanted to hear about my new career plan, so I was feeling isolated in my ambitions until I started going online and looking for help. I've found some great support in a Facebook group for moms doing MBAs. It's not the same as having your family or partner be with you all the way, but in some ways it's actually better, since we all share and learn from each other and I don't feel like I have to temper down what I hope to do when I'm done."

Hopping the Maternal Wall: Job Hunting on Maternity Leave

Earlier in the project, I wrote a blog post on the phenomenon of women looking for jobs while on maternity leave. I thought it was a fairly interesting but non-controversial post.

I was wrong.

Instead, I got a slew of venomous comments in response. Some were probably just the usual angry Internet trolls, but for others the idea of new moms using their maternity leave to find another role was genuinely offensive. For some it was the perceived unfairness of women getting a "paid" opportunity to find a new job, but for the majority the idea that a woman on maternity leave was trying to be strategic about her career was disturbing to their notions of motherhood. As one woman, whose perspective represented the tone of the majority of comments, wrote, "It makes me sick to think that instead of bonding with their precious newborn, the women you spoke with were polishing up their CVs." But as Rakhi Henderson told me, "Looking for a job on maternity leave is less dramatic than people make it out to be! Babies sleep and sending out some e-mails and doing some calls isn't quite neglect!"

But again, it speaks to the difficulty of being able to pursue what is right for your individual career and family—in spite of the larger expectations or norms surrounding motherhood. Although it might not be considered appropriate "new mom" behavior, Jennifer Berdahl, an expert in social power and status in organizations at the University of Toronto's Rotman School of Management, says job-hopping while on leave "could be a very rational reaction to the bias women often experience on the job after they return to work after a maternity leave."[22]

As Berdahl points out, research has shown that women often get tagged with the "mommy identity," and are less likely to get promoted or receive a raise after the birth of a child, "even holding constant their work hours, professional accomplishments and productivity." But starting fresh with a new employer, she says, has been identified as one way to avoid this bias, which is sometimes referred to as the "maternal wall."

"When women begin a new job after they have already become mothers, they are more likely to be seen as a valued new hire and recruit, and the fact that they are mothers . . . is just one of many background characteristics they were hired with, not a new and featured identity they have in that work environment."

Among women I interviewed in creative industries or those with a "youth" bias, maternal branding was a real issue. Helen,* an account director at an online branding agency in New York cites this as her reason for leaving her last agency. "I had been with them for about three years when I got pregnant with my daughter (now two years old). I came back after a six-month maternity leave, during which I kept up with clients and the office by checking e-mails regularly (even though I wasn't the lead responder) and coming in about once a month. But when I came back, I felt like something had changed. My ideas were regularly overlooked, clients were shifted out of my portfolio; it was subtle at first and then suddenly it wasn't anymore. I left and took a more senior role with one of my former clients. And although I talked about what happened with some female colleagues in the industry, I would never do anything formal about it. The industry is too small for that—and I'm happy where I've ended up."

Taking a Long-Term Perspective

Many of the women I spoke with used their maternity-leave time to take classes or to research and lay the foundation for what would become a new business or other venture. For others, the leave was an opportunity to reflect on what this next life stage would mean to them both personally and professionally.

Name: Angela Mitchell
Role: Partner, Risk Consulting KPMG
Children: Claire, 9; Chloe, 5

After returning from her first maternity leave, Angela Mitchell went from managing a group of three to a group of more than twenty. After she returned from her second maternity leave, Angela became an associate partner at the Toronto offices of the international auditing firm KPMG. Four years later she became a partner.

Each of these promotions came after she'd been away for a full year of maternity leave.

Unlike many of her colleagues, maternity leave was not the first time Angela had taken a scheduled pause from her career track. Five years after joining KPMG, she had taken advantage of the firm's work/life balance policy to spend five months in Barcelona with her husband. Angela purposely used time away from the office to recharge, refocus and affirm her priorities, and particularly during her maternity leaves, she considered her time well spent.

"I used that time to become really clear about who I wanted to be as a mother, as a wife and as a professional so that when I came back to work, I didn't feel conflicted about any of my roles." She credits this personal assessment for her post-baby career success.

"It's not that I never feel guilty, but that I have real clarity about the different roles and priorities in my life. I know why I'm doing what I'm doing and I believe this helps me to successfully manage the pull from the various areas of my life versus feeling like they are in conflict. As a result, I'm not afraid of setting boundaries with both colleagues and clients. I have a window each evening where I'm not available, and that's my time with my family.

"Family and career is not an either/or choice; it's about thinking long term and being clear about all your priorities and how you will balance them."

Consider:

› **Be deliberate with time away from your job.** Using maternity leave for professional advancement is controversial to many women I spoke with but can have practical and strategic benefits. If you're lucky enough to have a significant amount of maternity leave, once things settle on the home front (and they do eventually!) consider your career goals and what you can do during this time to advance them—if that feels right to you.

› **Reach out.** Maternity leave and the birth of a new baby can be a great time to expand and reinvest in your professional networks. A few months in, plan lunches and coffee meetings (even with the baby) with both current colleagues, those in other departments you're interested in and with past colleagues you always mean to see more of. Because you never know . . .

Announcing Your Maternity Leave: The Bellwether

For many of the women I interviewed, the reaction and response to announcing their pregnancy was a foreshadowing of what they could expect in terms of how their motherhood would be viewed and treated by their colleagues, managers and workplaces.

It used to be that the issue of maternity was considered fair game in interviews with women. If a woman openly planned on becoming pregnant, she might not be hired.

For instance, in an interview, Shirley Hoy, the longest-serving city manager in Toronto, recalled how when interviewing for a promotion with the city in the 1980s she was asked by the panel if she planned to have a family, because if so, that would be "disruptive" to her career.

"I think at the time I said that this is not an area that would determine my competency and they need to assess if I've demonstrated I can do the job," said Hoy. She didn't get the job and around that time, she and her then-husband made the decision not to have children.[23]

In Canada, a woman has no legal obligation to disclose a pregnancy, whether or not she is up for a promotion or a new job. Similarly, in the U.S., federal and state laws specify that an employer can't make decisions based on certain protected characteristics—one of which is pregnancy.

Yet keeping the news quiet for fear of a negative response is generally considered a poor strategy. If you think your employers are likely to discriminate against you because you are pregnant, you should probably assume that the situation will be exacerbated when they find out that you didn't share the news.

In *Lean In*, Sheryl Sandberg recounts how she once took a calculated risk and asked a prospective employee whether she was considering having children soon: "I understood that doing so could expose me and my company to legal risk . . . But I have also witnessed first-hand how they [discrimination laws] can have a chilling effect on discourse, sometimes even to the detriment of the people they are designed to defend."[24]

Despite legal protections, maternity discrimination remains a very real problem. For instance, despite strong legislation, one recent U.K. survey found that one in ten women were nevertheless replaced by their maternity leave covers, and the jobs of two in every five maternity returnees had changed when they went back to work—in almost half of these cases (45.5 percent) the change was for the worse.[25]

Name: Sandra Fathi
Role: President and Founder, Affect (a PR and social
           media firm)
Children: Danielle, 13; Jordan, 8

Almost anyone who's ever worked for someone else has probably had one of those days or weeks where you think, "Forget this, I wish I could just quit right now, go out on my own and start my own business." Six months after 9/11, when her daughter was just eighteen months old, Sandra Fathi went into her job one Monday and did just that.

"I called my husband from my desk and told him that I was going to quit and I didn't have a backup plan. But coming in that morning, I felt like I couldn't spend another day in an office where being a mother was something that I constantly needed to hide or compensate for." Sandra had discovered for herself that, regardless of employment law, what's in an organization's HR handbook or on its recruiting website, the reality of office culture, especially for working mothers, comes down to the unwritten rules and the environment created by colleagues and bosses. And it was watching the way her female colleagues on their maternity leave were treated that led Sandra to make the big jump.

Sandra had watched as two new mothers in her office, both established and strong employees, had been fired within the space of months. This, combined with her own still-fresh experience of being penalized for taking a three-month maternity leave (at a different company) after the birth of her first child, inspired her to make the change to start a business that subsequently became Affect.

Today, Sandra leads a team of twenty full-time employees with clients in technology, healthcare and professional services. Her agency is part of the Global Reach PR network with over thirty-five partner offices in fifty countries. But that Monday in

2002, she hadn't yet thought of any of this. Her motivation for leaving was simple: "I just wanted to be able to control my work culture and to create an environment where being a parent was a point of respect, something I had never personally experienced."

Sandra began her career in Israel as a reporter for the magazine *People & Computers* and later led marketing for several technology companies. After she and her husband, an actuary, moved to Dallas, Texas, Sandra made the career transition to public relations and joined the technology group of a global PR firm. "It was an exciting time to be in tech PR and I was working with clients like Ericsson and Microsoft and was more than happy to work the long days and nights that often went with the job.

"It was only when I got pregnant about a year and a half after I'd started that I noticed that our group at work had virtually no working mothers. My direct boss and most of my female colleagues were single. There were other women in the company with families, but they and their children were much older. With no relevant role models around me, I just did my best to hide my pregnancy and to avoid talking about it." This became increasingly difficult as the weeks and months went by. "I had a difficult pregnancy and was very sick, but I just kept going. I remember a client meeting where I literally had to run out in the middle of a presentation, throw up violently in the ladies' room and come back to complete the meeting as if nothing had happened."

Despite the difficulties, Sandra loved her job and her client work was going well. "I'd delivered some strong results and had regular positive feedback from clients and senior management, so I was looking forward to my annual review that year and wanted to make sure I had it before I went on maternity leave." But despite Sandra's repeated attempts to schedule the meeting, the review kept getting delayed.

Finally, time ran out and Sandra left to have her baby.

Three months later, right on schedule, she was back at work full time. With her mother-in-law living with Sandra's family for six months, she wasn't even worried about having to work evenings.

"Now my boss and the other managers were ready to have my review and so we met in my second week back. This was when they told me that despite the success of my work and excellent client relations, the fact that I'd been out of the office for three months meant that I wouldn't be getting either a raise or a promotion. They suggested that it wouldn't look right if I was promoted after being out of the office for so long. I was even told that I should have been more involved in work while I was on maternity leave, following the example that was set by a vice president in another division at the time who had even continued working from her hospital bed after giving birth.

"I was stunned. The fact that they made the twelve weeks I was gone seem like I was on an extended vacation, and not that I had left only because I was having a baby, made me wonder what I was doing there." Sandra's career frustration combined with the desire to be closer to more family prompted another move. Six months after their daughter was born, she and her husband were back in New York. Within months, Sandra had found another high-tech PR and marketing job in a different global firm. "Ironically, when I came on board, two other women in the group were leaving to go on maternity leave. In fact, I was hired to replace one of the women, who was planning to return to work on a part-time basis."

In the first month of maternity leave, one of the women was laid off. The new mother who had just planned to come back to a reduced schedule was let go two weeks before she was supposed to come back to work.

"I began to hate going in to work." Sandra recalls.

(Although a global firm, the particular office in which Sandra worked had fewer than fifty employees and so was able to use a loophole in the FMLA to avoid legal repercussion for their actions.)

Then 9/11 happened, and for Sandra, doing a job that devalued her family was no longer an option. "It was April 2002 when I started what was to become Affect. It was right in the middle of the post-9/11 economy, when so many businesses in New York were struggling." Sandra's former employer became her first client, contracting her to finish the work that she had been doing when she left.

"At first, my employer was upset that I was leaving. But when I suggested that he could cut costs by using me as a freelancer on a part-time basis, he came around quickly. It was a great 'soft landing' for me as a newly independent consultant, and it gave him a way to still get the results he wanted without paying benefits or having to train a new person."

After a decade in the industry, Sandra had a list of other contacts that she began reaching out to. "My first step was to activate my professional network. Anyone I had worked with or for in the last ten years received a call or e-mail from me letting them know that I was out on my own and would be happy to collaborate with them or provide freelance project support.

"From the first day after I quit, I treated my new unemployed status as a 'job.' This meant I never took my daughter out of day care or looked to save money by reducing her hours, since I planned to continue working full time."

As the workload increased, Sandra began hiring former colleagues as freelancers, many of whom were new mothers looking to stay involved with their old professional selves but have more flexibility.

By August 2002, just four months after quitting her job, Sandra had enough regular client work to hire her first full-time employee.

"I was in marketing, so I immediately understood the need for lead generation. I created a website and a company newsletter, wrote bylined articles, issued press releases and began networking and speaking in professional forums."

That day, when Sandra left her job, she had been relying on the fact that her husband's stable income would tide them over while she built a new career and business for herself. Then, three months later, he was laid off from his job in the financial sector.

"The unexpected financial hardship completely eliminated any semblance of security we had. The fear of being two unemployed parents with a mortgage, car payments and a child in day care drove me to work harder in that first year than I ever worked in any other job. In many ways, that was probably what made the company grow so quickly and successfully."

Three years after she had started her business, Sandra became pregnant with her second child. This time, though, she was prepared. "I knew what to expect. I planned with my team for the reality that I might be sick quite often and have to work from home a great deal.

"Emotionally my second pregnancy was much easier. I had an incredible level of control and I didn't need to worry about what other people thought. But it was also physically harder. Being self-employed meant that I was back at work two weeks after my son was born. This time there was no maternity leave."

Balancing the demands of her growing business and family remains a challenge. "Right now we're at the juncture where I know what I need to do to grow the business to the next level, but I'm deliberately delaying until my kids are a bit older.

"Eleven years after I started, a driving force for me is still creating a work culture where employees really see that balancing an outside life, whether for family or other interests, is something that we support and genuinely respect. I've actually turned away clients that I feel might compromise this commitment.

"Looking back, I do think that like many young professional women, I was blindsided by what happened when I was pregnant. I'd never considered what to look for in a work environment or how to successfully manage my professional ambitions with changing needs and priorities. I think that if we want more women to professionally succeed after having children, we need to prepare them for that life phase as part of their professional education, something that they think about before they actually need it. Before I had my daughter, I never scrutinized an employer or an employment opportunity based on the treatment of women and more importantly mothers in the workplace. Although I had the strength and opportunity to leave my employer, not every woman is able to follow that path. Working women not only need to demand more from their employers, they need to know that they deserve it. It's not that being a mother requires concessions at work; it's about having an employer that values and respects who you are as a human being and provides you with the environment and tools that you need in order to be successful in the workplace."

The Business of Breast-Feeding

The societal and medical push to get women to breast-feed has been gaining ground. In 1980, the rate of women who breast-fed "at least some period of time" was 54 percent—by 2004, it was up to 75 percent.[26] I'll admit that I never breast-fed any of my kids, and I have to say I was in awe of some of the stories I heard of women balancing work demands with their commitment to breast-feed, from stories of responding to e-mails while attached to a hands-free pump, shipping milk overnight while on business trips, or racing to day cares or to meet nannies to keep to a feeding schedule.

Many pediatricians recommend that babies be breast-fed for the first six months of life, with the American Association of Pediatrics encouraging breast-feeding for one year. The World Health Organization recommends that women continue breast-feeding to complement other foods until the baby is two. While the breast-feeding literature often references the cost savings of breast versus formula, new research suggests that breast-feeding actually does come with its own cost: a long-term negative impact on a mother's earnings.

According to the study, published in the April issue of the journal *American Sociological Review*, women who breast-feed for longer than six months see a steeper decline in their earnings in the first year of baby's life than women who breast-feed for a shorter period or who formula-feed. (Note: I was unable to find data on whether or how this study would apply in countries like Canada where a year of maternity leave is possible. However, common sense would suggest that the financial impact should be significantly less.) The earnings gap persists for at least five years after the baby is born.

The study used data from the National Longitudinal Survey of Youth, a long-term survey that included interviews with American women from 1979 to 1994. The researchers took data from 1,313 women who had their first child between 1980 and 1993, were employed before having their baby and didn't have multiple births.

The results of steep earning declines in long-duration breast-feeders held even after controlling for factors such as age, immigration status, race, region of the country, education, marital status and number of subsequent kids.

The researchers' analysis compared changes among women, so it's not easy to give a simple percentage of income lost by feeding choice.

The primary reason given for the earning discrepancy was that, over time, breast-feeding moms worked less, although the study didn't discuss why this was the case—whether moms who plan to breast-feed long term might also plan to leave the workforce from the beginning, or whether moms who breast-feed long-term find their workplaces unsupportive and either choose to leave or get pushed out. Not all that surprisingly then, the study also found that the husbands of women who chose to breast-feed longer were higher earners than husbands of non-breast-feeders.

(From: "The Hidden Cost of Breast Feeding Revealed," by Stephanie Pappas, *Live Science*, April 26, 2012, http://www.livescience.com/19934-hidden-cost-breast-feeding.html)

Ramping Up versus Temporarily (but Strategically) Treading Water

Throughout my interviews, I also heard many stories of mothers who deliberately chose to take on roles post-baby that they were overqualified for, or to stay put where they were as a strategic (and usually temporary) way to navigate an especially trying or difficult life phase—like getting used to life with a new baby or expanded family.

Research shows that over 16 percent of highly qualified women have declined a promotion as a way to manage work and family, and another 38 percent say they have deliberately chosen a position with fewer responsibilities and lower compensation than they were qualified for, in order to fulfill responsibilities at home.[27]

This included the strategy of trying to stay "below the radar" so they weren't put in the position of having the stigma of having to decline a promotion.

One working mom of three, a brand manager for a large services company in London, put it this way: "I can do my job in my sleep, which means I'm not stressed, I can leave on time and I never have to take work home. Is it ideal? No, but it lets me keep my hand in the work world, make some decent money and still manage the kids. My plan is to ramp up to something more challenging when the kids are older."

Consumer-goods manufacturer Unilever is one example of the private sector's deliberate efforts to accommodate the reality that successful careers don't necessarily have to be defined by a relentless race up the ladder. Instead, Unilever is proactively encouraging women (and men) to make the career choices they feel comfortable with, rather than choosing the career options they feel pressured to want or accept.

"Previously, women in marketing often felt the pressure to move 'up or out.' Instead, we are now adopting a more flexible approach, which lets talented women move at their own pace and makes it OK to just stay at a certain level," says Alison Leung, a mother of two and Director of Marketing, Foods, at Unilever Canada (a position she reached after starting her own family). "In the days after we announced this policy, I received a call from a woman in another department who told me how relieved she was. She had recently been offered a promotion that she felt she couldn't take for personal reasons but she had been so stressed about letting her mentors and manager down on this front that she had been considering just leaving."

What Sheryl Sandberg refers to as leaning back, the Wharton Business School describes as "plateauing"—a growing lack of appetite for the corporate climb—but what is missed in this discussion is that choosing to pause on the "climb" doesn't necessarily mean that the individual won't be interested in continuing when the time feels right.

Name: Zabeen Hirji
Role: Chief Human Resources, The Royal Bank of
           Canada
Children: Two teenagers: a daughter and son

"I would like to debunk the myth that a woman's career has to suffer over the long term just because her trajectory might change after children.

"I have two stories to tell.

"The first is that while on my first maternity leave in my mid-thirties, I was offered a significant promotion. This was a role in a business I hadn't previously worked in, to be the Regional Manager for our credit card operations in Central Canada. The role was pretty senior (it was one level below vice-president). By all accounts, this was a 'stretch move' that would take me out of my comfort zone. In fact, I was the first person to go into such a role with no prior experience in the credit card business. I accepted the role, but I also had the courage to ask if I could delay the start date to a few months after my return to work from my four-month maternity leave. I felt that I needed the time to adjust to being a mother with a busy career and once I'd done that, I would transition into the new role. Since the person I was replacing was retiring, he was able to delay his departure date and I was able to stagger my return to work and the new role.

"Fast-forward two years and I was on my second maternity leave. This time I planned to take a year off. Unfortunately, some issues arose at work, and my boss asked me to consider returning earlier. While there wasn't undue pressure, I felt a strong sense of loyalty to RBC and to my boss who had been very supportive. So I agreed to come back after six months. A few months later I was offered the role of vice president in our technology group. I had some tough choices to make, so I prepared my balance sheet to help me decide. The pros were I would learn about a new area (technology); it was a significant promotion (i.e., vice president, and at a pretty young age); and I would be able to leverage my knowledge and experience in the credit card business and operations.

The cons were I couldn't get excited enough about the work; and more importantly the timing wasn't right for me to take on a new role that would require more time and energy, as I now had two children under the age of three. The risk-reward equation didn't work for me and so I turned down the promotion.

"A year later (in 1997), I was offered a vice president role in human resources and this time the choice was much easier. I would learn about a new area, it was a significant promotion and I was very excited about the role and the work. As well, having worked in so many different parts of the organization, I really felt I could make a difference. Personally I was ready to take on more—my husband and I were in a better routine at home, and I had kind of figured out how to integrate my work and life without feeling a sense of guilt. What's interesting is I subsequently turned down a promotion to a Senior Vice President role in one of our businesses because I had made the decision that I wanted to remain in human resources. I took on more and more responsibilities, and was appointed Senior Vice President in 2001, and in 2007 I was appointed as the Chief Human Resources Officer and joined the bank's senior management committee in 2009.

"Success is about choices—having choices and making choices. I encourage women (and men) to broaden their experiences early in their careers, so that they have a strong portfolio of skills and experiences before they have children. In my case it meant taking lateral moves, and in fact I even took roles at lower levels, just so that I could learn about new areas and have more choices in the future.

"I also caution people against fixating on a singular definition of career success, or of measuring yourself against someone else's yardstick. You be the judge of your own success. For me, this meant I also had to be clear about how I would measure my success as a mother. I reprioritized things at home; for example, things no longer needed to be perfectly organized, and I sought outside help for whatever I could afford to.

"We made some unconventional choices. For instance, we decided not to over-program our children with extracurricular activities. Why? So we could spend quality time together on weekends. My husband and I gave up much of our social lives; we pretty much only did things that included our children. Would this work for everyone? Probably not, but it worked for us. We are still very close as a family and I think the significant time we spent together contributed to that

"My leadership approach has changed as a re~   ~eing a mother—I am more flexible, more op~   ~verse ways of thinking and solving problems ~   ~re understanding and empathetic about the ~   ~nges my colleagues and staff face with ~   ~as to work/life integration. I recently asked my daughter for her perspective. She told me that there were times when she was in elementary school that she wished I was like the other mothers (going on all the field trips, picking her up from school, putting homemade cookies in her lunches, etc.). However, now she is glad that I had a busy career because she is so much more independent and has learned to make her own decisions. As for me, I'm glad I chose to pursue my career while raising our children, and by and large I think I made the right trade-offs. What I did give up, though, was time for myself. There are always some sacrifices to be made."

Temporarily and deliberately choosing to "plateau" can be a legitimate and strategic way to both stay in the game and adjust to any parenting challenges that might be going on at any given time.

After all, careers have an increasingly longer span and one decision no longer defines their full narrative or success. Consider that in 2006, when Sheryl Sandberg was 37 and had been at Google for five years, she turned down LinkedIn founder Reid Hoffman who was offering her the chance to be the CEO of LinkedIn. While she wanted a more challenging role, she also wanted to have another child and so she passed on the job.

Name: Rachael Ferenbok

Role: Legal Counsel, Office of the Vice President, Research, Innovations and Partnerships, University of Toronto

Children: Gabrielle, 5; Sam, 3

"My decision to return to work after my first maternity leave was in part financial but also in part because an extended absence from the workforce would likely render me unmarketable in the future."

While previously Rachael was a lawyer at a large global firm, she decided that wouldn't be the right place for her after she had her children.

"With a young family under foot, I was absolutely certain that I would not be able to balance or manage the unpredictability of children and a demanding job.

"In 2008, my daughter was a year old and I started looking for a position that could potentially meet my needs. It took me a couple of months to find my current position and over the last five years (and another baby later), it has been near perfection. I am very lucky, though, because my boss is great and trusts me completely to do my job. As well, the University of Toronto has progressive policies in place that encourage work/life balance and contemplate alternate work arrangements.

"My position is unique because I do not manage people and my 'clients' are physically located in a different building. These factors allowed me to negotiate working off-site two days a week. On those days, I forward my work phone to my home and always have e-mail access. I can log into my work computer from home as well. Modern technology along with the right workplace has made the arrangement successful and allows me to stay closely connected to my family, my home and my community.

"I believe there are some great options for mothers who are seeking a balanced family/work life, but looking in the right places and with an open mind is key.

"I advise women who ask me about balancing careers and young families to decide what would make them happiest over the next few years rather than career aspirations over the next few decades. A position that can accommodate the family schedule is a great opportunity, in my view. Over time, I will make decisions more heavily weighted on my own career aspirations (whatever they may be) but it will likely involve staying within the University of Toronto. The university offers great challenges and a spectrum of career opportunities—and tuition for my kids is an added bonus!

"I do not feel frustrated or benched in comparison to my former colleagues who have become law firm partners, because there is simply no comparison to be made between a legal position within the broader public sector and a law firm partner. In any event, a meaningful comparison requires a consistent definition and measure of success."

For Rae Ann Fera (see page 193 for her full story), returning to a job that she knew inside out just made sense after the birth of her first daughter. At the time she was the editor of *Boards*, an advertising trade magazine, and it was a position that she had held for almost nine years. "When I decided to return to work, I relished going back to a job that I knew I could do with my eyes closed—since as a new mom, I was pretty sure I couldn't parent with my eyes closed."

Critics argue that if women had better support systems (both at work and at home) these types of decisions or trade-offs wouldn't be necessary. Some certainly wouldn't have made the decisions to delay a promotion or stay in a comfortable but less challenging role but many others might—and this needs to be acknowledged as a legitimate choice.

As so many of these stories illustrate, having a successful and fulfilling career actually doesn't require a relentless devotion to "moving forward," constantly "leaning in," and instead recognize that it's also OK to just stay put, scale back or combine some variant of the two. Staying in a role that is comfortable while navigating early motherhood or other family or personal demands is also a reasonable strategy for continuing to earn a paycheck while balancing life on the home or personal front. Today, 80 percent of families in the U.S. no longer fit the male-as-sole-breadwinner mold. Instead, more than half of American women are their family's breadwinners.[28]

While the media tends to frame the issue of working or staying at home as an either/or choice for women, the reality is that with today's costs and economic uncertainties, few women (or men) really have that option. "From a career progression perspective, I can hear the career counselor in my head saying I should be applying for a promotion within my organization or looking for a new job—I know that," said Tanya,* a project manager at a mid-size environmental nonprofit in Vancouver. "But the truth is, this role pays well and it doesn't stress me out. I'm a single mom, so I feel like I really have to balance out what gives me the best financial return with the ability to enjoy my family and manage my home life. Others might not see that as a success, but for me, it is. I like what I do, am still building my career, just at a different pace than I might have otherwise, and I get to be a less stressed mom for my kids."

Are We Too Focused on Maternity Leave?
In discussions on work/life balance or female talent retention, maternity or parental leave tends to take center stage.

Since maternity leave is the big and often unknown jump into the world of motherhood and all it involves, it's understandable that there is a high level of focus on what and how the transition is managed. But is it possible that we are too focused on maternity leave? Among my interviews with women who had older children, this theme regularly resurfaced.

Karen,* a mother of two teenage daughters, and a research lawyer in Boston, had these thoughts: "Yes, newborns and little children are challenging, but these are the stages where quality child care can really fill the gaps. Babies need to be held, fed and changed and it is possible to outsource that well. What this debate hasn't evolved to reflect is that you really *can't* do that with teenagers. This is when they are making the big life choices and need parents to help them or at least be around to try. When my 14-year-old daughter had some personal issues last year, my husband and I both had to take unpaid leaves of absence to navigate them with her. Both our employers let us do this but I can't say they were incredibly supportive—the way they would have been if it was for a younger child."

Increasingly, it seems that where the focus needs to be is on finding more flexible work options that allow men and women to juggle all the stages of parenting and family care—especially with regards to elder care.

"How are we going to remain competitive when we aren't paying attention to the fact that we have a huge number in the most productive stage of the career cycle having to deal with kids, elder care, demanding jobs and unrelenting e-mail?" says Linda Duxbury, co-author with Christopher Higgins of *Balancing Work, Childcare and Eldercare*, a study that surveyed over 25,000 professionals, knowledge workers and managers.[29]

Among the findings were that women are twice as likely as men to be working and "sandwiched" between raising kids and caring for aging parents, and three times as likely to be providing elder care alone. But significantly, a big shift is occurring among "Generation X" men, who are equally involved as caregivers and in some ways feel the stress and emotional strain more acutely than the generation before.

Elder care is the work/life balance issue that child care was thirty-five years ago, when employers finally realized that "family-friendly" policies, from compressed workweeks to flexible schedules, were needed to attract and keep employees. The difference is that the elder care issue has a much broader reach since, as Duxbury frames it, "People can choose to have children but they can't choose whether or not to have parents."

Paternity Leave

"If you want to change the impact that potential maternity has on how women are viewed, then you almost have to go down the Scandinavian pathway,[†] which is to legislate that parental leave has to be split between both partners," says Beatrix Dart, associate dean of the Rotman School and executive director of the Rotman Women's Initiative.

"Gender imbalance in the workplace can only be solved through drastic measures. Until then, women will always be seen as primarily

---

[†] In 1980, only 5 percent of Swedish fathers took parental leave. Andrea Doucet, a Brock University professor who holds the Canada Research Chair in Gender, Work and Care, pointed out in a recent op-ed for *The New York Times* that "[Ten] years later, it was just 7 percent. It was only when nontransferable and well-paid leave for fathers (also referred to as the 'daddy month') was introduced in 1996 that uptake quickly rose to 77 percent. A second 'daddy month' was implemented in 2002 and the numbers have risen to above 90 percent."

responsible for taking care of children. Whether you like it or not, [there is] a bias or a stereotype in [employers'] minds: I wonder if she'll get pregnant? If you make it mandatory that parental leave is split, that question is gone," said Dart.[30]

Globally, paternity benefits vary widely. For instance: American fathers who qualify are eligible to take twelve weeks *unpaid* leave through the FMLA. There is no federal paid parental leave program in the U.S., and just 17 percent of employers provide paternity leave with pay, according to a 2010 benefits survey from the Society for Human Resource Management. In the U.K., as of April 2011, new fathers are eligible for six months of paternity leave; however, a survey of 1,500 dads done by the think tank Demos found that only one in ten men would take more than two weeks.[31] The primary reason cited was that paternity leave covers less than a quarter of their salary. Australian fathers can share up to fifty-two weeks of unpaid leave with their partners. And in Canada, both new parents have the right to take parental leave of up to thirty-five or thirty-seven weeks of unpaid time off work.

Legal entitlement to paternity leave is the first step—changing cultural norms is the next challenge. Currently, the number of fathers using formal paternity or parental leave benefits remains low. A study done by the Boston College Center for Work and Family, *The New Dad: Caring, Committed and Conflicted*, asked fathers how much time away from work they had taken after the birth of their most recent child. More that three-quarters of fathers in the study took off one week or less and only one in one hundred took more than four weeks off.

The association between the parental leave and a person's perceived commitment to his or her career remains powerful. Consider the public commentary and uproar that occurred when Colby Lewis of the Texas Rangers took a game off to be present at the birth of his daughter. His commitment to his work, level of focus and loyalty to his team came into question, for simply stepping out of the rotation to be with his family for this one occasion.[32] Rob Williams, chief executive of the Fatherhood Institute, a national think tank in the U.K., says, "There is a stigma around men taking time out to care for their children. We do think that when a man asks for any time off to spend it with his family he is almost coming out as not a committed career man.

"He risks looking less reliable than his colleagues. The reason men don't take time off now is partly regulation and partly financial. It is much easier for a woman to ask for flexible work than a man. You can change the structure of leave but you can still have that cultural block."

Of my interviewees' partners who were not engaged in the primary caregiving role or who didn't have careers that could flexibly accommodate an altered schedule, fewer than 20 percent had taken a formal paternity leave. Instead, most of the fathers I spoke with, particularly those in professional, corporate or organizational roles said they felt most comfortable using vacation time to carve out regular pockets of time at home.

Similarly, my husband, Rana, never took an official paternity leave—he was never really offered one. When we had our first son, he was running a media company in London; with the second and third, a nonprofit in Toronto. The nature of those roles meant that although he couldn't take full time off, he was able to control his time and schedule—working flexibly and remotely. It was an arrangement that I think worked better for both of us than just a few focused weeks, since it made it possible for us to move closer to being genuine co-parents. Greater flexibility like this is perhaps a more sustainable model than the existing focus on an intense period of maternity or paternity leave.

Dan Leighton, author of the Demos Report, *Reinventing the Workplace,* believes that increasingly, flexible working will emerge as the only real option to address the social challenges of shared parenting as well as an aging population, since "as it stands, parental leave is expensive for the employee, the employer and the state."

THREE

Reinvention

Few life events have the power to alter our sense of self so profoundly as becoming a mother.

Until then, although we play a variety of different roles in our community, peer group and family, our identity is primarily influenced by our career, work and aspirations.

Motherhood can throw that clear sense of who we are and what we are about into a total state of flux. Stacey, a mother of three and creative director for a clothing brand put it to me this way: "Even if you wanted to be pregnant and, like me, were actively trying for some time, motherhood is such a change that I think you should consciously allow yourself to mourn the end of the person you were so you can then shift into the person you will become."

She's right.

For a generation of women that has spent so much time cultivating, developing and investing in who we are and who we want to be, the idea of losing control of our identity can be upsetting.

However, it can also be incredibly empowering to have the chance to create or cultivate entirely new aspects of our identity as part of this life change. Rebecca Woolf is an author, businesswoman and founder of the hugely popular blog *Girls Gone Child*, where she chronicles that identity shift with a positive perspective that at times feels almost subversive—given how accustomed we've become to a focus on all the negatives associated with motherhood. Rebecca is now 30 years old and the mother of four.

"Motherhood helped me define myself. I was younger than (I thought!) I wanted to be when I got pregnant and I was told by most that having a baby would end my writing career, would rob me of my twenties and life as I knew it. But parenthood made me ambitious. Made my husband ambitious. Suddenly we HAD to get out of bed in the morning. We HAD to work and to make it happen for ourselves because someone else was depending on us! A little human was completely reliant on me and I had to deliver! I had to take care of him, you know? Whereas in the past, it was just me . . .

"I am a better woman because of my kids. I'm a better wife. I'm a better writer and business person and friend. I am stronger and more ambitious and far more ME than I ever thought I'd be," she tells me.

Maternity and Reinvention

Having children often prompts, if not a complete career evaluation, then at least the desire to reflect on who we are, where we are and what we are doing in both our professional and personal lives. Some women do this deliberately; for others, it sneaks up more gradually. The reassessment can be the result of practical needs, such as looking for new options to manage child care and work or increased financial demands, or it can be prompted by their new parental responsibilities, leading them to change how they see themselves and their choices, and perhaps to reconsider whether the career path that they may have chosen several years before actually reflects their current goals and values.

My Story: An Accidental but Much-Needed Reinvention

I always viewed my career as an essential part of my identity, even when I was struggling to figure out who I was and what I wanted to do. And yet it wasn't until I became a mother that I managed to give my career the focus it needed to actually come together. Before my first son was born, I had made all kinds of classic yet oh-so-obvious professional mistakes. For some reason, I didn't seem to think that my *real* career had started yet—it was somewhere in the future, waiting to happen, and in the interim, none of this actually *counted*.

Having a child completely shifted that skewed perspective and it changed how I saw and presented myself professionally. Time took on a new meaning—there is no better marker for the passage of time than having a child ticking through developmental milestones. Seeing my son grow and change really brought home to me that there was no magical future where I was going to finally become an adult and do the things I wanted, but that it was about *now*.

Day-to-day time management also shifted for me. I had to work faster and more efficiently because of day-care pickup times, bath times and bedtimes; and for the first time since I'd left home, I no longer felt that a bowl of cereal and some chips could be counted as dinner (for the record, now that we have three kids, dinner for them is often cereal—but with scrambled eggs and fruit on the side).

In all, having a child made me finally grow up, and with that came many professional and career benefits. My experience certainly wasn't unique—this theme was echoed in so many of my interviews:

"I never anticipated that becoming a mother would help me professionally, but it did. I've always looked much younger than I am and often had a hard time getting taken seriously by our older board members and clients. I don't know if I changed after my daughter was born or they just changed how they saw me, but I felt like I suddenly had far more authority and respect around the office."
—Carol, Financial Services Analyst (James, 8, Cindy, 6)

"I found becoming a mother changed how I carried myself professionally. I always used to be really worried about whether or not people at work liked me, but after my son was born, this seemed to matter less. I wanted them to respect me and my work but cared much less about how 'popular' I was at work."
—Denise, HR Manager (Jodi, 10, Jane, 7)

"When I had my first child, it was like I was suddenly no longer the fun 'girl' in the office, and at first, that was hard for me—until I realized how that old persona had been undermining my professional reputation all this time."
—Samantha, PR Account Director (Chloe, 6)

Forced Reinvention

Undergoing an identity crisis comes with the territory for most new mothers, says Jacqui Marson, a psychologist specializing in motherhood issues. "In my research, the overwhelming majority of women say having children is the best thing they have ever done, but that no one warned them about the profound sense of loss of who you are that comes with it."[33] Motherhood not only changes how you see yourself but also how others see you—and not always in a positive way. For women in the public eye or those whose careers are built on them being seen as trendy or "cool," reconciling those traits with society's entrenched perception of what a mother should be can present an additional challenge.

Name: Erica Ehm
Role: Creator and Publisher, YummyMummyClub.ca
Children: Josh,13; Jessie, 9

"After I had my son I was essentially washed up career-wise. I was no longer young or hip. Physically, I was heavier. My old career was done and now I had to completely reinvent myself."

Erica Ehm made her name in the 1980s as a video deejay (VJ) on MuchMusic. She interviewed rock stars, reviewed concerts, did the odd acting job and along the way also wrote her own songs (which won her three Canadian Country Music Awards).

"Motherhood completely changed how others saw me—but it also really shifted the prism that I had on my life and world. Becoming a mother altered everything for me—how I saw work, my career, myself, my relationships—all of it. That said, I had a hard time with the transition from career woman to new mother and then finding a way to bring the re-launched career part of my identity back again."

"Being a VJ was done. Instead I had to restart by doing freelance work like contributing to a kids' magazine, writing for kids' theatre. I wrote a play, *Caillou's Big Party*, and when that sold out in the theatres, I was commissioned to write *The Big Comfy Couch* and then *Caillou's Big Book Club*.

"Working again helped me adjust to motherhood. But I still constantly felt like everyone else around me was such a good mother and yet I couldn't seem to figure it out. I started speaking to other moms around the supermarket and in my neighborhood, and I discovered most of them were experiencing many of the same difficulties, but everyone was acting like they were OK. It made me want to create an online space where women could share these challenges instead of just keeping it all to themselves." So, seven years ago, Erica founded YummyMummyClub.ca as a platform for other moms. Today it's a business with close to twenty staff who all work from home, a platform that hosts close to fifty blogs as well as a series of webisodes relevant to moms. "My work, my family and my business are completely intertwined. My husband is an entrepreneur who also works from home and we have a part-time nanny, so there's a seamless integration of all of the different parts.

"The beauty of parenting is that there is no right or wrong, just what works or what doesn't for each child at each stage. Women need to take that same approach to their careers and families, finding and being confident about what's right for them as their careers, lives and dreams shift, and being open to reinvention and changes that happen. The only real lesson is that there's no right way to do this."

A Catalyst for Change

Many women I spoke with said that their children gave them both courage and motivation for their career or life reinvention, pushing them to the next project, stage or goal. However, for me it was Michelle's story that best exemplified this ideal of never viewing her children as anything other than a positive catalyst for change in her life.

Name: Michelle Lochan
Role: Owner and Managing Director, MarketStart
Children: Mahayah, 15; Maykah, 13; Masahda, 11; Makhai
           and Makeda, 5

Michelle is a mother who has successfully redefined and re-launched her career over the years. When we met, she had just been recognized as the 2012 MicroSkills Entrepreneur of the Year for her current business, MarketStart, a consultancy specializing in strategic planning and marketing for small businesses and nonprofits. Since becoming a mother, Michelle has held executive positions in advertising and executive recruitment, as well as founding (earlier) a marketing and communications consultancy.

"I never saw any of my children as obstacles or burdens. Even in the toughest times, they were the reason I was determined to make things work for us." Michelle says she was always a strong student and ambitious about her career. "But I knew early on that I wanted to be a wife and mother also and I felt ready, much earlier than any of my friends, to go down that path."

After studying sociology and anthropology at university, she worked in executive recruitment. After just six months she was managing a team of 15 writers and administrative support personnel. "I came in when the firm was building and soon they became one of the top three recruitment firms in Florida. But, while I enjoyed the work, I didn't enjoy the environment and it didn't feel like it was enough for my life." At 23, Michelle married her college boyfriend and was soon pregnant. "Neither of our families was very supportive of our decision to start a family so soon and so young. My mother was especially worried, since this didn't fit her image and expectations for me." Michelle's mother, an immigrant from Trinidad, had always worked while raising her family and Michelle was confident that she would be able to do the same.

"My position at the recruitment agency was guaranteed for three months and I had planned on going back to work full time. But time with my daughter made me reconsider what I wanted to do—and I realized that what I wanted was more time at home." So she left, and spent the next eight months retraining in graphic design. "The timing worked out really well—it was right when graphic design was really just emerging and so the opportunities were everywhere. Within months, through word of mouth and my professional network, I started to build a strong freelance practice." It seemed like the ideal combination: she could control her time while earning a good salary, and she could work from home. "I really enjoyed the creativity and sense of entrepreneurship, but just eighteen months later, I was being recruited for a new position. I was asked to be a director for a new online college." Michelle's new role involved overseeing the design and implementation of the recruitment strategies. "It was too good an opportunity to miss, and so I found day care for my daughter, who was two and a half at the time, and spent the next two years there." She loved the start-up environment and the sense of purpose that came from making education more accessible. Her enthusiasm showed in the results. "I was able to exceed the enrollment target I had been given by more than 200 percent, which felt good, especially since I felt that the career wins would secure my job—since I was now pregnant again."

After the birth of her second daughter, Michelle was back at work after three months and both children were in day care. During this time, her husband had gone back to school to study computer networking and had subsequently gotten a well-paid job on a cruise line. "It meant much more money but it also meant that he would be gone for months at a time."

After several months of coping with full-time work and being the only parent at home, Michelle considered her options and then decided to take some time off with her kids. "I loved being at home with the kids and having some time to refocus on what I thought was next for my family and myself." However, her husband's long absence was hard on her marriage. "The foundation wasn't there, and although I knew I wanted to be a wife and have a strong family and marriage, neither of us was sure of what it would look like or how to make it happen."

Still, they tried to make it work and soon Michelle was pregnant with their third child. "My third pregnancy was a time of spiritual renewal and transformation for me. I joined a church and renewed my faith, which became a real anchor for me." With three children, she faced the dual challenges of wanting to be financially self-sufficient, while continuing to be able to control her time (she was homeschooling her children to provide them with more of an Afrocentric curriculum). "It was with my third child that I realized that entrepreneurship was the channel that would allow me to meet my career, life and financial criteria."

And so, when her third child was four and while she was still homeschooling, Michelle reinvented herself again and started In the Black Marketing and Communications. "When I got my first big contract I was able to put them in a small home-based Afrocentric private school and then focus fully on building the business." It came together quickly. "Just after I incorporated it, I landed three big contracts, so it was successful and profitable right from the start."

The kids were doing well, Michelle was enjoying creative, fulfilling and financially rewarding work. Her relationship however, was becoming increasingly rocky. "Looking back, I think my husband had lost his way, and what I hadn't realized was that he had also been mishandling our finances. And so even though we were both earning a good living, and had been for some time, we were now in severe financial circumstances." After several excruciating months they ended up selling their home, and Michelle left her husband and moved from Florida to Toronto to be closer to family. "Initially, I tried to keep the business going but it became difficult. I realized that I needed an operational structure in place to allow me to step away from the day to day." So, to her incredible disappointment and frustration, business slowed down.

"Between the changes in my business and my marriage ending, it was like everything just came crashing down around me." Then Michelle found out she was pregnant again—and this time she was expecting twins. But, determined to recreate the life she wanted for her kids, Michelle enrolled in a micro-skills community resources program that provided child care and support while she got to work on her new consultancy business, MarketStart. She is once again running a profitable and successful business, and has recreated the life that she wanted for her family.

"Even with school-age children, child care remains a challenge. For after-school care, I do use the services of an in-home child care provider because we have a specialized [vegetarian] diet and she is able to manage that better for me and the children. Prior to that I was a part of a collective of women that were all involved in either business start-ups or furthering their education, and so to meet the irregular hours that these activities required, we all shared the responsibilities of caring for each other's children based on our availability. Around this time, my parents also retired and so could help if the kids were sick or couldn't go to school for some reason. I gave my eldest daughters the gift of babysitting training so they can help me and earn some extra money. Also, my ex-husband now takes his responsibilities seriously and has set a great schedule for raising them as well.

"When I have to travel, I hire a full-time nanny to live in my home for the duration of my trip. Running my business and family requires a significant amount of structure. Since trying to wing it leaves me feeling very stressed, I plan my weeks in advance, allowing for some flexibility so I can adapt to changes should an opportunity come up. I have now even rented office space to separate myself further from home, because otherwise I can easily start folding laundry while on a conference call.

"A sample day looks something like this:

5:00 a.m.	Up
5:30 a.m.	Start creative writing (3 pages)
6:30 a.m.	Social media updates and e-mail
7:30 a.m.	Children up and readied for school
8:30 a.m.	Walk the children to school
8:40 a.m.	Breakfast and action planning

9:30 a.m.	Client work, sales contacts (2 per day), seek marketing opportunities
3:30 p.m.	Stop work
4:30 p.m.	Children home, and evening activities begin: dinner, homework, showers, etc.
8:00 p.m.	Gym (3 to 4 days per week)
10:00 p.m.	Bed

"I constantly tell women that PATIENCE is key. You cannot rush a child to grow, so use the time to grow as well. In this rat-race culture where achievement defines success, I see motherhood as an anchor that has you tethered. It refreshes your perspective and provides focus and purpose."

Many women I met shared the sentiment of having fallen into a career or happened upon a job that they just stayed with, although it wasn't aligned to their interests or original plans. For several of them, parenthood became the catalyst to make them more conscious and deliberate in the choices they were making.

Mothers and More, an American organization for stay-at-home mothers, found in a survey that about 71 percent of its members plan to return to work—but the survey found that more than one-third do not plan to return to the same occupation, and another third are undecided about their career path, suggesting that their previous jobs were just something they were doing versus a calling or long-term career they were building. Of course you don't need to have a child to face these questions, but for many, it's often a significant drive towards acting on some answers.

Reinvention and Purpose: Why Am I Doing This?
For the past decade, we've been hearing how employees at all levels are increasingly looking for meaning from their work. Once the bills are paid, the question "Why am I doing this and what does it matter?" looms.

It's not a new consideration. In 1946, Austrian psychiatrist Viktor Frankl wrote *Man's Search for Meaning*, in which he argued that our deepest hankerings are not sexual (sorry, Freud!) but are actually the lust for a purpose in life. Which raises the question, do you have to love your career or job to be successful?

Of course not. Lots of women I spoke with are happy to earn a good living in a position with decent hours—and use the rest of their time to focus on their families, community involvement or personal passions. After all, children and family are probably the most common way to create meaning in life. As a result, many women and men find themselves relieved (at least for the first few years) of the pressing *need* to find "meaningful" work. Work serves the primary function of providing for their families, and their home lives become their source of identity and purpose.

It's an approach that needs to be reaffirmed—particularly against the constant cultural message to follow your dreams in a more extreme way. "We need to remind people that it's OK to learn to love what you do, especially if it works with the rest of your life. People put so much pressure on themselves to find a 'soulmate of a career' and this simply isn't realistic and practical for many. There are, in fact, many ways to love what you do instead of only insisting on doing what you love," advises Alexandra Levit, a mother of two and best-selling business and workplace author. (Her recent book, *Blind Spots*, addresses common workplace myths.)

For others, if work wasn't meaningful before children (and if they have the financial option) staying home becomes the right choice. In her research among highly qualified and professional women, economist Sylvia Ann Hewlett, author of *Off-Ramps and On-Ramps: Keeping Talented Women on the Road to Success*, found that almost 30 percent of women who leave their jobs after they have children do so because they find their work not satisfying or meaningful (for women in business and law these numbers are even higher, 52 and 59 percent respectively).[34]

In a society where most of us spend roughly 1,800 hours a year at work, the desire to find a role or career that has meaning—especially once you have kids—can be very important. Anu, a mother of two, who left a thriving real estate career in Houston to train as a nurse, told me, "I decided that if I'm spending time away from my kids, I want to feel that it is for something that really matters, that I can believe in a bit more beyond just the commission or next paycheck."

Name: Catherine McKenna
Role: Executive Director, Banff Forum and Co-Founder, Canadian Lawyers Abroad
Children: Madeline, 9; Isabelle, 6; Cormac, 4

Canadian Lawyers Abroad (CLA) the organization that Catherine co-founded, is a nonprofit that brings together legal talent to support the rule of law, good governance and human rights work in partnership with organizations in Africa and Asia and with Aboriginal communities in Canada. "I went to law school and focused on international law because I wanted a career where I felt like I could have a positive impact on global events," she begins. While her other friends from law school were applying for jobs at the big Toronto and New York firms, she went to Indonesia to work for a law firm in Jakarta and then went on to work for the United Nations in East Timor (right after the East Timorese voted for independence from Indonesia). "I was working with Timorese and UN colleagues to negotiate a new treaty between East Timor and Australia relating to resource development and I couldn't believe how outnumbered we were. Australia and the oil companies involved literally had teams and teams of lawyers. The East Timorese had four people, including me, and I was a relatively recent law graduate." It was this experience that would later spark the idea that would become Canadian Lawyers Abroad.

After working at the UN, Catherine and her husband Scott, who worked with the Canadian Foreign Service, decided to return home to Canada, to Ottawa, where Scott's job was based. Here Catherine faced the reality that she was unlikely to find exciting international legal work in their new city. Catherine joined one of Canada's top law firms and was regularly clocking in the standard ten-hour days, six days a week. She and Scott bought a house, got caught up in some renovations and started planning for a family. Although she missed the excitement and feeling of making a difference that her work for the UN had provided, the law firm job paid well and had excellent benefits.

It was on her first maternity leave that Catherine initially got the chance to pick up on the idea that she'd had years earlier while working in East Timor. "I had no real idea what maternity leave was going to be or should be like. But what surprised me about it was, that for the first time in years, I wasn't just going and going or working until the wee hours. I actually had some time on my hands to think. And I thought of all my friends sitting at desks in big firms and how they probably would have loved to be involved in some small part of the East Timor negotiations, and what a profound differ- ence their involvement could have in other places." And so, during her first six-month maternity leave, she and a friend launched Canadian Lawyers Abroad.

It was a long journey from that beginning to where Catherine is now, running CLA full time.

After her first maternity leave, she returned to her law firm job. Determined to keep CLA going despite her long hours, she negotiated for a four-day workweek, although, as she recalls, ". . . everyone advised me against it, pointing out that I would be working five days a week and being paid for four. But to me, it was still better than working seven days a week and being paid for five. Still, the transition back was really hard. My husband was traveling a lot, the baby wasn't sleeping at night, the corporate law department was busy and finding child-care arrangements that worked with my hours seemed impossible." She also noticed that it had become harder to ignore the doubts she'd previously had about the work she was doing. "Strangely, through all of this, I continued doing what I could for CLA whenever possible. It had become an outlet from the rest of my life, something that I controlled and felt ownership over—my refuge." She kept working and building CLA on the side, evenings, mornings, weekends and whenever she could snatch a moment throughout her day.

She also looked for child-care arrangements that worked for her family. "By now I'd realized that the most important thing I could do for both myself and our family was to invest in child care that took away some of my stress and worry. I needed to create the space for me to do what I believed would ultimately put all of us in a better position as a family." Catherine started with a nanny share and then eventually she and Scott hired an amazing nanny who has now been with her family for almost eight years. "The continuity of child care and having someone that we all know and trust has been one of the best investments we've ever made."

Two years later, she had her second baby. On this maternity leave, Catherine took nine months, during which she worked on building CLA by applying for funding and sponsorship, speaking to student groups and sourcing suitable projects through her networks. Logistically, having full-time help made going back to work easier once her maternity leave ended, but emotionally, Catherine found it even harder to deny that her career ambitions were changing. "With two kids, I had less time than before and so how I spent that time began to matter even more to me."

Meanwhile, her husband had left his career to start a nonprofit, Building Markets (formerly Peace Dividend Trust), an international organization that assists humanitarian missions to be more effective and efficient on the ground.

"I'm less of a risk-taker," Catherine says, "so with Scott now doing Building Markets full time, I felt like I had to 'stay on course' so to speak. So, I kept CLA to something I was doing on the side."

Her compromise was that she left her law firm job and took an in-house legal job at a large company. Here, unlike at a private law firm, she wasn't required to bill client hours, which gave her more time to continue to grow CLA's reach and operations. "When I left the law firm, everyone thought that it was because of the new baby, that I couldn't handle the hours and expectations any longer. My former colleagues treated me as though stepping away meant that I had failed, lost my edge. And yes, wanting to get away from the ten-hour days was part of why I left, but it was less about that than everyone seemed to think. It was really that my children made me realize how quickly time was passing, and that I had one life, and this was not how I wanted to spend it. Although my colleagues at the law firm wouldn't see it like this, I actually became *more* ambitious after my children were born. I was less willing to settle for work that had little meaning to me, work that was just a way to pay our bills."

Although Catherine had moved to a job with better hours and a bit more freedom after her second maternity leave, she was increasingly feeling the pull to make more of a difference in the world. "My eldest is a real worrier about things she hears on the news or learns about at school. As a result, issues like the environment or homelessness became less abstract to me, since she made them very real. And I think she was the push for both my husband and myself to say, 'Well, what *are* we doing to have a bigger impact?'"

Two years later she was pregnant with her third child.

Soon after her third maternity leave, Catherine took the plunge that she'd wanted to make for a while. She left her day job as a lawyer and now runs CLA full time. "It's amazing to be able to focus on it fully. Running my own organization also comes with other benefits that I hadn't considered before: the flexibility to control my time so I can go in and read to my daughter's class or watch my kids' swimming lessons." She admits that she still worries about the risk and that, financially, she gave up a lot, including a pension and good salary. But, she says, "Scott and I feel that our family will get the most benefit from having two parents who are engaged and believe in the work they are doing."

Now that she is full time with CLA, Catherine has big plans for what she hopes to achieve with the organization, including expanding CLA's work with Aboriginal communities and organizations in Canada and finding ways to create new partnerships with the legal community.

"After almost ten years of just having a job, I feel like I'm now on the right path again, piecing together my ideal career, where I do meaningful work and keep a variety of options open for further down the road. My advice to other women is that we all need to stop thinking that we need to be amazing at everything we take home, professionally or personally; we just need to keep doing it and working on staying in."

(Update: Since we first spoke, Catherine has now also taken on an executive role at the Banff Forum, a network of emerging leaders committed to public policy, and is also teaching first-year graduate students at the Munk School of Global Affairs at the University of Toronto.)

Consider:

› **Start with small steps.** Going for your dream job or career doesn't have to be an overnight decision or a full-time commitment. Consider how some freelance or volunteer work can help you to practically start to work towards your dream career or role.

› **It's never too late.** Financial commitments, life, children and other obligations can all conspire to slowly (or maybe dramatically) lead us away from our essential selves and true goals. But delays are not denials—get back in touch to what it is you've always wanted by taking the time to understand why you want it.

› **Control who is setting your goals.** Don't let former colleagues, friends or family define the framework or benchmarks for your personal ambitions. Let their perspectives and opinions go. It's your career and your life, so set your own targets and success points.

› **Don't be afraid to admit what you really want.** Be open to and unafraid of how your children might change the values and perspectives that you bring to your career. It can be scary, but it's also an opportunity to connect with what your true purpose with work could be.

› **Be open.** Look for conscious and tangible ways to expand your world of possibilities and avoid immediately discounting "unconventional" choices.

Name: Donna Bishop
Role: Founder and CEO, Green Beauty
Children: Dylan, 9; Audrey, 5

Before she became a mother, Donna hadn't yet found her professional sweet spot. She was working at a PR firm, but "despite being promoted quickly and achieving regular career advancement, I felt like I was just going through the motions professionally. Not unhappy but also not feeling satisfied or fully engaged."

When she became pregnant with her son, Donna saw it as a chance for a change.

"I don't think I really had a plan when it came to work. I wanted to 'be successful' but had trouble articulating anything beyond that. After Dylan was born I was inspired to take something that had previously been a hobby and turn it into a profession."

A self-described "makeup junkie," Donna regularly did her friends' makeup for weddings and special events and so she decided to build on this interest. Soon she began a career as a freelance makeup artist. She admits that after years in an office, there was the appeal of a career that was just "'the task at hand'—no client updates, no reports, no project management." Not working, however, was never an option for her. "Working made me a better mother because it made me feel accomplished and competent and happy in a way that motherhood did not. And let me be clear, I was not an unhappy mother; but I think for women who have worked in a career prior to becoming a parent, there is an itch there that needs to be scratched."

Donna was enjoying being a makeup artist, developing a healthy roster of clients and having a job that felt like "fun" when two-year-old Dylan was diagnosed with cancer.

"It all happened very quickly. I'll never forget the date: Sunday, October 15, and we were playing in the living room when Steve (my husband) felt a lump on Dylan's left side. It looked like he had an egg under his skin that was poking out. First thing on Monday morning we went to the walk-in clinic close to our house, not really knowing what to expect. The doctor looked at Dylan's side for a second and sent us straight to the hospital. We were quickly moved up through the hospital food chain from intern fellows to regular doctors, then specialists and finally the head of pediatrics. We spent the night in emergency still in the dark about what the specific diagnosis was."

The next morning they were told Dylan had a Wilms tumor. This is a rare kidney cancer that primarily affects children. "We met with the head of oncology, who told us Dylan would need surgery—on Friday. The tumor and his left kidney would be removed and then he would start chemotherapy. We went home that afternoon to wait, and I remember Steve weeping as he drove and Dylan, oblivious, singing 'Baby Beluga' in the back seat. The surgery went as well as we could have hoped. After five hours we found out that he was going to be fine, that the tumor was only stage two and stayed intact while it was removed, so no cells had spread.

"I remember we skipped Halloween that year. Dylan's first chemo appointment was on November 1. Steve and I turned off all the lights and hid in the basement with a bottle of red wine, still trying to come to terms with what was happening. Dylan had eighteen sessions of chemo over the next six months. This was minimal compared with what most cancer patients require. That said, it meant taking him out of day care and limiting his exposure to crowds, as his immune system had weakened significantly. So no stores, no friends coming over or going to other people's homes.

"Of course my work took a pause, although occasionally when my mom was with Dylan I would go see a client, just to have a sense of normalcy. It sounds clichéd, but a health crisis, especially one involving your child, really puts everything— and I mean *everything*—into perspective. When Dylan was diagnosed with cancer I just kept thinking, 'My God, you feed your child organic, you nurse them as long as you can, you clean with eco cleaners and STILL a young child gets cancer? This is insanity.'"

Dylan still goes for yearly checkups but thankfully is now fine.

"After what happened with Dylan, I wanted to do something to feel like I was making a difference. So I turned to the beauty industry that I both know and love so much. At this time the questionable nature of the ingredients in makeup and skin care products was just starting to get attention. I started researching and the more I learned, the more I was struck by how even people who are so careful about what they and their families put in their bodies just take for granted that what we put *on* our bodies is safe. Propelled by my family situation and armed with this growing knowledge base, I worked to make my makeup eco/green and toxin free."

This was the start of Green Beauty, which now includes an online site for beauty products and a flagship salon in Toronto (with additional locations underway). By the time Green Beauty launched, Donna had had another child, a daughter, who was just over a year old. "Green Beauty had been months in the making. My working, and hence sleeping, hours became highly unconventional during that time. I pulled a lot of late, late nights and would sleep with Audrey during the day and then be bright-eyed for after school and dinnertime with the whole family."

One of the challenges in having people share their success stories is that there is a tendency to gloss over the journey, specifically the day-to-day struggles that are always a part of life. But Donna was comfortable sharing not only the business hurdles (for example, having to deal with an incorrectly installed eco toilet in their spa that subsequently leaked into the dining room of the restaurant below) to her own struggle with severe postpartum anxiety after each of her children.

"Overcoming postpartum issues was the biggest challenge I made it through. The first few months after each child was born were actually harder on me personally than Dylan's cancer. I had postpartum anxiety—that's different from depression. I had crippling panic attacks and high anxiety. The day often seemed too insurmountable to get through. Without medication and an incredibly supportive husband, who knows where I would be? It impacted everything. There was a time when I had to avoid the computer because just the idea of turning it on made me anxious. Once the meds began to work things got much, much better. I felt like myself again and could focus on work and family stuff."

Reinvention after becoming a mother was never intentional for Donna but a natural evolution. Since its launch, Green Beauty has grown from an online boutique run out of her basement to a full-service spa and hair studio with five staff. She's also a green beauty and fashion expert with regular appearances on a popular Canadian afternoon talk show, frequently speaks about the need for greater awareness of the ingredients in personal care products, and is a key cabinet member for the Environmental Defense, Just Beautiful campaign. Even with so many balls in the air, Donna retains a strong sense of perspective on it all: "I often remind my team and myself that, 'we are not saving lives here'—meaning nothing is truly that urgent. After what my family went through with Dylan, few business- or career-related issues can stress me out. It's all solvable. I am not talking about slacking off or procrastinating, but I have found freedom in embracing that sometimes things can be done later. This philosophy has meant I manage my time well, I have no regrets about how often I see my kids and my team feels appreciated and not overburdened.

"I think that for so long motherhood was seen as the pinnacle of female accomplishments. Today, while being a mother is an incredibly important part of our lives, it's not the top of the pyramid. There is no pyramid. I see it instead as a Ferris wheel and each seat is an element of a woman's life— meetings, birthday parties, groceries, holidays, school trips, client meetings, doctor appointments, drinks with your BFF, date nights (which Steve and I do every Thursday night)—that you address different aspects of your life in that moment, but all the others are an equal priority, at that time."

Name: Jill*
Role: SVP, Global Engineering Firm
Children: Two sons, 11 and 9; one daughter, 8

Jill got back on the fast track at work after almost eight years out as a stay-at-home mom. "Now, I'm really glad that my career has come together so well and feel really grateful that I was able to not just get any job but to really go back to building what I'd started and then thought I wanted to stop." After graduating with a master's in mechanical engineering, Jill was hired by a large oil company. "It was a great role for me, with lots of travel, great mentors and really interesting work that I enjoyed."

Five years after she started, she was selected for their management training program, which included the opportunity to do an executive MBA. It was here that she met her husband-to-be, a mergers and acquisitions lawyer at a big firm. Two years later they were married, and a year after that she was expecting their first son. "Both of us were really committed to our careers when we met and I planned on going back to work after six months, which I did."

But after her second son was born, she decided to take some time off. "I just felt like the kids weren't seeing enough of either of us, and my husband was both completely unwilling (and I suppose unable) to cut his hours back. We didn't have much family support at the time and so I decided to spend the year at home, and then see how it went from there."

The adjustment was hard at first. "Moving my work wardrobe to the downstairs closet actually made me burst into tears. It felt like I was physically putting a version of myself away." Soon, Jill was pregnant with their third child. "There was a lot I missed about work at first, but I did love being with the kids and gradually I began to enjoy being involved in the school and with the other mothers." Soon her intentions of keeping her hand in the game slipped away. "I had initially planned to do some consulting work once our third was in nursery, but to be honest, we were doing fine financially and without that as an incentive, it was hard to find a reason to shake things up."

Unfortunately, that soon changed. "Just before we were going to celebrate our eleventh anniversary, my husband told me that he had been seeing another partner at his firm, and that he was moving out to be with her. And yeah, he wanted a divorce. I was completely blindsided; I'd never guessed anything. Why would I? I thought we had a great marriage, we rarely fought and the fact that he worked long hours was nothing new but something I understood.

"I felt like my entire identity was gone overnight. Since I hadn't worked in years, I'd started to almost subconsciously define myself and my own identity as it related to him and the kids. Now that he was gone, yes, I was still a mom, but who else was I? And what was I going to do now?"

Although the settlement they reached on child support was fair, it was also going to mean a significant lifestyle change for Jill. "Well, now I had the financial incentive I'd previously lacked, but even before anything was decided in terms of the settlement, I already knew I had to get back to work." The challenge for Jill was that she had let both her professional networks and CV lapse in these intervening years.

"I remember walking down to the closet where all my old work clothes were, thinking I should get some stuff dry-cleaned so at least I'd have something professional to wear to any informational coffees or lunches that I set up and just opening the door and crying and crying, thinking, 'How did I get myself into this position?'" Jill had an excellent education and CV, but it was out of date. Realizing she had to start somewhere, she began by calling and e-mailing around. "I couldn't afford to feel uncomfortable, so I got in touch with everyone I'd ever worked with. This led to some small contracting work, which was a good transition back into the work world for me and gave me some recent items to put on my résumé."

Eventually she picked up a few more contracts, then a regular consulting gig. Three years later, she was offered a full-time job at her current company and, last year, received a promotion. "The gradual ramp up actually worked out really well. It gave me the chance to both settle the family and to settle myself again. I'd forgotten that I was actually really good at what I did—and that I used to love it! To be honest, this position is an even better fit for me than my previous role. It allows me to combine business and analysis with the technical side—and it's much more lucrative, which, to be honest, feels fantastic after being dependent on someone else for all those years.

"I would tell other women who find themselves in a similar position to start somewhere and just rely on the fact that you are more experienced and more capable than the initial gigs you might get, but that your talent and potential will come through—and also that if you think it's not really being recognized, don't be afraid to move on."

Consider:

> **It's OK to want to do something different.** Many at-home parents discover new interests and change career paths when they return to the workplace. In fact, a study by the Wharton Business School found that only 39 percent of mothers took the same kind of job as their previous role on their career re-entry.[35] If you have been out of the workforce for some time or feel ready for a post-motherhood career change, start with an honest assessment about what's most important to you now and why. "I didn't find the right role for myself until I let go of my own limitations on what I thought my career should be and how it should look—even though it wasn't what I wanted any longer," says Mary, a former financial consultant and mother of three girls in Florham Park, New Jersey, who just finished retraining as a figure skating coach and has plans to open her own school.

> **Use social media.** Even if you haven't worked in years and have completely stopped meeting with former colleagues and supervisors, social media is a low-barrier way to reconnect and put the word out that you're looking for the next opportunity.

> **Look around.** If financial priorities don't require you to take the first job on offer, then frame this time not as a job search but as an exploratory time to consider the types of work that you might be interested in (which might be different in form and content than your prior positions). Instead, make your goal to meet as many people from as many different industries and organizations as possible—and see where that leads.

> **Don't get hung up on the money.** If you can afford to do so, be open to roles that might be different in pay and status than your last position. "I advise women that nothing is permanent," says Jill. "So if it's a freelance project that might have previously been too junior for you or a consulting gig that pays almost nothing, but it gets you in the door, then take it. It's not the forever and ever role, but these are stepping stones back."

Reinvention: As Part of a Team

It used to be a fairly common arrangement for husbands and wives to work together—on the farm, in a small store or in some other type of venture. And it seems that the idea of a family business continues to have a strong appeal. According to the U.S. Small Business Administration, 90 percent of the 21 million small businesses in the U.S. are family owned. Family businesses, including those run by married CEOs, account for 50 percent of the U.S. GDP, and 35 percent of the Fortune 500 companies.[36]

A joint business venture means every part of your relationship is affected by the fact that you live and work together. Lindsey Donner, who co-founded a business with her husband in 2009, less than a year after they had gotten married, describes it this way: "Starting a business is risky. Starting one with your spouse is outright nutty. You're gambling your finances, your mental health, your retirement funds, your personal happiness—and the most important relationship of your adult life."[37] And yet, the benefits, especially for parents, are significant. A joint venture means increased autonomy, greater flexibility, a reduced or eliminated commute and the ability to integrate child care into your workday.

Name: Sonia Klinger
Role: Sales and Marketing, OrangeRed Painting
Children: Mattia, 3

I initially interviewed Sonia for her story of achieving post-baby success in the young, male environment of Red Bull Canada. About a year after our conversation, she contacted me to say that she had decided to leave her job and instead join her husband's business. "My decision to leave my job was a difficult one. I had been working there for seven years, and it became a part of who I was. But for the past couple of years, I had been doing a great deal of thinking about what the next career and life step for me would be."

In 2009, Sonia's husband had co-founded a commercial and residential painting company, OrangeRed Painting Inc.

"One night when I was talking with my husband about what I wanted to do and our shared plans, it suddenly dawned on us that I should join their team and help with marketing and sales to try and grow the company even more. My husband and I had worked together before—we actually met at our previous job. Back then, we made the decision that what happens at work stays at work. And that remains true today. But that's not to say that it's all peachy. There have been times where we have disagreed on certain work situations. It's hard to separate work from the personal but you have to.

"My advice is to make sure that you are honest and lay the groundwork before you make the decision to work with your partner. My husband and I did a lot of talking about this and we outlined the pros and cons. It took me months to actually make the decision, but I am happy that I did. I have more control over my schedule and there's something very power-ful about both raising our daughter and building our busi-ness together."

(Update: Since we spoke, Sonia has also started her own public relations company, Ruby Tangerine PR.)

If Sonia's updated story represents a more common path to reinvention in a joint business, the husband-and-wife team of Ayesha and Parag Khanna is an example of a new and emerging model. They are part of what urban studies expert and author Richard Florida first identified as the "global creative class."[38] The term refers to artists, writers, architects, those in knowledge sectors such as management consultants and engineers, and those whose creativity is a key factor in their work and whose work allows them to be less location bound.

Name: Ayesha Khanna
Role: Founder and Director, Hybrid Reality Institute
Children: Zara, 4; Zubin, 2

Ayesha and Parag Khanna are both authors in their own right and recently published their first joint book, *Hybrid Reality: Thriving in the Emerging Human-Technology Civilization.* They are also the co-founders and directors of the Hybrid Reality Institute, a research and advisory group focused on human-technology co-evolution and geo-technology. "I always had an entrepreneurial spirit, but before I met Parag, I usually undertook small business ventures on my own—editing and publishing a magazine, investing in a restaurant, starting a consulting firm. All of this was only done on the side while I maintained a full-time career in technology and innovation strategy on Wall Street.

"One of the things that attracted me to Parag was his sense of adventure and love of traveling. After we got married, I became bolder in following my ideas and in reimagining how my career could work. I decided to work virtually, and often part time, so I could join Parag on his work trips, which continued during my pregnancy and after Zara was born. We always took turns looking after Zara while the other one went out for meetings or took conference calls, often in the middle of the night, depending on which time zone we were in compared to our clients.

We truly felt that even though we were working in different fields and on different projects that we were very much on the same team when it came to managing work and family.

"When Parag and I first met, we were doing completely different things—he was working in geopolitics and I was working in technology. We used to talk about our interests and we were both very curious about the other's specialization. One day, we were walking home from dinner and I mentioned to him my interest in starting an institute on emerging technologies. Parag was very supportive and said that he thought there should be a deeper examination of these technologies in a geopolitical context as well. We talked about it for months and eventually decided to co-found the Institute together.

"We spent the next three years writing our joint book while also continuing to work on other individual projects. We worked together intermittently, which was good for us since I think working every single minute together on the same project would be challenging given how much time we already spend together as a couple and as parents. The advantage of working together is that your partner has a full appreciation of your work and how much time it takes. The disadvantage is that we often have meetings together, so it's hard to split up the time with the kids. Two years ago when our son, Zubin, was born, we started taking a trusted nanny with us when we traveled so that we could be sure the children were happy and safe while we both worked.

"Last year, Parag and I spent a year in London with Zara and Zubin—they joined me while I worked on my Ph.D. on intelligent infrastructure at the London School of Economics. The structure of our lives and workdays is very fluid. On the one hand, we have an incredible amount of flexibility in terms of where and how we work. But on the other hand, being entrepreneurial means that you don't leave your work at the office.

"It's not a lifestyle that's for everyone, but it really works for us."

Consider:

› **Get started working with your partner.** If you're considering working with your partner, keep in mind that strong communication skills and patience should already be staples of your relationship. Ideally the arrangement should be something you want to do as opposed to something you have to do.

› **Have an "out clause."** A three- to six-month trial will show you how and if it's working. Then you can reassess whether moving forward is the right strategy.

› **Find ways to maintain your individuality.** Working and parenting together can take a toll on your sense of self. Remember that everyone needs alone time—and that includes making sure your partner gets some as well.

› **Think about using separate work spaces.** Work independently part of the time whether at home or in your office, or just choose different coffee shops—a little physical distance can really help make things easier on a day-to-day basis.

› **Be clear on who does what.** Ambiguity on your roles can be great on the home front, but from my interviews I regularly heard that carrying this over into your workplace can be a disaster. Instead, spell out what each person's responsibilities are and try not to overlap with each other so each of you has a definite sense of ownership.

Reinvention through Re-education

In stories throughout the book and on the website, numerous women have talked about their decision to return to school after becoming mothers. Some upgraded their degrees or skills, some finished a program they had started, and others decided to completely retrain in a new profession. It's a growing trend and today nearly one-quarter of undergraduate students in the U.S. are also parents.[39]

Name: Helena Spence *
Role: Student, Ph.D. in management systems
Children: Two daughters, 6 and 5

"I had my kids before I started my Ph.D. and waited till they were both in school full time before I went back . . . Both my husband and I felt that having someone at home with the kids in the early years was a priority for us, and so what we agreed on was a five-five plan. I got the first five years home. He gets the second five. Then we both work once our eldest is ten. Our hope is that five years out of the workforce isn't too damaging career-wise to either of us, and this way, neither of us absorbs a full ten-year hit, while still giving our kids—and frankly ourselves—that nesting, nurturing time.

"In many ways, when it comes to integrating career and motherhood, there is no better 'job' than being a student. My time is very flexible. I work long hours, but I can work them in and around the kids' schedules. I can't always be present. But I can always be present when it matters. A banking friend once said that when she hires, she prefers to hire moms. Moms, she said, know how to prioritize, know how to use their time effectively and know how to multitask. They deliver.

"I think it's true. Since becoming a mom I'm much better at identifying work that doesn't need doing. I have 4.5 hours a day in which I can be Mom—from 7 a.m. to 8:30 a.m. and from 5 p.m. to 8 p.m. I make the other hours that I'm working as productive and goal-focused as possible. Compared to me-before-kids, I get similar results with fewer work hours by strategically identifying what not to do and by not dithering with the to do's. I'm a much more efficient worker.

"That said, during crunch periods for me, my husband ends up working triple time. I try to support him through his busy projects with the same generosity that he gives me. I achieve these goals maybe 20 percent of the time. But when I do pull it off, our days are filled with laughter and joy instead of tension and bickering, and the laundry always gets done eventually."

Consider:

> **Volunteer first.** Before committing to a program, try volunteering in the chosen field so you know if the pros of retraining or additional credentials will outweigh the cons.

> **Take a close look at the syllabi and textbooks, then make your decision.**

> **Audit classes to see if the course is right for you.**

> **Look at online options.** According to the American Association of University Women, more than 60 percent of online students today are women and the majority of them are over 25.

> **Find services.** Look for schools with programs for parents such as campus day cares and financial services.

> **Make friends with other student mothers.** Several mothers told me that making friends with others in the same situation made a huge difference for them. "It was a real support system for me to have a community of other student moms. We would have playdates for the kids while we studied and swap cooking duties and just help each other out," said Michelle Gibson, a single mom of a six-year-old daughter, who recently completed an MS in project management.

Motherhood: A Whole New World of Opportunities

Motherhood means a whole new world of issues, subjects, products and services that suddenly confront you. For many women, these new interests, involvements or circumstances also lead (either intentionally or unintentionally) to the start of a new career. They may spark entrepreneurial and "mompreneur" initiatives (which I look at in greater detail in Chapter Four).

And the new experiences or circumstances of motherhood may open up new skills or career paths that they had previously never considered.

Name: Nada Arnot
Role: VP Marketing, Kaplan
Children: Owen, 8; Fred, 4

There is such a premium placed on having a plan—knowing where your career is going, what you are trying to achieve, and when you want (or hope) to have reached your goal. But don't overlook opportunities, interests and obstacles that you never anticipated! They will come up along the way.

Nada Arnot and I were roommates and close friends as undergraduates. At the time, she was focused on policy and thinking about a career in government. Now, some years later, she's a successful marketer with over thirteen years' experience in digital marketing, a field that didn't even exist in our student days.

Raised by an immigrant single mother who put herself through engineering school and went on to a successful career, Nada had always been ambitious about work. "Kids and family always seemed like something that anyone could do; it was what *else* were you going to be and do that was always emphasized to me. My first 'real' job after graduating was as an analyst and then as a policy strategist at the Government of Canada."

Then, in 2004, she moved with her husband to New York. "I was three months into my marriage, in a new city, when I discovered that, contrary to what we'd been assuming, the visa I was on didn't actually allow me to immediately look for work." This put policy work out of the question. "I just kept thinking about what I could do to keep myself from going stir crazy and killing my career. I thought about learning to trade futures or writing—I was just looking for anything."

That's also when she found out she was pregnant. "I was glad when I found out I was pregnant because it gave me a sense of some kind of purpose and direction during that time."

Nada started with the usual rounds of research, books and websites about pregnancy, learning about what to expect. There was of course no end of resources available for her— but nothing that resonated with or for her husband.

She sensed a market opportunity.

Four months into her pregnancy, she launched The Funky Stork—a website dedicated to the modern expectant father and new dad. The process of launching and building The Funky Stork gave her a completely new set of skills, setting her on an unexpected career path in the emerging sphere of digital marketing. "I started blogging and doing paid sponsorships for the site, liaising with PR agencies, getting payments for reviews and freelance contributions—way before any of this became the norm for 'mommy bloggers.'

Four years after its launch, she sold The Funky Stork. By then, she'd started several other sites, including a site for surfers (which she also sold) and another called GroomGrove, which she still manages. Two years after Owen was born, she had her work papers and decided to apply online for a post she saw advertised at NBC.

Remarkably, Nada got a call for an interview the next day. "It was like the role was written for me—it combined technical skills with marketing and they were looking for someone with an entrepreneurial background." She got the job and became the Senior Search Marketing Strategist at NBC Universal. "I loved it and it was a huge career jump for me." In the two and a half years she was at NBC, she managed the online marketing program for over forty-five NBC web properties, including MSNBC, SNL and Bravo. She also scored some big career wins, including managing a multi-million-dollar search engine marketing program that generated millions of incremental revenue for the company. In the 2008 downturn, NBC laid off thirty-two of the forty people on her team. Nada, meanwhile, was promoted to Director, lead Audience Development and Digital Marketing and moved to the iVillage websites.

Here too she delivered. Collectively, the digital strategies accounted for 54 percent of the overall monthly unique visitors to iVillage.com, 25 percent of which was exclusively from social media marketing. Her second son, Fred, was born while she was at iVillage.

"I was gone for twelve weeks, and when I returned, I received my promotion. That was a big turning point for me. It was also very different from my experience with Owen, when I didn't have a work visa and couldn't find an employer to sponsor me."

While she was at iVillage, she was recruited for an agency role at RF Binder, a boutique public relations agency belonging to Ruder Finn.

"I was actually very happy with my position at iVillage, but the opportunity at RF Binder was something I couldn't turn down. I was recruited to start and lead their digital practice, which meant that I would be responsible for a significant part of the agency's business." At RF Binder Partners, Nada became the Chief Digital Officer (SVP), which meant that she oversaw digital marketing and social media strategy. She grew the practice group from two to thirty people working on brands like Dunkin' Donuts, JOHNSON'S Baby, Hershey's, and Irving Oil.

Nada was making a name for herself in the industry. In 2012, she was nominated for five digital awards and was being recognized for her ability to quickly deliver online results for clients. Soon Nada was overseeing over thirty digital accounts plus managing new business. "I was also working sixteen-hour days consistently, I felt like my home life was fraying and I was frustrated by the lack of control that I had over the programs. I was looking to go back in-house where I could manage a full-scale program end to end, and at that point Kaplan got in touch with me about the role I have now.

"Careers are rarely ever linear, particularly for women. Having children and managing a household often means that we need to make sacrifices and adjustments to our careers at various points in our lives. However, in hindsight, these 'interruptions' in my career trajectory were critical in propelling me forward. They gave me the opportunity to reflect on what I really wanted and to focus on developing the skills I needed to succeed. That said, the interruptions were not easy—I was concerned that they would become permanent, which caused me a lot of stress. I think this is normal, and women who feel the same should know that they are not alone.

"Take this time to press reset—you will often come out stronger and more successful if you do."

Reinvention: Beyond the Maternity Years

Since having children—and especially that first baby—is such a life catalyst, much of the cultural and media focus is on what does or doesn't happen career-wise in the immediate few years after becoming a mother. However, reinvention happens throughout our careers, with new opportunities and ventures continually emerging, and very often our children directly or indirectly influence these choices and changes.

For the past four years now, Heather,* a Chicago editor for a financial reporting firm, has been enjoying a new phase of her professional life. "It's a renaissance for me! I'm not worried about hustling home for the kids or even what's for dinner. I haven't felt this free since I started my financial services career, almost thirty years ago.

"I started my career as a financial consultant, and to keep my hand in while raising our three girls I did part-time work, consulting work. As they got older I increased my hours, and by the time they were in high school, I was working full time—but it was once they left home that I felt fully free to take on an editor role with the late nights, the client events and the travel. I always worked in some capacity, but this is the most challenging and enjoyable role I've ever had. I tell my girls that 'having it all' can happen, and one way to do it is to stagger it over the long haul instead of trying to cram it all in at once."

According to Phyllis Moen, a sociologist at the University of Minnesota who studies work/life balance, women in the empty-nest phase of life talk about how they now work long hours without worry, or have finally taken a job requiring lots of travel or have started a business making the most of their newfound energy and with more evenings available for networking. "There is greater focus on their career. People that I've interviewed say things like, 'Now, this is my time.'"[40] Just as baby-boomer women redefined what young motherhood looked like—blending family life with professional aspirations—now they're redefining the empty-nest phase. They're building careers when, in earlier generations, women at their age would have been considering retirement."

Sitara Hewitt, star of the hit television series *Little Mosque on the Prairie* and mother to three-year-old son Rowan, told me how her mother's journey, ". . . inspires me to look outside what others are doing in terms of their careers and instead pursue anything that interests me, both personally and professionally."

Name: Dr. Farida Azhar Hewitt
Role: Contract Professor, Geography, Wilfred Laurier
          University; author of *The Other Side of Silence: The
          Lives of Women in the Karakoram Mountain*
Children: Four daughters

"I'm a human geographer, and my research focused on
women in traditional, premodern villages and their experience with 'development' and 'modernization.' When I went
back to resume my studies, my daughters were 5, 15, 17 and
20. My oldest daughter was in university. My husband is a
geographer, and since 1961 his research in glaciers and
landslides has taken him to the Karakoram Mountains, so
when I chose a site for the fieldwork portion of my MA thesis,
I looked to this area as well and decided on a village in Nagir,
in the Northern Areas.

"Tara, my youngest, accompanied me on these research
visits. We learned to speak Balti so that we could talk to the
women (we already knew Urdu, the official language of
Pakistan, since I am Pakistani) and lived with them in their
family homes. Let me say from the beginning, that it was my
husband who encouraged me to go back to school, and without
his encouragement I might have been content with an MA and
certainly never ventured into doing a doctorate or writing a
book! But once I had started, one step followed the other.

"Tara was in kindergarten when I entered university, so she
was in full day school every other day. On the alternate days,
if I had a class, I could leave her with a friend. I would go to
class and rush back. By starting my master's part time, it was
much more manageable to do. More challenging was doing
all the readings and writing essays. That was done between
the hours of 2 and 6 a.m. By going to bed early, I was able to
concentrate then—no phone calls, demands or problems to
solve! However, I could always be relied on to fall asleep in
front of the television, or in the waiting room when Tara
started ballet and ice skating. My other two daughters who
were at home became quite independent about making school
lunches, doing homework, keeping their rooms tidy, sorting

their laundry and so on. I still shopped and cooked dinner. We always ate together.

"It was difficult to go back to school after twenty-five years away from student life—back to reading vast amounts of material, sorting through and analyzing all that information and then writing papers. The main benefit was that I was more mature, had lived life, and was more knowledgeable and interested in world affairs.

"I would say that the main thing others can learn from my experience is that it is never too late to start learning. I was 51 when I got my Ph.D. and started teaching. A whole new world had opened up for me and I loved it. My daughters supported my efforts wholeheartedly, and were proud of me."

Name: Julia Deans
Role: Chief Executive Officer, Canadian Youth Business
           Foundation
Children: Ben, 21; Penny, 19

When we spoke, Julia was starting to contemplate her next role. She and her husband were also about to be empty-nesters, as their younger child was leaving for college in Pennsylvania. "I decided to take on this CEO position because I was ready for a big leadership challenge and loved the idea of expanding an already successful nonprofit to help even more young entre-preneurs launch businesses and create jobs."

Julia had recently stepped down from her position as the CEO of what is now Civic Action (previously the Toronto City Summit Alliance), a coalition of business, government, academic and community leaders working to address eco-nomic, social and environmental issues of the fourth largest city in North America. The convening role followed naturally from the volunteer work that she did at her children's school and came about after she had spent over four years out of the paid workforce: "The volunteer work that I had been doing really helped prepare me for this leadership position."

In the seven years that Julia was at the helm of the group, it launched numerous projects to improve the Toronto region. These included working on an initiative to place more than six hundred people from underrepresented groups on boards across the city, creating a new international arts festival and cross-sector partnerships that have improved commercial building energy efficiency and green procurement.

She became a regular speaker and media spokesperson—all of which was a significant departure from her previous career.

With joint degrees in law and public administration, Julia started working as a litigator in Toronto. "I had my first child in my second year of practice, took six months off and then went back full time. Two years later, we had our second child and I did the same thing.

"My grandmother had been a senior civil servant and my mother had always worked, so I had a very personal template for working and raising children. It's not that it was easy, but I didn't expect it to be and I felt that for me it was important to do it anyway."

Soon after her second maternity leave, her husband, a management consultant, was transferred to Hong Kong.

"It actually worked out really well for us. My law firm also had an office there, so I was able to continue my career with them—but with the added advantage of now being in a place where having significant household help was both incredibly affordable and commonplace." When the head office decided to close the Hong Kong satellite office, Julia again lucked out with the timing. "Coincidentally, it was right when my husband was being transferred to Singapore, so I helped close down the Hong Kong operations and then moved the family over."

In Singapore, Julia realized that she didn't want to join another law firm. "I took some time to settle the family and then found another role building up the Southeast Asian operations of a U.K.-based legal recruitment firm. "I loved the idea of helping put people together, I liked lawyers and knew many of them and, most of all, I wanted the experience of running a business."

Going back to work, especially in a demanding role like this, was not the norm for wives in the expat community. "I had to constantly justify myself and my decisions," she remembers. After two and a half years, the business was sold to the owners of Monster.com.

Soon after that, she and her husband moved back to Toronto.

"Again, I decided to take some time to establish the family. My husband was working and traveling constantly and the kids were six and eight, so I wanted to make sure they were adjusting well to the move before I decided on what to do next."

It was at this time that she got really involved in her kids' private school. "I was involved in the committees and the parent association, and ended up leading the lecture committee." The lecture committee presented a speaker series designed for the school's parents. "I realized that we were doing quite a bit of work for a very small audience and that, if we opened it up to other schools' parents and advertised it a bit, it could become something quite significant.

"We built it up and drew some big crowds in with topics like reading and bullying."

Her energy and drive on this project also suggested to her (and to several of the other parents) that it was probably time for her to go back to work. "I knew pockets of people but my professional network was fragmented since I hadn't lived in the city in ten years, and the three years I'd spent out of the workforce had taken a toll on my confidence."

She had one interview with a recruitment firm like the one she had previously worked at, and the reception wasn't all that welcoming. "The interviewer was extremely skeptical of my abilities and kept saying that, after four years out of the workforce, did I really think I had something to offer? It wasn't a big boost." Julia also wasn't sure if she wanted to go back to law or legal recruitment—or maybe after all this time, try something completely different.

But the success she had achieved in her volunteer program and the strength of her past experience hadn't gone unnoticed. A friend suggested that she meet with David Pecaut, who was the Chair and founder of the TCSA/Civic Action.

"We hit it off immediately and I was drawn to the role. It was essentially a start-up. When I began they had $7 in the bank and the role was fairly ambiguous, but David was exceptional and his vision was inspiring. As well, I had always been a policy person. I had studied public affairs at Columbia and was very drawn to the chance to work on issues that impacted so many people in the city: from diversity, to arts and culture, the environment and neighborhood building."

From the start it was a more than full-time role, but one filled with interesting and intellectually charged situations. "I'm a stimulus junkie and I knew from the start that this was not going to be a routine job. I was ready and willing to do what needed to be done. I was willing to be flexible on the salary but I also explained that I needed to have more than the usual amount of holidays. I was hoping for eight weeks so I could spend as much of the summer with my kids as possible—I got ten."

I asked her how she had managed to balance an intensely public schedule, including many evening events, with the needs of her teenagers. "As you get older and more senior in your career, it becomes much easier to carve out the space you need to focus on the kids. You realize that if you take time for your family, the world is not going to come to an end. Your employer isn't going to fire you or even lose confidence in you as long as you continue to deliver. So I would take the time that I needed. The kids were always first."

When the founder passed away, it was Julia who navigated the organization through larger and more diverse projects, taking on an expanded budget and remit as well as increasingly high-profile national and international roles for herself and the organization. Julia wasn't the only one who reinvented her career away from corporate life to more of a public service position. Her husband also decided that he wanted to take the opportunity to spend more time with their kids. "As our eldest came close to entering his last year of high school, my husband realized that he didn't want to miss out on time with them due to his travels and work schedule and so left his consulting partnership to be with the kids for two years. It worked out very well, since I had a really hectic time at work, and he was able to coach both children's basketball teams, teach a class, write a column and really be with the kids after school and in the evenings. He just loved it and it was possible because I had gone back to work in this new role."

Consider:

› **Respect your unpaid work.** "Women so often downplay their volunteer efforts and successes—and they shouldn't. My four years of volunteering was the perfect place to learn skills that really helped to make me successful in my last role. I always say that volunteering actually shows so much more about your abilities than paid employment—it's much harder to motivate unpaid people to do work than it is to manage paid staff in a business setting." advises Julia.

› **Focus on what you can add.** Don't fixate on what you can't do in terms of hours or skills. Instead, change your focus to what you can offer to add value and direct the conversation along these lines. "When I speak with other women looking to ramp up or get back into the workforce, I always emphasize that they need to focus on the skills they do have and what they can offer and not the reverse—which is what often happens."

Reinvention: The Privilege of Having a Plan

We all want advice on how to plan for success. What's often overlooked in this is that the ability to plan is actually a real privilege—it assumes a sense of certainty and control over our lives. Each year, approximately 250,000 newcomers immigrate to Canada.[41] The U.S. admits approximately 1 million legal immigrants each year.[42]

For new immigrant mothers, post-baby success is a postscript to the larger struggle to establish themselves in a new country. As part of my research, I had the opportunity to interview and speak with many immigrants, both recent and more established, about their experience immigrating and what they had had to do to reinvent themselves. These women faced financial challenges and the uphill battle of having their credentials and previous experience either completely overlooked or discounted, all while adjusting to and trying to navigate new cultural norms.

Name: Bushra Aafaqi
Role: Digital Marketing, SEO, Campaign Manager
Children: Faaz, 6; Zoya, 2

When Bushra and her husband, Arshed, immigrated to Canada in 2005, she had an MBA from Malaysia and high hopes of being able to get a good job. "After months of submitting CVs I realized that it was useless. My education and previous experience wasn't from a place they recognized, so it was meaningless. The only jobs that I could get interviews for were at call centers or in service positions.

"My husband was in a similar situation. He had an engineering degree and was able to secure an engineer position but with a small company and with no hopes of career advancement." Bushra's husband decided he would need to upgrade his skills and went back to school part time—while still working full time. Bushra ended up taking a call center job and becoming pregnant with their first child. It was after their son was born that she decided she needed to return to school as well. "I realized that to build the life we wanted for our family, I was going to have to get a set of Canadian credentials." She re-enrolled in an MBA program at Ryerson University and was given a full scholarship from the Ted Rogers Foundation for academic excellence and leadership. In addition to that, she worked as a TA to help with the bills and her son's day-care fees. She recalls that, "It was very *very* difficult, but I felt like we had no choice; we needed to do this to establish ourselves." Their one-year-old son went to a home day care where he often stayed from early morning till late in the evening, since in addition to their work hours they also had an hour-long commute. "I kept reminding myself that I was doing it for him, that this was what we had to do to give him the life I wanted him to be able to have."

Bushra ended up graduating as one of the top students in her class and got a good job as a project manager in a U.S.-headquartered digital analytics company. After being in her role for seven months, she got pregnant with her daughter. By that time, her husband finished his Master's from the

University of Toronto as well, and after taking a full year of maternity leave, Bushra moved companies and into a more senior role at a digital advertising company (Mediative, a part of YPG). "I would say that after we attained our respective degrees and found better opportunities, things started to come together for us. I was able to move my eldest son to a Montessori school, we had more regular hours and we bought a house. Now, both my kids are going to a Montessori school, and my son will soon be starting grade one.

"Motherhood has its ups and downs. However, it should not be the end of your career, and your career shouldn't be the reason for not starting a family. In a country such as Canada, where most of us are given and are able to take one year maternity leave, career and kids should not be either/or options. I'm planning on continuing to upgrade my skills and am taking some online courses. I feel like since we've come this far, I shouldn't stop now."

Name: Ratna Omidvar
Role: President, Maytree
Children: Ramona, early thirties; Yasmin, late twenties

The issue of helping immigrants is one that Ratna Omidvar both works on daily and has also lived herself. Today she is president of Maytree, a private foundation that promotes equity and prosperity through its policy insights, grants and programs. (I know it well, since I worked there for two years.) Under Ratna's leadership, Maytree has been recognized for its commitment to developing, testing and implementing pro-grams related to immigration, integration and diversity in the workplace, in the boardroom and in public office. A gifted speaker and writer, she has been recognized with honorary degrees from Canada's top universities and is a Member of the Order of Canada.

In 2010, *The Globe and Mail* named Ratna as one of the "Nation Builders of the Decade" for her leadership in creating practical employment programs for new immigrants, for helping them engage politically, and for building the business case for diversity in the eyes of both companies and government.

After the revolution in Iran, Ratna, with her husband and one-year-old daughter, fled Tehran, crossed the border into Turkey on a bus, then took a flight to Istanbul and then on to Munich. Canada was the default choice: "Australia was too far, the U.K. was too imperialist and Germany didn't offer any permanence," she recalls. They arrived in Canada in June 1981.

In a speech called "Letters to Canada," she chronicles her experiences as a new immigrant. She describes the daunting search for work, where without Canadian work experience there were few opportunities available. "They look at me earnestly and ask me slowly, 'Do . . . you . . . speak . . . English?' I am stunned at the question. Me? Top of the class in English Lit, member of the university debating team. It dawns on me slowly that I am just another brown face to them." She writes about the quiet grimness, the gray despair, of doctors, lawyers, engineers, who now work in factories or drive taxis, and her own personal struggle about whether she should change her name to make it easier to break into the job market. "I had qualified as a teacher of German as a second language in Germany. But even I realized that no one in Canada would want to learn German from an Indian who had just arrived as a refugee from Iran. So I took what I felt was the only course open to me—I reinvented myself. I don't say this to pretend that I had a clear formula; quite the opposite.

"In retrospect it felt like the game of snakes and ladders, up four, down three—I was a sales clerk selling tubes and pipes, I was an assistant to a film production company where I learned to make the perfect cup of coffee, I tried my hand at working for a writer, I thought about becoming a real estate agent . . ."

Within six months of arriving in Canada she began volunteering at her daughters' day care. This became the start of the community engagement path for her. Soon after, based on her own experience and that of other immigrants, Ratna decided to tackle the issue of the wasted talent of immigrants by creating a proposal to provide employment counseling for immigrants. The proposal was successful and they were awarded $75,000 to set up Skills for Change, an organization that for the past thirty years has offered employment referral and training programs for immigrants.

"One thing led to another, and my path as a social activist emerged, took shape, grew and flourished, and here I am today."

Consider Ratna's advice:

› **Don't sweat the small stuff.** "I see so many mothers today, literally losing themselves in worry about the small details, and I think because they have everything else, they can worry about all things, but I don't think it's helping them—or their children."

› **Embrace risk with open arms.** "I know it is scary, but it is only by opening yourself to the possibility and reality of failure that you will grow and find and reach the depths of your own capacity. And when you find them, you will be in wonder of yourself."

› **Don't let the perfect stand in the way of good.** "I often think that the pursuit of perfection in our lives holds us back from being excellent, because we are so frightened of not being perfect. There is something rigid about perfection, and it gets in the way of being good or very good. In the immediate next few months, remember that there is no such thing as the perfect résumé, the perfect interview or the perfect job. You can always recover from failure, but I don't quite see how one can recover or go forward from perfection."

› **Action trumps inaction any day.** "We live in a world that is dedicated to describing, redescribing and re-redescribing problems, instead of progressing to imagining and implementing solutions. Your action may not lead to nirvana, but remember that great work is done through small steps that create incremental change and ultimately lead to the solution."

FOUR

Staying on the Ladder

Acording to the latest numbers released by the U.S. Department of Labor, the largest groups of employed women are secretaries, nurses, teachers and cashiers (in that order). And in the first three occupations, women represent 80 percent of all those employed—indicating that for the vast majority of working women, not much has changed in the past fifty years or so. This chapter examines how working moms are doing in the professions and industries representative of the sampling of women that I spoke with.

In her book *Off-Ramps and On-Ramps*, Sylvia Ann Hewlett describes how from the 1970s to the 1990s, providing equal access was the approach to creating gender equity.

The belief was that once women had an equal access to opportunity and enough time was allowed to pass, the recruitment pipeline would fill with female talent that could then be promoted up, creating a gender balance at the senior levels.

Except that this didn't happen. Instead, women remained stuck in the middle.

As Sheryl Sandberg points out, ". . . the blunt truth is that men still run the world. While women continue to outpace men in educational achievement, we have ceased making real progress at the top of any industry. Women hold around 14 percent of Fortune 500 executive-officer positions and about 17 percent of board seats, numbers that have barely budged over the last decade. This means that when it comes to making the decisions that most affect our world, our voices are not heard equally."[43]

Further research found that keeping women in the running for senior corporate roles, particularly after the birth of children, requires addressing the dual impact of the "pull factors" (defined as those centered or arising from within the family) and "push factors" (which are centered at work).

Pull factors include parenting expectations, child-care issues and partner support; push factors are gender bias in the office, a lack of networks, and expectations around face time. I would add that the lack of relatable role models is also a factor—it becomes difficult to work towards goals that seem unattainable or too removed from where you currently are.

In *Lean In*, Sheryl Sandberg (somewhat controversially) argues that, "We [women] hold ourselves back in ways both big and small, by lacking self-confidence, by not raising our hands, and by pulling back when we should be leaning in . . . We internalise the negative messages we get throughout our lives, the messages that say it's wrong to be outspoken, aggressive, more powerful than men. We lower our own expectations of what we can achieve."

As a result, she says, many women are quietly checking out of their careers, sometimes years before they actually start a family. She believes women rarely make a sweeping decision to give up work to look after children, but instead make a string of choices (influenced by these push/pull factors) that propel them towards that end result.

The Business Case for Talent Retention

Corporate organizations have been launching and supporting a variety of initiatives to try and attract and then retain female talent, including flexible work options, mentoring programs, women's leadership training, child-care support and coaching. These efforts have very little to do with fairness and everything to do with business. In 1997, McKinsey & Company (the global management consulting firm based in New York, NY) concluded a year-long study involving seventy-seven companies and almost six thousand managers and executives. Their findings became the groundbreaking report *The War for Talent*, which found that the most important corporate resource over the next twenty years would be talent, and that as the demand for talent went up, the supply of it would go down. A decade later, the firm released *Women Matter*, a study that established that companies in which women were strongly represented on the board or in senior positions were also the strongest performing, measured by both the return on equity and operating margin.

Since then, study after study has regularly reconfirmed the apparent link between gender equity and success. For instance, Pepperdine University conducted a nineteen-year annual survey of 215 Fortune 500 companies that found that companies with a high ratio of women on the board or in senior positions are, by every measure of profitability (whether equity, revenue or assets), also the strongest performers—outperforming the industry average by 116 percent in equity, 46 percent in revenue and 41 percent in assets.[44]

Similarly, the independent research organization Catalyst also found that companies with the greatest representation of women in senior management positions performed the best—in fact they had a higher return on equity and a higher total return to shareholders by more than one-third.[45] There is an even more immediate business case to be made for retaining female talent: the cost of replacement. The total cost of replacing a senior manager who leaves is on average three times that person's salary.[46] According to other estimates, in certain knowledge-based companies the cost is even higher, an incredible 500 percent.[47] Certainly in law firms, the conservative estimate is that it costs from $200,000 to $500,000 for the firm to replace a second-year associate.

Changing Jobs

I have never worked anywhere on a full-time basis for more than fourteen months, and so I found the number of women that I interviewed who had been with one employer (albeit in different roles) for between ten and twenty years (or more) incredibly striking. For these women, there seemed to be a direct link between their post-baby success and the continuity of being with one employer—with many attributing their success in part to having built up an established professional reputation that could be strategically leveraged to help overcome challenges either at work or at home.

While staying long term with one employer certainly seems to have its advantages (for both the employer and employee), it's a tactic at odds with the larger trend. As of 2010, the average American has had eleven jobs just from the age of 18 to 46.[48] We now move through more jobs in a decade than executives did in a lifetime thirty years ago. Even against the backdrop of the recession (when people tend to stay with the jobs they have) and with the profound shift that has occurred in the employer-employee relationship, the culture of job changing is nonetheless here to stay. Companies are going to continue to be rigorous about their cost management and efficiency drives, making reduction in their workforce a normal part of doing business. Meanwhile, in the face of potential layoffs and increasing career alternatives, and without the prospect of secure pensions, individuals are becoming less loyal to their companies.

The average worker today stays at each of his or her jobs for 4.4 years, according to the most recent available data from the Bureau of Labor Statistics, but the expected tenure of the workforce's youngest employees is about half that.[49] Ninety-one percent of those born between 1977 and 1997 expect to stay in a job for less than three years. Strategic job hopping is an important part of career development, although knowing when and how often to make the change is an individual balancing act.

The Corporate Climb

Even as career pundits and industry leaders discuss the need to shift away from the metaphor of "the corporate ladder," the corporate climb nevertheless remains the foundation for private sector organizational life. (For the record, I much prefer the metaphor that Sheryl Sandberg uses, that careers are a "jungle gym" and not a ladder—since while there is only one way to the top of a ladder, there are multiple ways to reach the top of a jungle gym.)

Name: Tuula Jalasjaa
Role: Managing Director and Head, Dundee Wealth
          Retail Advisory Network, Scotiabank Global
          Wealth Management
Children: Lauren, 12; Rachel, 9

Tuula has worked in the banking and investment industry since 1997. She is now responsible for the overall investment management distribution of over $17 billion in assets. She became a vice president after her second child turned one and was promoted twice in the time after her maternity leave. Tuula is also the Chair of the Board of Scotia Asset Management US LP, sits on the Board of Directors of ScotiaMcLeod Financial Services Inc., and is Chair of Scotiabank Wealth Management's Advancement of People Committee, and also manages to fit in a close involvement with the United Way.

So what's her secret? "The biggest hurdles that I see for most women are in the high expectations we set for ourselves, that we can (or even should) do it all and have it balanced at all times with both work and family, and that around all of that we should also always be happy. We try to do it all and then we feel guilty when we can't. I think that women are often our own worst enemy, setting the bar so high and not accepting that it can't always be perfectly balanced. Some days work will have more focus, and other days it will be your family. If we can accept this, we will feel more successful with both our family and career goals, and our definition of success on both fronts is what counts.

"I never considered not staying fully in the game, to be honest. I'm naturally a type A person; I'm very energetic and motivated, but in order for women to maintain a competitive and healthy level of professional ambition, I think it's essential to work for an organization that gives you continuous opportunity for both development and to take on bigger challenges. In order to want to work towards the next opportunity, you need to believe that it's actually attainable for you. I think it's also important for women to take on strategically high visibility projects whenever you can—other people in your organization need to see you as a contender for the senior roles and opportunities."

Tuula was extremely candid when she discussed being pregnant at work. She was conscious that in her business environment (which is predominantly male), it was important to handle maternal matters carefully in order not to undermine her credibility. "Even though I was personally thrilled to be pregnant, I tried not to draw attention to it. Being pregnant wasn't something I needed to actively share or discuss in a work environment, and I met the same expectations at work that I did pre-pregnancy. I also made sure to reinforce to people that I wasn't planning on taking an extended period of time off and would be back before they knew it. With my first daughter, I took eight months. With my second, I went back part time to work on a special strategic project after three months, and then full time after four months.

"I think it is OK to share baby pictures and milestones sometimes, but when I came back from maternity leaves, I was careful not to have my 'new mother' status overshadow my work accomplishments and initiatives. Working in a male-dominated environment, I was sensitive to maintaining a work persona that was professional, and I stayed focused on my work and career goals. Yes, I was a mom, but at work I was an executive and that came first. You can't lose your professionalism just because you are a mom, and in any case, your family isn't in your office, so there's no need to bring that with you.

"My advice for young women would be to not worry that having children will ruin your career. There will never be a 'perfect time,' so have them when you personally feel the time is right. You can have children and a successful career! For newly returning mothers, I would say that it can be overwhelming at the beginning, but like everything else, you will adapt and it will get easier over time. Don't be afraid to ask for help from family or friends or get support at home.

"Women also still tend to take on more at home and with the kids. If you can, get help—it's hard to work the demanding hours often required with successful careers and manage everything else. This often leads to higher levels of stress, which can cause women to rethink their career aspirations and turn down bigger jobs in fear of overload.

"I'm trying to enjoy life to the fullest—my career is going very well and my two daughters are thriving. Next for me at work is hopefully a bigger role that challenges and fulfills me just as much as my current role."

Name: Jane Allen
Roles: Partner, Deloitte Canada, and Global Leader
               Renewable Energy/Chief Diversity Officer
Children: Two daughters, 24 and 20

In most other companies, Jane's two roles would be divided between two people. "Really they are two completely different full-time jobs," says Jane, "since it's not like one is in any way related to the other, but I personally enjoy the mix."

It also has a strategic business advantage. The culture in professional services firms, whether strategy consulting, law or banking, reflects a business model built on billing. "When the firm established this position, it recognized the need to have an experienced partner in the role to provide credibility when speaking with different practice groups about how diversity and talent retention matter to their business practice. The reality is that I wouldn't be listened to the same way if I was just speaking from a diversity perspective. This way, they appreciate that I understand our business and that I face the same challenges of meeting annual bottom line targets."

Her own post-baby experience and success as well as the past five years that she's spent spearheading Deloitte's diversity and women's leadership initiatives uniquely position Jane to be able to comment on this issue and the hurdles that women continue to face. "Part of the reason that this is still an issue is that the structure of most workplaces is based on a decades-old, pre-technology model where men worked and women stayed home with the kids. Men would work long hours, go home to their families in the evening and climb the corporate ladder in a very set way. We still haven't reached the tipping point of having enough women in positions of influence to significantly shift these expectations and to say that the focus of our business is going to be on results rather than face time, and that there are many ways to get the results we want and still live successful lives."

Deloitte's internal research suggests that the majority of women are also looking for templates that they can practically apply to their own lives and careers. "There's a perception among young women that there are few role models for them—they don't see women successfully managing their careers and their lives that they feel they can relate to," says Jane. "I also think that to a degree, we hear so much about the difficulty in managing work and family that women are increasingly anxious and subsequently the issues surrounding work and career seem insurmountable.

"I don't think the issue was quite as difficult for me though. Even as an adolescent, I always knew that I wanted to be financially independent and I always planned to have kids and a career. My parents immigrated to Canada when I was two, and from the beginning both of my parents worked full time. My mother didn't have the opportunity for higher education, but she always worked full time as a bookkeeper and instilled in me the importance of working.

"For myself, after having had so many years of education, I couldn't imagine just throwing that all away. I was 33 when I had my first child and at the time, I was working as the assistant dean for executive education at University of Toronto Business School. I had followed a mentor from the provincial government to the university and then when she left, I ended up assuming her role.

"I always knew that I didn't want to stay in this role long term, but the university was a great environment and had a great maternity policy for that time, so I did. Having my first daughter was the personal and professional catalyst for me to think seriously about what I wanted to do next." Jane took six months off to be with her daughter, then hired a nanny and launched a consultancy based on her earlier experience in the energy sector. "From the time my first daughter was six months to when she was fourteen years old, we had some kind of nanny help, both live in and live out.

"When I first launched my practice, I had a roster of contacts from my government work and soon I came across three other independent consultants doing similar energy contracts, and so we would work together to pitch larger projects focused on the strategy, research and analysis of the sector."

During that time, she also had her second child. "Although this time, as a business owner with clients who had pre-set expectations, I had a different type of maternity leave—I slowed down but I didn't stop." After another five years of running her business, Jane was starting to think about the next step. "The flexibility was great, but I was getting tired of having to do everything on my own, from pitching the business, managing the clients to ordering the paper clips."

Coincidentally, around that time, she began a conversation with a partner at Deloitte who mentioned that they were hiring people with her background in energy consulting. "I was interested; I was ready for something that was a bit more stable and where I didn't have to keep worrying about where the next project was going to come from. But at the same time, I was clear about some of the parameters I was interested in." Among them was the desire to work from home (they suggested she first get known before becoming flexible about her office face time) and a disinterest in travel.

"What helped is that the business model was very quantifiable—you had to deliver new business and then deliver to your clients—so in a sense there was an expectation that if you were in the office too much, something was wrong since you should be with your client or soon-to-be client. Even with help, the early years were crazy on the home front. The girls were three and seven when I joined Deloitte as a senior manager. My husband had an equally demanding job he was commuting to, and when the kids were little there was a lot of messy scheduling. I had lists for everything and often felt like I had hundreds of items that I had to juggle."

The work front also had its challenges. "The years of having my own business had taught me how to hustle, to make the cold call, get a meeting and close the deal. But I wasn't willing to travel for projects and I also tried to leave each day by five to make it home in time for dinner with the kids." This caused some frustration with her male colleagues. "Many of my male colleagues were based outside Toronto but would come in for the week to work. Since they were out of town and away from their families, they had an expectation that we would work late into the night together and then go for drinks and dinner.

"Deloitte does regular 360 reviews where you hear the feedback from your team, and it bothered me to hear that even though I was delivering the business and meeting the clients' needs, the fact that I wasn't willing to regularly adjust my schedule to theirs was such an issue. But you put up with it, and you counter it by doing a good job and staying focused on what matters to you. It helped that I always thought and still believe that too often the people coming in early and staying really late on a constant basis were present but not using their time well, and that they just don't understand the long-term benefits of setting limits."

Five years after she joined, and with the endorsement of all the other global partners in the energy practice group, Jane became a partner. "It was a big moment. Particularly at the time, there were an unbelievable number of hoops that we had to jump through to make partner. You needed a sponsor to bring your recommendation to the table, a partner to present you to the larger global partnership committee and to support the case, you needed to submit every project review, every sale, every contract that you'd achieved—as well as market analysis to prove that there was a market to buy what you would be selling as a partner."

Success was contingent not just on work and billings but on finding and cultivating relationships with the mentors and champions required to make it through. "All my mentors were men—partly because they were the ones in the position to help—and they did so just by casually demystifying the partnership process, sharing what I would need to do to get ahead, and lending me the confidence that of course I'd make partner. It wasn't an if but a when. . . . Their support meant a lot to me since it showed that they were invested in me and valued my contribution."

After a decade with the firm, Jane started to get restless at work. "I met with a coach over the period of a year, and for me the real learning was that it's OK to tell people that I was looking for something else—I'd thought that voicing this would be interpreted as me not being committed versus that I was just ready for another challenge."

The same partner who hired Jane now suggested that she take on her diversity role (with the caveat that she would continue her practice work). She's now been in this dual role for over five years and is thinking about what's next for her career. "I now regularly speak to younger women about career planning, and I like to stress that as difficult as it can be at the time, you have to accept that you can't plan everything. I would tell women to continually invest in themselves and not to lose their ambition. Of course, it will be hard at times, but it's best to just expect that and try to remember what you wanted when you spent all that time and money on your education."

Consider:

> **Invest in your professional relationships.** As Jane stated, it's the professional relationships that you organically build that provide confidence and insight—and will prove to be the most helpful over the long haul. This means less focus on the formal mentorship and instead investing in real relationships. For working moms in predominantly male environments, building the social capital to create reciprocal relationships is inherently more challenging—simply because mentoring and sponsoring relationships naturally form between individuals with common interests or shared backgrounds.

> **Don't get caught up in labels.** Develop the relationship but focus on the content and the returns that you both are getting.

> **Always think about what you can bring to the relationship.** (A new perspective on an issue? Material you've read or recently learned?)

> **If a formal mentoring program exists, get involved.** Or see if you can help establish one. A recent study showed that women who found mentors through a formal program were 50 percent more likely to be promoted than women who found mentors on their own.[50]

Academia

At first glance, an academic career seems like a strong choice for having both an interesting work life and being free from some of the strictures of corporate culture. For instance, in her *Atlantic* essay, "Why Women Still Can't Have It All," Professor Anne-Marie Slaughter (a law professor, she is also Dean of Princeton's Woodrow Wilson School of Public and International Affairs) discusses the benefits of academic life for the working mother—including the ability to usually set your own schedules and the ability to generally work remotely.

Currently, according to data from the research organization Catalyst, of women in academia in the U.S.:

> 32.2 percent are in non-tenure-track positions,
> 23.9 percent are in tenure-track positions and
> 44.0 percent are tenured.

Of women in academia in Canada:

> 36 percent are in non-tenure-track positions,
> 43.3 percent are in tenure-track positions and
> 30.9 percent are in tenured positions.

However, many of the same issues that plague the private sector are evident in academia, with men and women showing radically different developments regarding their future careers over time. For instance, at the beginning of their studies, 72 percent of women expressed an intention to pursue careers as researchers, either in industry or academia. For men this number was 61 percent. By the third year, the proportion of men planning careers in research had dropped from 61 percent to 59 percent. But for the women, the number had plummeted from 72 percent in the first year to 37 percent as they came closer to finishing their studies.[51] This sharp drop was attributed to women over time concluding that the characteristics of an academic career, including the increased impediments they would encounter, were unappealing and disproportionately greater than those faced by their male colleagues. The research found that women more than men see greater sacrifice as a prerequisite for success in academia and associate their available role models with a series of negative perceptions.

Gender discrimination is particularly pronounced in the hard sciences. In one study, physics students, after being given a lecture, were asked to judge their professor's competence. Half saw a man deliver a lecture and the other half saw a woman. Both were actors who delivered an identical script. Despite this, the students (both male and female) all judged the male actor as being significantly more qualified.[52]

"It feels like an uphill battle," said Kerri, mother of a seven-year-old boy and a five-year-old girl, who is currently completing a toxicology Ph.D. "What makes it harder in an academic setting, well, at least for me, is that I would have expected it in the private sector or corporate world, but I just assumed a higher level of equity in a university." Recently, during an assessment with her supervisor, Kerri was told that ". . . my problem was that I was throwing myself into my work like I'm a single guy. You are no [name of male colleague]. You're a mother and this isn't sustainable." Moments later, in reference to a male colleague with kids, her supervisor continued, "I'm sure [colleague's name]'s a great father and all, but you're a mother. It's different."

The irony is that Kerri's supervisor is a woman and mother, and the male colleague being referenced has more parenting responsibilities than his wife. "Also, let's note that the accusation is that I was throwing myself into my work like a single *guy*. Not a single person. Not a single woman. A single *guy*. Even in academia, women are expected to lean back from the get-go."

Name: Sarah Feldstein Ewing, Ph.D.
Role: Assistant Professor, Honors College/Center on
Alcoholism, Substance Abuse and Addictions
(CASAA), University of New Mexico
Children: Behr, 4; Elliot and Amy, 10 months

"There is a bit of a cultural expectation that you should wait
until you are tenured before having a child. I'm the first
woman to have been pregnant and to take maternity leave at
the Honors College. While academia still struggles with young
mothers, most of my friends at other universities are doing
the same thing I did—just going for my family as I work
towards tenure since your biological clock is right in the midst
of the process.

"That said, going up for tenure as you are building your
family is difficult. It's a fairly set process and it's the time
commitment, combined with the 'publish or perish' environment coming up against the demands of a young family that
also need your attention. It's true that some universities will
give you an additional year working towards tenure, but in a
competitive environment, as good as it sounds, it's often not
ideal since it backfires, with colleagues and senior department
heads resenting the exception being made.

"There's also a lot of traveling in academia, which can be
tough. Right now I do what I can remotely, and end up doing
a lot of twenty-four-hour trips where I pack everything into the
one full day. Before the kids, these trips would be spread out over
a week. But the flexible hours of academia and the opportunity
to pursue a topic that I care about is also incredibly exciting."

Medicine

For the past thirty years, the number of women in medical school has
been steadily growing. In Canada, women outnumber men at most
medical schools with a 57 percent enrollment, and in the U.S. women
make up 47 percent of the students.[53] The increase of women has been
responsible for some significant changes in the profession—including
improved work/life balance for all doctors, the rise in doctors doing
international aid work and improved patient communication skills.

A doctor's choice of how, where and what to practice will profoundly impact the layout and structure of his or her career. For instance, private practice offers more control but with the additional stresses of running a business; hospitals and academic environments allow doctors to train the next generation of practitioners as well as pursue research, but the combination is challenging and time intensive. In addition, while many challenges that doctors with children face are common across the professions (fatigue, time constraints, working mother guilt, the impossibility of leaving work issues at the office)—others are unique to the profession, including the issue of non-traditional work schedules and patient obligations.

The common theme is that despite the growing number of women within the profession, at the senior levels they remain vastly underrepresented for their numbers.

"We seriously need to get more women in top positions. The upper management structure needs to be changed," says Dr. Noni MacDonald, the first woman to be named a dean of medicine in Canada when she was appointed to the role at Dalhousie University in 1999. "There's too much internal politics that is often not attractive to women. Women often just turn away. I still see it very much as an old boys' club." As well, despite the overall increase of women in medicine, their professional aspirations have remained remarkably static.

"What's interesting is that there has been a minimal change in the percentage of women choosing particular specialties," says Dr. Ann M. Renucci, a corneal and external disease specialist in Grand Rapids, Michigan. "Women tend to gravitate to nonsurgical specialties and primary care, such as internal medicine, pediatrics, family practice and ob-gyn."[54]

Name: Alison Ashmalla
Role: Family Doctor, Riverdale Community Health
          Center
Children: Dylan, 4; Kristyn, 2

"I went into medical school at the University of Toronto when I was 21, I graduated at 25 and then I did my two years of residency, and what I noticed during that time was that there were very few good role models for female specialists—they just didn't seem to have very much control over their sched-ules and very limited options for balancing a family. I knew I wanted to have kids and wanted to have a bit more control over my work schedule." And so Alison decided to go into family medicine, particularly since her husband was pursuing a very intensive specialty (he's a lower gastrointestinal surgeon and oncologist).

"It wasn't an easy decision, particularly in a competitive environment like the University of Toronto, where choosing family medicine was pretty much seen as a 'soft' option." In Canada you can either be a salaried doctor, working for someone else at a clinic, or you can run your own practice, taking on all of the responsibility for overhead, staff and billing—which essentially equates to running a small business.

Just as she did with her decision on family medicine, Alison decided that when she balanced out the pros and cons of each, she preferred the option of working at someone else's clinic. "I decided to work at a community health center. Although it pays much less than private practice, it's also really rewarding work. Many of our patients are quite high-need and you get to know them very well." Although the practice is composed predominantly of women, many have no kids and Alison admitted to a certain measure of guilt at having to leave her patients' care to colleagues. "When I announced my first pregnancy, one of my colleagues bluntly told me, 'I'm happy for you, but not happy for what it means to me.'"

She also deliberately opted to have her kids close together (they are just fourteen months apart). "I figured we knew we wanted to have two, so we should do it quite soon and then be able to move on to the next stage.

"Family medicine is odd in that my career over the next ten years or more will essentially be the same as when I started. Although as the kids get older, I'm looking forward to engaging more on social justice topics related to the patients we see, such as refugee- and poverty-related health issues." Alison acknowl-edges that ". . . we have fallen into pretty gendered roles, since with Shady's schedule, I do more with the kids, but I enjoy what I do and don't feel the need to compete. I have a set schedule

The Myth of the Medical Meritocracy

Medicine seems like it should be one of the few careers in which men and women working the same hours and producing comparable results in similar specialties would be paid and promoted equally. However, a study published recently in *The Journal of the American Medical Association* reveals that medicine may not be so meritocratic after all.[55]

Researchers analyzed the professional trajectories of almost two thousand mid-career physician-researchers. Chosen because of their similarity to one another in professional interests, aptitude and ambition, the doctors in the study each had received a highly prestigious research grant early in their careers and worked not in private practice but in academic medical centers. The researchers examined a wide range of career factors, including the number of hours worked, professional achievements, leadership positions, marital status, parental status and salary. What they found was that a male doctor's annual salary averaged just over $200,000 and a female's averaged about $168,000. Like previous researchers, they found that the female doctors tended to be in lower-paying specialties, have fewer publications, work fewer hours and hold fewer administrative leadership positions.

But when these researchers ran the numbers again, this time adjusting for differences in specialty, publications, academic rank, hours worked and leadership positions, they found that the expected average salary for women *still* fell behind that of their male colleagues. The male doctors made over $12,000 per year more than the women.

"We really didn't expect to find such a substantial unexplained difference," said Dr. Reshma Jagsi, lead author and an associate professor of radiation oncology at the University of Michigan. The reasons for this income difference are most likely the same ones that impact other industries. This includes female doctors negotiating less aggressively than their male peers, and an unconscious bias that leads to women being paid and promoted less. "Medicine is not immune to these biases."

where I work from 8:30 to 4:30 on Tuesday, Wednesday and Friday, plus one Saturday a month. I usually do some paperwork, letters and that kind of thing on my days off but it's pretty flexible. This arrangement really works well for me."

Name: Dr. Rachel Wald, MD, FRCPC
Role: Staff Cardiologist at the Toronto General Hospital and Hospital for Sick Children
Assistant Professor, Departments of Pediatrics, Medicine, Obstetric/Gynecology and Medical Imaging, University of Toronto
Children: Benji, 6; Zachary, 3; Joshua and Tamar, 5 months

When Rachel and I met, she was in the middle of the fourth month of the five-month maternity leave that she was taking after the birth of her twins, although she admitted she still worked from home on her research and patient e-mails. A few months before, she had been awarded a Canadian Institutes of Health Research grant to coordinate a unified heart disease research and treatment program in fourteen hospitals in eight cities across Canada. "It took me three summers of work on this over-four-hundred-page proposal—so it's fantastic news!"

Even though she'd just had twins, this project would now be added to her regular workload. Rachel's area of expertise includes pediatric and adult congenital heart disease, pregnancy and heart disease, and cardiac imaging. "I knew since I was in grade twelve that I wanted to go into medicine and I absolutely love what I do. Survival into adult life for patients with congenital heart disease is a relatively recent development in medicine, so I get to be right at the forefront of the research and developments—which is incredibly exciting.

"But I also always knew that I wanted a family and didn't see why, with the right partner and support, I should have to choose between the two." Rachel's first son was born when she was 32 years old and had just started a staff position at Boston Children's Hospital. After two months of maternity leave, she was back at work. "It was exhausting since my work hours were incredibly long and I was up a lot of the night breast-feeding." With her second son, she took four months of maternity leave.

When I asked her about the women she went to medical school with, she agreed that some systematic changes need to be made. "Amongst almost a dozen of my doctor friends who are women, only two (including me) are still practicing full time. For me, having an equal spouse helps [her husband is also both a staff physician in the Division of Nephrology and an assistant professor in the Department of Medicine, also at the University of Toronto]. We both understand the demands we are under and have a real respect for what the other one does. It also means we're pretty good about being fifty-fifty parents. We work from eight to six, but then both log on after the kids are asleep to finish up our administrative work and e-mails, and then wake up at four or five in the morning to work on our research and publications.

"Everyone thinks that the hours in medicine and especially in specialties like ours make it non-conducive to family life [she's expected to be on call twelve weeks a year and in the hospital one weekend a month] but I see my sister [a tax lawyer] and her hours are much worse because she has very little control over her schedule—in comparison both Ron and I know our schedule about four to six months in advance, and so the weeks we're on call, we can plan ahead.

"I do think that my academic career is moving at a slower pace than my male colleagues', since despite my research I don't travel or attend as many conferences as most of them do. But I also know that I'll get to the same place as them but just on a slightly different timetable. I know another doctor who still comes in twice a week at 85, so I'm not sure that long term the time matters that much!"

Law

Law firms, particularly large law firms, remain stark examples of the gender gap in leadership. Schools in Canada and the U.S. have for years graduated classes that are almost evenly split between men and women. Large law firms duly absorb these new associates in almost equal numbers, and then a few years in, the gender split completely skews as women leave in large numbers.

According to data from research organization Catalyst, in the U.S.:

> in 2012, women made up 31.1 percent of all lawyers;
> women were 45.4 percent of associates in 2011;
> only 19 percent of equity partners at firms are women; and
> the trend continues in the academic sector, where only 20.6 percent of law school deans are women.

Similarly, in Canada the disparity is stark: despite now making up 39 percent of the profession in Ontario, and 31 percent of lawyers in private practice, women account for only 21 percent of law firm partners. Female lawyers are more likely than men to leave private practice after five to seven years and are much less likely to become an equity partner—issues that law firms are struggling to address. "You have a given population of people who were significantly motivated to go through law school with a certain career goal in mind," says Bettina B. Plevan, a labor and employment law specialist at Proskavar Rose in New York. "What de-motivates them to want to continue working in the law?"[56]

Perhaps the most important answer to her question is the fact that the path to partnership is usually approximately eight to ten years into practice. This often overlaps with a woman's time frame for starting a family: family-friendly work arrangements become more appealing. Time requirements, billing targets and a culture of face time are also contributing factors. The cost of this attrition is significant (in part because, according to estimates by the Law Society of Upper Canada, replacing an associate at that level comes at the approximate cost of $300,000 a year).

As a result, the legal profession is trying a variety of programs and initiatives designed to retain female talent. One is a maternity leave buddy program, which Tara L. Piurko, a partner at McCarthy Tétrault LLP and mother of two children under six, used during both her maternity leaves to keep in close contact with her practice. She and a selected work buddy regularly met for lunch, often with her baby in tow. "My maternity buddy seemed like a surprising choice to many. I chose a male corner-office partner with no kids. My reasoning was that I wasn't looking for help on how to be a mom or even a working mom; what I wanted was to stay up to date on the profession that I had invested so heavily in." In their regular communications by e-mail, phone or in person, she received updates from him about her files, her co-workers and her clients. As her return-to-work date neared, she spoke with him regularly and then began working two to three hours, a couple of times a week, to slowly get back on track. "I didn't want to show up at the end of my mat leave and try to hit the ground running. I knew it wasn't going to work," she recalled. "I was transitioning my baby to day care and I thought, 'I need to transition myself and my family back to work.'" Not long before her second maternity leave, Tara made partner.

"There is an observation that women who go off on maternity and then parental leave who are in the private practice of law can lose traction. And in a law firm, if you lose traction, it's hard to get your mojo back and be on the radar of the senior people who transfer the work around the office," explained Katherine Pollock, an employment law partner at Fasken Martineau DuMoulin LLP and their gender diversity officer.[57]

Name: Kristin Taylor
Role: Partner, Cassels Brock
Children: Beth, 11; Grace, 9

Kristin's career has followed what used to be considered the "right" path to professional success. First you make partner, then you can think about kids. Now in her nineteenth year of practicing employment and labor law, Kristin became a mother almost a year after she applied to be partner. "It wasn't actually planned that perfectly, especially since we had a miscarriage in between, but I became a partner and got pregnant within weeks in early 2001. I was the classic workaholic until then and I was worried about how I was going to keep working the kind of hours that I'd been putting in all this time.

"With my first mat leave [about five months], I did some work while I was off, but I worked strategically by categorizing my practice into two kinds: clients that other colleagues could take care of and clients who could not be delegated, whom I would continue to focus on. It wasn't a lot of work. I would check in once a day, most days, but it meant that I wasn't isolated and the work connection gave me confidence and allowed me to transition back much more easily.

"The reality is that in an industry built on clients and client service, it's a disservice to yourself and all the work you've put in to fully step away for an extended period of time. It's absolutely critical not to fall off everyone's radar, because the nature of the industry means that you can't just waltz in and expect that everyone will stack files on your desk. I didn't consider it an imposition, but an investment in myself and everything that I had already built.

"It helped that at that time, I had been at my previous firm [then Fraser Milner Casgrain, now Dentons] for the duration of my career and so my manager was supportive. There was a trust that I would figure out how to make my new family work with my existing practice if I just had the time. So I did it in stages. First I came back a few hours at a time, then a few days and so on."

Even with that, Kristin acknowledges that she felt defensive when, post-baby, she stumbled with her billable hours. "I really tried to view the issue from the lens of an employer and not as an employee, and would encourage other women to do the same. We need to take more of an ownership mentality. Just the way we want firms to make a long-term investment in us, we also need to make a similar long-term investment in ourselves." She credits this shift in perspective as allowing her to have the confidence to reimagine her workday.

"I realized that I didn't have to do what the person in front of me was doing. I knew I was committed long term to the firm and my career and so how I did it wasn't the most important thing anymore. I knew I didn't want to sit at my desk from 8 a.m. to 7 p.m. anymore and so I tried a number of different combinations. As a result, although my physical hours in the office were less than my peers, I made up for much of it at home."

With her second child and maternity leave, Kristen also focused on writing, publishing and keeping her professional profile up, both within the firm and within the profession more broadly. Today, her schedule differs slightly from that of her colleagues but better reflects the needs of her family. "The trade-off is that I usually work a second shift from home once both kids are in bed. I take calls when I'm out of the office and my BlackBerry is usually close at hand. Although you can technically be billing a client from anywhere—which is the one great and perhaps only advantage of the billable hour— the truth is that face time still really matters in the legal profession. The culture has been slow to change on that front, but I do think partners are starting to appreciate that face time can be overrated. This is particularly so once a lawyer has established a reputation of reliability, excellence in work product, trustworthiness, etc.

"In a lawyer's early years (whether that means post-graduation from law school or having recently changed jobs), networking is critical and face time is essential (since this is how you actually get assigned work to meet your billable hours targets). As well, many files, particularly transaction and litigation files, are staffed by teams and require a significant level of collaboration, and so it's just easier and more effective to have everyone in the room at the same time." She adds, "There's no set balance at any level or stage though. I re-evaluate each month to see where I need to place more of my time and attention. If something big is coming up at work or with the kids, then I try and adjust my schedule and commit-ments around that. It's not perfect or exact . . . [but] my girls are thriving and I love what I do."

Creating a New Precedent

"It's definitely time to rethink the frame of how a legal career should look. The majority of young associates believe that they need to first establish themselves professionally and gain some significant trac-tion—which is of course understandable. But the truth is, in the early years, you are actually far more dispensable in that the client is never actually asking for *you*. And this provides an element of flexibil-ity and freedom that isn't really possible quite the same way further on in your career," says Kate Broer, a partner in the litigation group at the global law firm Dentons. Broer is co-chair of Dentons' National Diversity and Inclusion Initiative and mother of two girls aged seven and five.

Name: Monique Ashamalla
Role: Associate, Heenan Blaikie LLP
Children: Micah, 11 months

Monique had just started her legal career when she found out she was expecting her first baby, and she was at the end of her pregnancy when we first spoke: "My plan is to take nine months leave before returning to work. I don't feel like I've been met with any hesitation in terms of my family's decision to take this step now. My colleagues have been very supportive and accommodating."

Monique thinks that a variety of factors are leading to this shift. "I feel that the unwritten rule used to be that you didn't have a baby until you became a partner, but that's definitely changing. Lawyers are entering the practice older than in the past, with many of them having worked or having done a master's degree in addition to law school. While law is a consuming profession, people seem less prepared to sacrifice family for career outright. I am finding this to be true not just for women but for men. Perhaps there is also a growing sense among young females today that they can do it all and do not have to postpone one for the other. I feel like, between my colleagues (among whom there are numerous other young parents) and my own parents, I have been given a lot of examples of how to manage both." (Update: When I last checked with Monique, she had returned to work after taking ten months' leave.)

I came across many more stories of women in law who were more successful post baby, and while the focus of the discussion still centers on what women in large law firms are or aren't doing, many of the women I spoke with had created successful careers for themselves at mid-size or small firms, in house, at nonprofits, or in policy or government. Many of their stories can be found in other sections of the book.

The Tech Sector

"Mentoring is key to expanding opportunities. Young women need to see mid-level and senior tech industry women succeeding. Last year, I attended a networking event where I spotted fewer than a dozen women among several hundred attendees. The 'woman in technology' keynoting the event was a celebrity marketing organic baby products, while a male colleague explained the underlying business model on her behalf. It's discouraging, and a missed opportunity, for young women not to encounter role models to spotlight the path towards leadership in the industry," wrote Perry Hewitt, the chief digital officer, Harvard University.[58]

Hewitt also points out that the answer to the standard question— "Where are all the women in tech?"—is that they are hiding in plain sight. There are many qualified women in the tech sector but we don't hear their stories, and their numbers are very low. For instance, while women hold 56 percent of professional jobs in the U.S., they account for 25 percent of information-technology positions and are founders of less than 8 percent of tech start-ups, says the National Center for Women and Information Technology. According to a recent study by the Institute of Engineering and Technology, women account for only 6 percent of the engineering workforce. This proportion has risen by just 1 percent since 2008. The latest figures from the *Computing Research Association Taulbee Survey* suggest that less than 12 percent of computer science degrees were awarded to women in 2010 to 2011.

Delving into the companies listed on a recent *Forbes* Top 25 Hottest Tech Stocks, the statistics gathered on senior management teams showed no women held CEO positions, 13 percent of the senior managers were women, and 1.9 percent of the women senior managers held a technical position. Similar statistics can be gathered from the Fortune 500 companies: 16 percent of the senior leadership teams were women and only 1.7 percent were women in senior technical positions. Most women who hold senior management positions have come from sales, marketing, finance, legal, or human resources; they rarely come from engineering or product development areas.

The good news is that the possibilities remain endless when it comes to the tech sector. For a start, according to the U.S. Bureau of Labor Statistics, tech and IT jobs are expected to grow by over 22 percent

through to 2020; and even better, this generation of women is growing up with technology seamlessly integrated into their lives, vastly
increasing the likelihood that they will choose careers in technology.

Name: Lauren Bacon
Role: Entrepreneur (Co-founder, Raised Eyebrow Web
             Studio), business coach, tech start-up advisor and
             best-selling author, *The Boss of You*
Children: Alec, 18 months

"I'm a self-taught web designer and coder who built my first
website in 1995 and landed my first full-time job as a coder in
1997. In 2000, I left that job to start my own digital agency,
which grew over time to a staff of nine. After my son was
born (at the end of 2011), I stepped away from that business,
selling my shares to my co-founder (who is also a mom, to a
three-year-old). Since that time, I have been focusing on doing
more writing—my business partner and I co-authored a book
for women entrepreneurs, *The Boss of You*—as well as advising
tech start-ups and coaching entrepreneurs and leaders.

"I grew up in a pretty conventional 1970s household: my
mom stayed home with my siblings and me until all of us were
in school full time, and then she went back to work part time,
as a receptionist, so that she could be home in the mornings to
get us off to school, and back in time to greet us when we
came through the door. My dad worked very long hours and
was the primary breadwinner, and while he baked muffins
once in a while and picked up after himself, he still delegated
most of the household responsibilities to my mom.

"I've always been very career-focused, so I actually didn't
plan on having kids until I met my partner, David, and he told
me he very much wanted children and started grilling me on
why I didn't want any. No one had really challenged me on it
to that extent before, and I was pretty smitten with him, so I
started to examine the assumptions I'd made up to that point.
I realized that I had internalized the roles my parents had
played, and even though my mom eventually had an extremely
successful career (she became the executive director of a

nonprofit housing society that manages a large portfolio of buildings in Vancouver), I had internalized this outdated idea that in order to be a good mom, I needed to put my career entirely on hold.

"Meanwhile, David had grown up with two parents who were exceedingly dedicated to their careers—both scientists—and they had always had nannies, so he had a very different point of reference. And I realized, hey, his family is really close-knit and healthy, so maybe there are some other ways of making this work. Which, of course, I'd always known intel-lectually—I know tons of people who grew up with different family environments than me who are happy and healthy—but for whatever reason, it was hard for me to imagine hiring a nanny or putting my kid in day care, and continuing to focus on my work alongside having children.

"So that was the most profound shift that took place for me: moving from seeing motherhood and career as more or less mutually exclusive, to a more nuanced view. (And as I said, this is *not* how I saw the choice for other women, just a weird dichotomy I had within myself. I thought *I* needed to care less about work in order to be a good mom.)

"Now, my primary framework is what I call 'oxygen-mask parenting,' like the in-flight safety demos; you have to put your own oxygen mask on before you help others. Or in other words: happy parents, happy kids. I really see working moth-erhood as a gift, because it's helped me get very, very clear on the work that matters most to me. I ask myself regularly: Is this oxygen-mask work or blah work? If it's blah work, I try and minimize it, because that's getting in the way of me being present with my son. If it's oxygen-mask work, then I believe it makes me a better parent because I am fulfilled and happy—and because it gives my son a great example of what meaningful work and a fulfilled life look like.

"I would say that the challenges we face in the tech industry are for the most part common to all male-dominated environ-ments: The predominance of men's perspectives has a ten-dency to make women feel like we must hold ourselves to men's definition of success. Layer on top of that the fact that the tech sector is still young and attracts a lot of people under the age of forty; the odds are good for many women that their boss will be a guy under thirty who hasn't really given much thought to starting a family, let alone creating a family-friendly workplace. A huge number of tech companies, particularly start-ups, are very small and don't even have an HR department or much in the way of employee benefits.

"There's also a prevalence of 'always-on' thinking; when you work in an environment where things are happening 24/7, it can be difficult to set and maintain boundaries between work time and non-work time. It's not impossible—most of the moms I know in the tech sector have wrestled with this and have figured out how and when to unplug in order to be present with their partners and kids during off hours—but it does take real discipline. Of course, this is true in every sector, now, but I'd argue that it's more intense in the tech sector.

"The flip side is that tech affords some wonderful opportunities for parents who crave more autonomy and flexibility: Many tech companies have employees who work from home at least part of the time, and in my experience, they often let people set their own hours as well. This is particularly true for people in technical roles; if you're a coder, you probably don't need to attend a lot of meetings, and if you'd like to work from 6 p.m. to 3 a.m. and spend half the year overseas, no one's going to get in your way. I'm always bothered by the notion that there's one right way to do anything, and so one of the biggest things that I would like to see shift is to see more women in leadership roles, i.e., founding their own start-ups and demonstrating that there are viable alternatives to the stereotypical all-work-all-the-time start-up founder burnout highway.

"I would also love to see more dads in the tech sector owning up to the fact that they crave greater flexibility as well. So long as women are outnumbered by men in tech, we face an uphill battle when it comes to getting our perspectives heard, and we very much need male allies. Again, I think this is starting to happen more, and it's very gratifying to see that. But there's still a long way to go."

Keeping Going: Success in the Middle

It's in the middle of the corporate climb that women feel the most pressed and are most tempted to look for alternatives and even consider stepping out of the workforce if they can.

The reason is that they don't yet have the perks of C-suite seniority and often have young children and partners who are also at a similar career stage (which increases the family stress).

Name: Tracy MacKinnon
Role: Senior Tax Manager, Deloitte
Children: A daughter, 5; a son, 3

"A year after returning to work following my second maternity leave, I was chosen to participate in the Step Up program, which is a leadership program for high-performing senior managers in our firm. This recognition meant a lot to me and has changed my own approach to my career. Prior to the coaching and mentoring I received in the program, I was a bit passive. I felt that if I did a great job and let people know I was interested, my colleagues would give me the work and profile I needed to move my career forward. Now, I am much more assertive about creating those opportunities for myself instead of just waiting hopefully.

"For sure, some days are absolutely crazy and having such a full life can sometimes be overwhelming. One morning, due to an unusual snowfall, our day care was closed. I had a client meeting (and no way to contact them to postpone it) and my husband had an important board meeting. We didn't know what to do and were getting frantic. Luckily, one of my friends was home that morning and she agreed to watch my daughter (I was pregnant with my son at the time). That evening, my husband and I wrote out a long list of who to contact in a child-care emergency and in what order. We haven't needed it since, but it's reassuring to know that we have several backup plans in place if we need them."

For Tracy, organization and planning ahead has become the only way to manage it all.

"My days are busy and jam-packed, so I try to be prepared

for every eventuality, at home and at work. This has helped me enormously. If my nylons get a run, I have a spare pair at work. When I leave for work in the morning, I know what we'll be having for dinner and my cupboards are stocked so we have all the ingredients. My husband and I know the days we have appointments or when we each need to be in early, work late, or when we have some time to ourselves because it's all color coded (by family member) on our fridge calendar."

Name: Kathleen Collins
Role: VP Director of Integrated Solutions at DDB
              Canada
Children: Ben, 8; Max, 6

"My role is a combination of new business development, overseeing our account services group and helping with the management of the agency as a member of our management committee.

"Travel and nights out are a part of my industry (advertising). When work functions come along, I always make an effort to go. Sometimes it is only a brief appearance but some nights you just have to be there. The biggest challenge in new business development is the crunch right before an RFP (Request for Proposal) is due or before we head into a pitch. No matter how much you try to plan and be organized, there always seems to be more work than time to get it done. So my plan really is to try to stay on top of a pitch as much as possible. I try to arrange for extra help right before the pitch (my husband, or his stepmom, or a sitter). Travel can be hard, especially when the kids get upset about my being away. But the boys are getting older, so they seem less bothered than they used to be. My husband is traveling a lot right now as well, so when I have to travel, it can be a real challenge. I've learned to ask for help and I'm lucky enough to be surrounded by family, friends and neighbors who will say yes when we do get in a pinch! I have found that most people though, even those without kids, have been quite willing to accommodate my schedule—when I ask.

"When my two boys were young, the main thing I learned was to work as efficiently as possible. I can honestly say that focus means you can get more done in less time. As long as you deliver on work commitments and make deadlines, people usually aren't all that concerned about your hours in the office. But, of course, it isn't always easy. I've taken countless numbers of calls from home. Client service means being accessible to clients and your team. I often have to get back on the computer after the kids go to bed and there have been more late nights than I care to admit to, when something has to get done. I've worked on holidays (but always try to limit how much). And I couldn't tell you how many times I've called my husband to ask if he can take my pickup night so I can stay at work a bit later.

"I'd advise other women to talk to people in your office going through what you are experiencing. Ask for opinions of what works for others but recognize you have to figure out what works for you in your situation. Doing everything you can to be the person others can count on to get things done also goes a long way. So does finding a job you like. Since it isn't always easy to find balance, you want to enjoy it enough to make the sometimes struggle worthwhile."

Name: Caroline Butchey
Role: Director, Strategy Program Office, Global
          Banking, Scotia Capital
Children: Jessica, 9; Jaden, 7

In addition to her work and family (including a partner with a similarly hectic career), Caroline is also in the midst of finishing her MBA from Dalhousie. "Even when I wasn't exactly sure *how* I would do it, I was always confident that I would proactively continue to grow my career after my kids were born. It helped that I had built a solid reputation in the years before I had my children. During my maternity leave, I was encouraged to explore two more senior positions within the organization that were potential fits with my own career targets.

"While I was on maternity leave the second time, I stayed in touch with my colleagues at the office on an informal basis and reviewed the job postings online. I found out about two opportunities within the bank that were at a more senior level and applied for one, although it didn't work out. That happened in the early to mid-part of my maternity leave. Towards the end of my leave, I found out about a unique role that involved running an operations area involving fifty-plus people. It was daunting at first as I knew very little about the area, but I was encouraged to apply and was successful in getting the appointment. Scotiabank provided me with a four-month transition period, where I was given an opportunity to train with the individual that I would be replacing, and I remained in that role until 2010.

"This was a director's role, and so over the next five years, I was exposed to many key areas and developed strong networks and, most importantly, I was able to hone my leadership skills. In the end, the opportunity to 'make a difference' in this new and challenging role while further developing a large network of supporters was a significant turning point in my career. I loved my work and never doubted that I could find a way to maintain and enjoy both. I try to compartmentalize my life so that when I'm in the office, I'm 100 percent here, and when I'm with the kids, I'm 100 percent with them.

"For me, organizing and delegating are key to staying sane while managing a busy dual-career family with young children. I end up planning my full menu for the week while sipping my Saturday morning coffee and flipping through cookbooks and food magazines.

"Part of what keeps me going is that I really enjoy what I do. In 2010, I was encouraged to join the Executive Project Office as a leadership development opportunity, which was a real boost to my ambition and career. It is a highly engaging annual program that brings together approximately six to ten high-potential leaders from across the bank to work on key projects for a short period. I would say that it was like 'mentorship on steroids' since it really pushed us to go beyond our comfort zone.

"Just over a year ago, I took on a new role within Global Banking and Markets to assist with setting up a strategy office with a focus on execution. I am thrilled with this assignment and have had amazing opportunities to network with senior staff from all over the bank and have been given high-profile projects.

"Right now, I think success comes down to working extremely hard, being positive and networking constantly and thoughtfully while being patient as you think of your career as long term."

Consider:

These were some of the most common tips that I heard on how to manage the busy life stage:

› **Prevent burnout.** Take on only those work challenges that keep you engaged and excited.

› **Make time for yourself.** Use those personal days!

› **Make lists!** Write it all down.

› **Use apps.** Manage items more effectively.

› **Use a family calendar.** Update it weekly and hang it in the kitchen so everyone can see what's coming up and where everyone is.

› **Make having a social life a priority.**

› **Do as much as you can the night before work.** This will help to make mornings as smooth as possible. A rough morning for you or the kids can color the rest of your day.

› **Freeze a month of lunches.** One of my favorite tips (since I hate packing lunches) was from one mom of three who is an associate at a litigation firm and makes a full month of lunches the first Sunday of each month; and each night, she just takes them out to defrost!

Ambition and Motherhood: An Uncomfortable Relationship?

In their book, *The Arc of Ambition,* authors James Champy and Nitin Nohria describe the ambivalence many feel about ambition. "We see it as dangerous yet essential. We disapprove of those who abuse it, but we dismiss those who lack it. We see too little of it as a failing, too much of it as a sin. . . . Simply put, ambition is what makes us go. Ambition is the spirit of success, of striving for something worth achieving."

In the larger culture, ambition and women remains an uncomfortable pairing—and motherhood seems to exacerbate it further. Sheryl Sandberg describes this as the "leadership gap," and says that while many individual women are ambitious, the data clearly show that many more men than women aspire to most senior jobs. She wrote, "A 2012 McKinsey survey of more than four thousand employees found that 36 percent wanted to reach the C-suite, compared to only 18 percent of the women. When jobs are described as powerful, challenging and involving high levels of responsibility, they appeal more to men . . . and that even among highly educated professional men and women, more men than women describe themselves as 'ambitious.'"[59]

Sandberg does note that there is a start of a shift with the next generation—a recent survey of Millennials found that women were just as likely to describe themselves as ambitious, and a 2012 Pew poll found that for the first time among people between 18 and 34, more young women (66 percent) than young men (59 percent) rate "success in a high paying career or profession as important to their lives."[60]

What Sylvia Ann Hewlett found in her research on off-ramping and on-ramping with women's careers was that as women take time out from the workforce (usually for children) and face escalating demands at home, they also subsequently downsize their ambitions since they redefine what they view as possible for themselves. I would add that this is most likely helped along by our cultural reinforcement that motherhood is fundamentally incompatible with ambition, so women adjust and so do their employers.

In her book, *Necessary Dreams*, published in 2004, psychiatrist Anna Fels argued convincingly that ambition stands on two legs: mastery and recognition. To hold on to their dreams, women must attain the necessary credentials and experience, but they also must have their achievement and potential recognized in the larger world. The latter is often missing in female careers, and if women take some time out, employers and bosses are culturally conditioned to become even more skeptical about a woman's professional value.

A downsized cycle emerges: a woman's confidence and ambition stalls; she is perceived as less committed, then she no longer gets the good jobs or the plum assignments and this serves to lower her ambition further.

A vicious cycle is created of women feeling less ambitious, employers being unable to promote women who are not absolutely committed and invested in the endeavor, and then women failing to see the role models that would motivate or shore up their own confidence and ambitions. Of course, *ambition* is a highly subjective and personal term. What it means to each person changes over time and throughout various life stages. We need to remind ourselves that feeling or being less ambitious for a time doesn't mean it's a permanent state of being or anything to berate ourselves over.

News anchor and mother of two Reena Heer describes her own sense of ambition as in flux: "To be honest it changes. Some days I feel like I still don't have my old level of ambition fully back and then it's the complete reverse, where it's stronger than ever. And then I'll have a day where I just want to be with my family no matter what the professional costs are. We don't hear enough about this, but I tell women it takes time to get your confidence and ambition back after having a baby—how you feel a month, ten months or maybe even a couple of years after, is not how you'll always feel."

I certainly spoke with women who, although outwardly successful, felt that motherhood (especially recent motherhood) had taken a toll on their ambition and reinforced my belief that we need to make it OK to expand what success looks like and to be honest and supportive about the reality that what we might be ambitious for shifts and changes throughout our life.

Michelle,* a lawyer and mother of two, told me, "I think that motherhood dulls your ambition because you are no longer simply defined by what you do, and in the same vein, many people are not singularly focused on their careers, as there are so many other things that require your attention and focus. You can no longer go to every client opportunity, every lecture or take on every interesting case because that means that someone else will be putting your kids to bed, hearing about their days, and instilling their values into your children. Another issue is simply the sleep deprivation that comes with having kids. It is hard to care about your career when you have not slept through the night in a year."

Some women's frustration with themselves is also reflected in our collective misunderstanding that career success has to be a constant upward climb versus a longer-term understanding that careers no longer work in a linear manner. I was speaking about this on a panel, and one woman, a grandmother of two and mother of three (who went back to school herself when her daughter was 11) pointed out to me that men don't always feel relentlessly ambitious or career focused, since that's just not how life is, but with women, we always attribute lulls in our ambition or career climb to our children—whether that's accurate or not.

Easily, over half of the five-hundred-plus women I spoke with specifically mentioned that they felt more ambitious or more committed to career success after they became mothers (with ambition being defined far more broadly than just a raise or promotion and instead also including legacy projects, community impact, and feeling like a good role model).

Leah Eichler, a career columnist and the CEO of r/ally (a collaboration tool to help professional women achieve their goals), believes we are overdue for a change. "I think women need to get over the negative associations with ambition. *Ambition* is a good word. Somewhere along the way, women started interpreting *ambition* as meaning that they valued their professional lives over everything else. I don't think that's the case. I also find it frustrating that we teach our children—both boys and girls—to be ambitious, get good grades and be at the top of their class, but then, after they finish school and land a fabulous job, women are supposed to pretend they don't want it all anymore."

Name: Kyla Falkinder
Role: Consultant, HCL AXON
Children: Davis, 4; Charles, 2

When I first spoke to Kyla she was eight months pregnant with her second son. "I know I've become far more ambitious about my career since I had my first son. And I'm hoping I feel the same way after my second is born."

Now, two years later, she has spent a year in a job that she describes as her "dream job" as an SAP communications consultant for the global consultancy firm HCL AXON. "It has all the elements I was looking for: long-term growth, financial compensation, challenging work, and placing me on a path of even more growth and opportunity. I have always been ambitious about my career. And from a young age I was drawn to the idea of having a 'big job' and the ability to make serious money. I was lucky that my parents never pushed me into any one direction, so I was able to find what I really loved to do."

After completing her undergraduate degree, she did an MSc in mass communications and began working at a creative marketing agency. "My mother was a stay-at-home mother and I think seeing her frustrations was part of my motivation to make sure I found a career I loved and then really pursued it." However, it took a while for Kyla to go for the "big job" that she has always wanted.

"Before I got married, I was with a marketing agency for a few years and was already thinking that it was time to start looking for a more challenging role with greater potential. While I loved the work I was doing, it was a privately owned agency and as an account director, I had the sense that I had gone as far as I was going to go. But when I got married, I reconsidered it. Glen [her husband] and I talked a lot about whether we should have kids right away or whether I should pursue 'the awesome next job' as I called it then and that I felt like I was ready for. As much as I wanted to go for the job, I knew it could be healthier to have kids younger and I felt like there was no point pursuing my career full on, getting that dream job and then getting ripped out and away from the momentum of my career. So instead, I decided to stay where I was."

Maternity leave turned out to be hard for Kyla. "It was isolating and frustrating and even though nothing my husband said or did supported this, during that time I felt somehow less equal to him in our relationship. I adored my son but just wasn't that happy." But knowing she wanted two kids, she decided to have another child soon after the first so that "I could start the next phase of my career." Her second son was born just under a year later.

"I went to lots of mommy and play groups and found that I had to be really careful about feeling other women out before I referenced what I wanted to do or what my goals were, since there was a lot of judgment if you spoke too ambitiously about your career with an infant in tow. And most of the career talk I did hear was about finding some work to do from home or part time for a bit of extra income, which was the opposite of what I was looking for. I wanted to fully go for it career-wise. I respect stay-at-home moms—the months I spent at home on both my maternity leaves were so much harder than working in the corporate world. And even though my mother was always really supportive about my education and goals, there is a sense that she didn't fully expect me to be so enthusiastic about my career. But I find it very empowering to feel that I can financially provide for my family.

"With my second maternity leave, I knew I wasn't going to go back to the agency and that it was now time to find that next job and make the career jump that I had been biding my time for." Since both Kyla's father and husband are business owners, she was conscious of the effect that maternity leaves could have, and so she told her agency from the start that she wouldn't be coming back after her maternity leave. "I wanted to be fair to them, to give them enough time to find someone else, but I also wanted to give myself a real incentive to make sure I found my next role—the one that I had been waiting for all this time."

During her second maternity leave, Kyla forced herself to network beyond her comfort level. I'm not shy but I'm not a natural extrovert. I had to push myself to really get out there, make the calls, set up the informational interviews and just start talking to people about what I was looking for. I knew I didn't want to be on the agency side any longer, although it had been a great experience. I wanted to work more on business systems with aspects of creative rather than in a creative-focused environment. I wanted challenging and interesting work that paid enough to justify the cost of two kids in day care, with the prospect of both serious income and long-term growth prospects."

She set up informational interviews, which she hadn't done since she'd graduated. "I quickly realized that it's a completely different experience as a new mom of two. Interestingly, some of the most frustrating interviews I had were with a few men in their forties. These were contacts socially, so I also knew their wives and families. Most of them had stay-at-home wives, which I didn't think would be a big deal, but when I spoke to them, they didn't seem to believe that I really wanted to be back at work. Two of them suggested that I just keep Glen's books instead of trying to have my own career."

Kyla's experience brings to mind my own when I was pitching companies to support The MomShift. Frequently, these presentations were being made to much older and fairly senior men. To my surprise, it was these men, not the younger ones, who were often very receptive to the concept. Although many had had stay-at-home wives, a number of them now had grown daughters who were struggling with working-mom career issues. They told me with obvious pride about their daughters' elite educations and the promising careers they had embarked on only to feel like they had to stop or scale back once they had children. These dads were confused and disappointed—and suddenly an issue that they had never seriously considered before had become deeply personal.

As one man told me, "It made me realize that having her mother stay at home might not have been such a good thing—since she [his daughter] now thinks that the only way to be a good mom is to stay at home full time." Another said, "I keep encouraging her to at least try going back and she keeps saying that the environment won't be supportive, and it makes me wonder what I might have done in my own professional career to help change this."

For Kyla, although a segment of her network didn't seem all that helpful or supportive, the act of reaching out and talking about her goals helped make it even easier to expand out further. "I started to talk to people I met casually about what I was looking for, and one of those conversations was with my neighbor who then introduced me to her colleague's sister's partner, a communications consultant." This woman subsequently led to Kyla's new job and along the way became a close mentor.

When Kyla's second son was ten months old, she started her new role. "I went back to work earlier than I'd hoped, but I didn't want to miss out on the opportunity." The role is a two-year gig, with excellent pay, analytical and interesting work, in a management consulting position that allows her to gain the niche skills and experience that she and her mentor are hoping will lead to a much more senior level job next. Even though life is much happier and better, Kyla acknowledges that it's not easy. "We've learned to line up backup babysitters and be prepared. I'm lucky that Glen gets some flexibility in terms of his time, but he works long hours—days and evenings—and so it can feel like we are both always going and we have no time to relax."

But even still, now that she's on track and able to pursue what she was waiting for, she says, "Even with that, both of us, individually and together as a couple, are much happier."

(Update: Since our interview, Kyla transitioned from this contract role to a permanent IT Strategic Change Consultant position with McDonald's. She's also joined a hospital board and has been elected the Marketing Communications Chair.)

Consider:

> **Get personal.** Ambition is a very personal frame for our life—it's so much more than just wanting to be a CEO of a company or even wanting what you used to want or feel like you *should* want. Invest the time to genuinely define for yourself

what is driving or exciting you. Remember that it is normal for your sense of ambition to ebb and flow. And that's OK.

> **Break it down.** Little successes provide momentum, so break down your big dreams and goals into small, manageable and attainable tasks or targets. And then go from there.

The Myth of the Female Sector

An industry or workforce that is predominantly female should theoretically be one where it's easier for working mothers to succeed. However, this doesn't seem to be the case. As one career expert wrote on her blog, "It's never good for one's career to be in a room full of women unless you're a model or a stripper. Because women choose lower-paying work, which means that where there are all women, there are lower salaries."[61] Not only that, but it turns out that men actually do better than women in female-dominated industries. It's a phenomenon known as "the glass escalator."

"Men that enter female-dominated professions tend to be promoted at faster rates than women in those professions," explains Caren Goldberg, Ph.D., an assistant professor of management at American University's Kogod School of Business. "When you look at senior management, you tend to see men disproportionately represented. So while there may be less than 5 percent of all nurses who are male, you see a much larger percentage than 5 percent in senior-level positions like hospital administrators."[62] Research shows that men in female-dominated jobs tend to fare even better than men in male-dominated jobs, and they typically earn higher salaries, receive more promotions and achieve higher levels within organizations than their female counterparts.

Goldberg attributes the glass escalator, in part, to stereotypes about men and the characteristics of strong leadership—all of which work to a man's advantage.

"Research indicates that stereotypes about what a prototypical man is also match with stereotypes about what a prototypical manager is," says Goldberg, noting that men tend to be perceived as more assertive for instance. "And when you're in a female-dominated profession, there are fewer people that have the ability to match these preconceived ideas."

One such profession is PR. According to research by the Institute of Public Relations, 60 to 80 percent of those working in PR today are women. It's difficult to find a proven reason why women are a majority presence in PR, but speculation includes stereotypical generalizations of a gender affinity for communications and relationship building, the glamorized (although inaccurate) portrayal of the career (think of Samantha on *Sex and the City*, or the women in *Entourage*) or that women migrated to PR early on—since it was a profession that was outside of "traditional female" occupations like teaching or nursing but also didn't challenge gender stereotypes (or have the barriers to entry) as medicine or engineering do.

However, the hours are long and, as with most client-based careers, often erratic, particularly since PR involves dealing with media deadlines as well as client needs. New business development and client relations can also mean regular long evenings. As someone who spent several years in PR agencies of all sizes, I can attest that most of these agencies are staffed by fairly young women, but they are concentrated at the middle to bottom of the agency structure. Thus, the glass escalator is certainly in effect: the Public Relations Society of America, tracking the industry, has found that 80 percent of upper management in the industry is male. Even more troubling is that the 2010 Public Relations Society of America's Survey found that the average income for women in public relations is 60 percent that of their male colleagues. This is down from 2006 when it was 69 percent. So although the percentage of women in the industry is increasing, their wages are decreasing. In addition, women make up less than half the executive committee roles in most large PR firms, and only four women in the world lead agencies with more than $100 million in revenue.[63]

Global PR firm Edelman recognized this leadership gap within their own organization—68 percent of the workforce at Edelman is made up of women yet only 35 percent are in leadership roles. In response, Edelman launched the Global Executive Network Initiative (GWEN) to prioritize networking, recruiting, collaborating and career planning for women across the network. Richard Edelman, the global President and CEO, has committed the firm to reaching a fifty-fifty male-female ratio in leadership by 2016.

Says Edelman, "I'm ultimately going to turn the reins at Edelman over to my three daughters, whether as owners or managers. They will have to make their own decisions about work/life balance, about the right life partners and about where to live. What I want for them and for all of the women at Edelman is that they make the call about how far and how fast they want to rise in the organization and that they have the opportunity to thrive without having to choose between Edelman and life outside of work. I don't want Edelman women to, in the words of Sheryl Sandberg, COO of Facebook, 'leave before you leave,' to hold back in anticipation of children. I want Edelman to be the place where women can grow, succeed, choose to have children and come back to lead."

Name: Lisa Kimmel
Role: General Manager, Edelman Toronto
Children: Sam, 9; Chloe, 7

"I absolutely believe that a key component of achieving post-baby career success is in finding an organization committed to creating an environment in which women can succeed and move into the most senior ranks. Otherwise, no matter what you do personally, you're fighting an uphill battle.

"If I could sum up my post-baby success in two words, they'd be: career catapult. By this I mean I was promoted while I was eight months pregnant and then immediately upon returning from my second maternity leave. I do think this was due in part to my choice to be engaged (to an extent that worked for me) while I was on my maternity leaves. I kept on top of what was happening in my profession, in our business and with our clients. This meant that when I returned from my maternity leaves, I was able to immediately re-engage in my career and in contributing to the business.

"The biggest challenge—and subsequent realization—I had was that I can't try to manage both my personal and professional life together. By this I mean that when I'm with my kids, I need to focus on my kids. When I'm working, I have to focus on my work. By having that complete separation, I'm able to do each effectively. That said, I also make a point of sharing my work stories, experiences and challenges with my children so that they are aware of, and understand, my work and why it's important to me. I've also invested in having the best child-care provider possible for my kids. Given the amount of time that I invest in my career, it's critically important that I'm also investing in my kids' care. I'm continually amazed by financially well-off parents who try to 'nickel and dime' when it comes to their child-care provider's wages. To me, this is the most important investment you can make, so don't scrimp!

"Our nanny takes our kids to and from school, provides help and guidance with homework, bathes them, feeds them nutritious meals, and also ensures that they are socially and physically active when in her care. She also makes dinner for us (and does our groceries now that our kids are in school full time), allowing my husband and me to spend quality time with the kids when we're home rather than worrying about meal prep, etc.

"I think it's important for women to ask for what they want. Quite often, they don't. So if you want a promotion or need some flexibility to accommodate for your family circumstances, just ask! If you've earned the respect of your organization's leaders, then they should trust you to 'get the job done' in whatever way works best for you. As leaders, we need to create an environment in which women can succeed and feel comfortable telling us what they need to do their jobs well."

I had the opportunity to speak with other members of Lisa's team and I consistently heard how happy they were with her commitment to having women across Edelman share their stories, challenges and advice; they found the process inspiring, practical and helpful.

"As women, I believe that we have a responsibility to each other to be honest about the challenges that we face, and act as supporters in trying times," Lisa told me. "There is comfort in numbers, in knowing that we're not alone, and that other women in all likelihood are experiencing similar challenges. With a proper support network, challenges can be overcome and will allow you to 'have it all'—whatever that means to you, as it will be different from each woman, and whether it's all at once, or over time."

Name: Sara Gourlay
Role: Chief Operating Officer at Hill+Knowlton
          Strategies in India
Children: Jamie, 9; Bronwen, 4

"It's a grand-sounding title for a role that involves running two of our global accounts, running our three businesses across five office locations across India and driving client services across this huge market. I spend a great deal of time on conference calls at odd hours, travel frequently, deal with all manner of odd HR and operational issues (all of which are urgent) and develop strategies and concepts for existing and new clients.

"Before I had kids, I was mid–senior management level within the U.K. business. I didn't really think about having children as an issue in terms of work, which was incredibly naive in retrospect. The plan was always that I would go back to work full time and that my lovely husband would take a step back in his career to look after the children.

"Coming back after Jamie was born wasn't easy. There were some political issues that I had to wade through and I don't think I appreciated how emotional it would be. My role had changed while I was away, which happened without much discussion, and I remember struggling to juggle being a new mother; a changing relationship with parents, friends and my husband; and establishing a whole new range of relationships with clients and a new boss and a newly competitive environ-ment. I felt a bit left behind, because my world had been nappies and feeding for six months and I stupidly expected to go back to work and find that not much had changed.

"When I left for maternity leave, my boss at the time was a very supportive woman who had children of her own. She suggested that when I was transitioning back it would be good for me to work one day from home, and trusted that the work and the clients wouldn't suffer. Then she moved into a new role soon after my return, and a man was brought in to replace her. The dynamic changed dramatically and I felt huge pressure to be present at all times. The funny thing was that there was a male colleague that was at the same level as me (in fact, he'd been brought in to cover my maternity leave) and while it was never a problem for him to work from home or be late, it was for me. I'm not sure what prompted that, but it added immense stress to that time period.

"I'd accepted that I'd feel guilty for being away from the children—and I still do feel that—but I hadn't expected to feel that other people were expecting me not to cope with both roles. Most of my 'mommy' friends were stay-at-home moms or had decided to reduce working hours to accommodate their families. That really wasn't an option for me given I am both very career-minded and also I am the main earner for our family.

"As far as work went, somehow it wasn't quite appropriate to raise any concerns. This may be my interpretation of it, but there was a sense in my mind that I had to give the impression that nothing would stop me when it came to getting the job done. I seem to remember just pushing through it all.

"The combination made the initial years post-baby very difficult. It didn't help that the industry also hit a downturn in spending and the firm needed to make one of the two directors in the team redundant—and that was me. It wasn't handled well and I was given the impression that my motherhood was seen as a weakness by the HR team. I am glad to say that the team has changed since then.

"After that, we moved to the Middle East, where I led H+K Strategies in Qatar and Kuwait for over four years. It was a good move—the work was challenging and fascinating but with a better sense of family than I'd experienced in the U.K. My boss then was a single man living a very single-man life, but he was supportive of me as a mother, which helped me regain some lost confidence.

"I fell pregnant with my daughter during this time and had a very difficult pregnancy that was exhausting. In retrospect, I didn't help myself by keeping up a punishing level of work and self-expectation. The transition back to work after she was born was much easier, partly because we had live-in help for her first year and partly because she was a sleep-loving baby. Since then, she's lived in Qatar, Singapore and Dubai, and travel has meant I've spent a lot of time away. It isn't easy and I have days where I feel nothing but guilt that I'm not with them, but I know that when I am there she and my son have all my attention. My world is work and family, and right now I have very little social life and no hobbies. When they're grown and independent, that will come back, but right now, these two roles are enough.

"I wish I'd known that combining career and motherhood would get easier and that I would gain so much from mother-hood. In PR you meet some challenging personalities and situations, but nothing equips you for difficult times better than a toddler tantrum in the middle of a crowded shopping centre, or shows you how much stamina you really have like a long, sleepless night. I've become more patient and able to handle stresses.

"I've also found that I've grown in confidence. I'm proud of what I achieved and the experience I've built up through my career, but my absolute proudest achievement is a long and happy marriage and two children who are healthy, fascinating and brave."

I raised with Sara my observation that although in PR the majority of the workforce is female, this gender balance is not reflected in the senior levels.

"I know," she said. "I think historically when women have a family they stop expecting promotions, stop chasing opportu-nities, which is understandable in many ways. The client services nature of the industry can make it difficult for work-ing moms. I wouldn't have had the career I've had without my husband being willing to step back from his, and that decision is still unusual.

"I also think that men tend to be more open to changing roles, to taking risks and sometimes to moving to a foreign country without any assurances. Things are getting better, particularly in the U.K., but I'd be lying if I said I thought we'll see a lot of women heading up global agencies any time soon. I know very successful women who would rather fake an offsite meeting than admit they are taking time for their kids. We need to be realistic about our lives and not try to overcompensate just because we're mothers. Maybe we need to stop apologizing or feeling a need to apologize. For me, ambition is a necessity, not a luxury. I have to work and, because life gets more expensive, I have to keep progressing and earning more money. It would be nice to win the lottery to take that pressure away, but I think I would still have the drive to push and challenge myself."

Consider:

> **Look at the local culture.** During the course of my interviews, I regularly had the chance to speak with women at the same level and within the same organization but in different groups or offices—and frequently, their experiences were completely contradictory. While personality and individual perception were part of it, overwhelmingly it seemed that the primary influence on the interviewees' post-baby career experience was the result of the microculture created by their specific manager or leader.

FIVE

How We Work

A couple of years ago, I was asked to contribute a short article to a news website explaining which book I would most recommend to recent graduates and why.

My choice was *The 4-Hour Workweek* by Timothy Ferriss. The book promises to show the reader how to "escape the 9–5, live anywhere and join the new rich." It was a global best-seller.

But that's not why I chose it.

The best lesson in *The 4-Hour Workweek* is the overarching idea that we actually have an incredible array of options on how we structure our work lives. For instance, how you pay your bills and how you define your "career" aren't necessarily one and the same. The examples and stories in Ferriss's book all emphasize the idea that your work life and your life's work don't need to follow the model that most of us have grown up with. And even if you have no interest in actually outsourcing chunks of your life, or remote working or setting up online businesses that let you work from anywhere (some of his ideas) Ferriss helps you take a fresh look at the way things usually get done.

Which is good news, since the traditional career structure of regulated workdays, few if any career breaks or pauses, and an expectation for significant overtime and face time was always a poor fit for the majority of working mothers.

What Is a Career?

With company loyalty, pension plans and the eight-hour workday becoming less common, and 24/7 technology, multiple career changes, extended working lives and entrepreneurship becoming the norm, the nature of a successful career has never been more fluid.

Although the traditional career model still frames and dominates much of the career discussion and available advice, alternative ways of structuring work are beginning to move from the sidelines and into the mainstream. This shift is being driven by a few factors. One is that Generations X, Y and Z are staying in school longer and therefore starting their careers later and with different priorities and expectations.

The second is that Baby Boomers are increasingly reluctant to fully leave the workforce and are instead looking for ways to continue to work—just in different ways or roles. And unprecedented numbers of highly educated working mothers are having children later— often in their mid- to late thirties, at a time that is in direct conflict with the traditional "momentum phase" of a number of careers. For instance, a full 60 percent of highly qualified women follow non-linear career paths, immediately disqualifying them from the arc of the traditional career.[64]

As a result, necessity has meant that working moms are often at the forefront of creating new career models. Research has found that although over 93 percent of women who take time off from work would like to reconnect with their careers, 74 percent do so, but only 40 percent do so in a way that connects them to "full mainstream jobs."[65]

For many mothers who are returning to the workforce, the classic and fairly rigid 9-to-5 (or 8-to-6) full-time role is either not readily available or not a desirable option. Instead, they are increasingly redefining how their career or workday operates. By doing so, they are also creating templates that allow them more flexibility and empower them with the ability to better adjust work for family and vice versa. The following are the work parameters that most frequently came up in my interviews.

Control

I repeatedly heard women say that the change they were looking for was not necessarily to work fewer hours but to control *when* and *how* they worked. A recent survey commissioned by social networking website LinkedIn showed that women's definition of professional success has changed in the last five or ten years with work/life balance more highly valued than salary, position or even longer maternity leaves.[66] In part, the desire for new ways of structuring work is driven by the expansion of the workday.

One new mother who recently made partner at her Chicago consulting firm said, "It used to be that once you reached a certain level of seniority, some of the billing or client pressures were slightly relieved and the pace eased a little. Now making partner is like being told that the prize for the pie-eating contest is more pie. It's relentless and never slows down."

As a result, organizations and companies of all sizes are increasingly open to trying to find more sustainable ways of retaining talent over the long term and to provide employees with an increased level of control over their workday. Almost half of the women I interviewed had at some point in their career used one of the options below to navigate through particularly busy or stressful work/life periods.

> Flextime: flexible daily start and end times
> Remote work: either a partial or fully remote work schedule, which involves employees working from home or satellite offices
> Compressed workweek: a full-time work schedule condensed into fewer than five days a week
> Job sharing: two employees sharing responsibility for one full-time job
> Part-time or reduced schedule: employees working fewer hours than the standard workweek
> Freelance or consulting work

The first step to leveraging these options is often to reframe how you personally think a successful career should be or look. Deanna Matzanke, Director, Diversity and Inclusion, Scotiabank (an organization that offers all of the above flexible work options) acknowledges that, "Of course, it's an ongoing challenge to equip our people with the right skills to manage a diverse workforce that includes working mothers. But I think that sometimes the challenge is with our working mothers themselves who still believe that they have to do it all or have it all, and as a result they work themselves to the bone doing it when, in many cases, a flexible work program or initiatives might have been the perfect thing to help them manage their challenges.

"I advise women to exercise their creativity. There are many different ways of 'being' at work and 'being' a mother. Those two ways of being don't have to be mutually exclusive. Take a good look at the kinds of policies and programs your organization offers or that your community has in place. Talk to your manager about different ways of accomplishing your job that harmonize with your commitments as a mother. A conversation is always a great way to start—I always remind women that you don't know till you ask!"

Stigmatized Still?

When Yahoo and then Best Buy announced within weeks of each other that they were canceling remote working, it reignited the discussion on workplace flexibility.

Work/life balance experts were quick to point out that both companies were facing financial difficulties and that these were one-off events that don't represent an overarching backlash against workplace flexibility. Maybe so, but on an individual level and in hallways and offices across the country, flexible workers still fear penalties for their decisions.

Sheryl Sandberg, herself a strong advocate for a work culture that focuses on efficiency and results over long hours and face time, shares how it wasn't until very recently that she felt comfortable telling the world that she leaves the office to get home to dinner with her kids which isn't flextime but just the ability to leave at what was once the end of the normal workday. "It's not until the last year, two years, that I'm brave enough to talk about it publicly," she admits.

If someone with her profile and position is still nervous about acknowledging any deviation from the expected (extended) workday, then it doesn't bode well for men or women in less exalted positions. The culture of face time is now so powerful that even as a freelancer, I would feel apologetic for leaving at 5:30 to go pick up my kids—even though I rarely left the office for lunch and usually had roles that were structured around me delivering a set piece of work. None of that matters; it's still difficult to be seen as the first to leave the office.

More than Just Changing the Workday

Apart from rearranging the structure of their workday, many successful working moms I interviewed have also changed how they structure their careers. This included taking on consulting work, embarking on a portfolio career (where they are working between two or more different organizations to make a full-time career) and of course, entrepreneurial ventures.

This is what author and economist Sylvia Ann Hewlett called the "second generation" of policies that, no longer just for working mothers, are moving towards redefining the way all of us view, plan and move through our careers. "Yes, flexible work can carve out partial relief in the here and now, but flexible work arrangements don't deal with the longer-term recalcitrant problems and what is needed is greater appreciation and understanding of an arc of career flexibility that takes into account the span of a woman's work life—which is nonlinear and that allows people to scale back and then come back," she explains.

For those with the ability, the office infrastructure and support, one approach is to look to bring more home into the office. Shortly after she banned employees from remote working, Yahoo! CEO Marissa Mayer was hotly criticized for building a nursery (at her own expense) next to her office in order to bring her then four-month-old son into the office. While few of us have that option, many moms I spoke with mentioned the benefits of entrepreneurship or work-from-home options that allowed them, in their own way, to merge rather than separate work and family. I have done both and have found that my current arrangement of having a home office with live-in child care is the one that allows me to work but also feel involved with what my kids are doing.

Amaryllis Fox, CEO of Mulu, an online social network that allows women to share product recommendations and donate a percentage of the revenue to charity, frequently has her four-year-old daughter, Zoe, in the office and traveling with her. "She's grown up with the Mulu team as her extended family," says Fox, 31. "It's wonderful for her to see what we all do here."[67]

Work from Home

It is nearly three decades since pioneers promised "telecommuting" would change our working lives, and the technology to make that change—tablets, mobile phones, Wi-Fi—is ever more pervasive. And yet, the prevalence of the face-time culture means that flexible and work-from-home scenarios remain the exception and not the norm. For a working parent, it's hard to overstate the benefits of being able to do your job from home even one or two days a week. The time saved on the commute, face-time meetings and all the rituals of office culture means, for many, getting more done on the work, home and child front.

What I noticed is that among the women I interviewed who successfully worked flexibly and who were not consultants or otherwise self-employed, virtually all had been with their organizations for a significant length of time. This seems to reinforce what the studies say: that if you give people flexibility, you win their loyalty. Or maybe it's also that employees with banked years and an established reputation are also the ones who successfully negotiate and retain flexible work arrangements.

Name: Lee Anne Bocz
Role: Senior Manager, Communications, Deloitte
Children: Daniel, 16

Lee Anne's role combines national communications strategic plan development, and writing and editing firm communications. She has a team of six who report to her. For the past nine years, ever since her son was diagnosed with autism, Lee Anne has also been homeschooling her son. "The process around the diagnosis and then navigating what we needed after that was incredibly stressful both physically and mentally. At the same time, I had just started a new communications role with expanded responsibilities."

Deloitte is globally recognized as a leader for its flexible work options. However, as with all organizations, how these are implemented generally depends on the immediate supervisor and group. In Lee Anne's case, her boss at the time was not very understanding about the pull she was now facing on the home front. "I was battling the school board, the teachers and trying to find a good doctor. Autism was even less understood then, so it was a real struggle to try and get resources for him. As a parent, I was also trying to deal with this blow. An autism diagnosis forces you to change your original hopes and dreams for your child; I was having to explain his challenges to others who didn't understand why he acted the way he did, and search for options, alternatives and help (which are very hard to find!). In the midst of all that turmoil, I was also working full-time in a demanding job where I had just been promoted.

"In addition, a few times a week, my son's school would call to say he was having behavioral issues that they were having trouble dealing with. Sometimes he would try to run away when he was upset, and they felt like I was the only one who could solve these issues by talking to him over the phone or giving them advice-on-the-go. Needless to say, it was rather distracting to get called out of meetings at work to try to calm my distraught child down over the phone, or imagine where in the school he might be hiding so I could suggest where they search. When I look back on the work I did that year, I'm amazed that I accomplished as much as I did and didn't have some sort of meltdown myself.

"What I needed was time and flexibility to just sort out the situation. But when I explained the circumstances to my boss, she told me, 'Do what you need to do to sort it out, but make sure it's addressed by the end of the summer.'"

Meanwhile dealing with the school board was becoming an exhausting and uphill battle.

After a particularly difficult few weeks, Lee Anne and her husband decided to pull him out of school. They couldn't find any other options and homeschooling seemed like her only choice. "My husband (a teacher) had worked part time when my son was going into kindergarten and grade one, since we anticipated that it would be a difficult transition for him. This time we decided that, although he was the professional educator, I would be the one to take charge of implementing the homeschool plan—in part because there was no way he could work remotely, and from a financial perspective, in terms of benefits and pensions, it made sense for him to continue full time.

"It wasn't an easy decision however—I really thought I was going to have to decide between a job I loved and had invested in for the past decade and what I thought was best for my son. We didn't know what else to do at that point."

In a twist of fate, that August, just as she was preparing to resign, her boss was moved to another role. Lee Anne's new boss was familiar with her accomplishments in the organization and when he heard about her dilemma, he took a completely different approach. "I told him my problem and that I understood that I would probably have to resign in the coming couple of months. I couldn't believe his response, which was, 'Well, before you do that, let's see how we can make this work for you and for us.'

"To my amazement, he encouraged me to do whatever I needed to help my son, while giving me the freedom to work 'on a schedule of my choosing.'

"His willingness to support my unique flexibility requirements and his reassurance that I was an 'important member of his team' were incredible morale boosters, and sent a message to everyone that personal flexibility was important to him and our organization. Because of his actions and ongoing support, I still make a strong contribution at work and have been successfully homeschooling my son ever since. The flexible options created a win-win scenario."

The solution was that Lee Anne would work from home four days a week and come into the office one day a week. When working at home, her days were structured to allow her to work around her son's homeschooling, dividing her time between the two.

An average day for Lee Anne now looks something like this:

7:30–10:30 a.m.	Deloitte
10:30 a.m.–12:00 p.m.	Focus on my son, with a break for "recess" when I check urgent voice- and e-mails
12:30–1:30 p.m.	Deloitte

| 1:30–3:30 p.m. | Back at school with my son |
| 3:30–6:00 p.m. | Deloitte |

"I usually log in again after dinner to finish up any outstanding items, but I don't multitask. Instead I've learned to be very focused on what I'm doing at the time. I've also learned that it's important to remember that you never know who will be and where you will find your allies.

"I was also very careful about letting my team know that they could always reach me and accommodating special requests for meetings at times that didn't fit my schedule.

"I also made a point of talking about both my arrangement and my son's challenges naturally and often. I think it's important to be open about personal challenges—everyone has them and if we can bring our full selves to work and support each other, it's a much more productive and appealing environment."

A Constant Upward Climb?

As mentioned earlier, although Sheryl Sandberg's *Lean In* is a specific call to action for women to proactively go for the next rung on the career ladder, she herself turned down a promotion at LinkedIn because it was offered at the time she was planning to have a second child. Sandberg acknowledges that the frame of careers as a ladder that needs to be relentlessly climbed is an outdated analogy for how careers today can work.

Instead she proposes replacing the career-ladder metaphor with the concept of a career jungle gym (a metaphor she attributes to Pattie Sellers, the editor of *Fortune* magazine), since a jungle gym allows for lateral moves, for staying in one place and maybe at times for even a step backwards before leaping forwards.[68]

Name: Laurie Cooper
Role: Director, Customer Development Strategy,
          Unilever
Children: Nicholas, 17; Amanda, 16

"I think it's essential that we start to recognize different ways to have a successful career. The reality is, at times, you just aren't going to be focused on ramping it up, trying to make it bigger or securing the next promotion—and that's OK. In fact it's more than OK, because it lets you build your career in a way that also works for the rest of your life."

Laurie has spent more than twenty years working in consumer packaged goods, from foods to home and personal care products. She has worked in customer development, shopper marketing, finance as well as consumer and market insight. Her current role, and most recent promotion, brings together elements from all of the above. "I certainly didn't have a straight career path. After just over eleven years of working full time, I decided to stay home with my kids, who were then two and one.

"At the time, I was really challenged to feel great about what I was delivering both at work and at home. I was dealing with a long commute and the pace was crazy for everyone. I had gained agreement from my manager to work remotely at least two days a week, which had never been done in Unilever Canada before—so I literally wrote the policy on what was called 'tele-commuting' at the time. Even though this created greater flexibility, I was still quite conflicted. I recall picking up my daughter at the sitter on her first birthday. She was in a party hat covered in chocolate cake, and I realized in that moment that where I wanted to be was with her. And so I spent the next three years home with the kids and it was incredible. I was able to devote all my energy to building our 'family foundation' without feeling torn between priorities.

"When I talk about my career now, I tell women it's OK not to take a promotion if it doesn't fit with the rest of your life, just like it's OK to take a lateral move or even a more junior role. There's no right way to do this, but it's important to make decisions that you feel confident in and with. I decided to look into returning to work when both of my kids were heading to school full time and I was left wondering how to be productive with my time. That's when I reached out to a few people at Unilever who I thought would have forgotten me by then, but I was surprised to hear that there were opportunities available for me. I was quickly energized by the thought of getting back in the race and taking on new challenges.

"When I did come back full time, I decided to come in at a lower level than I'd been at three years earlier when I left. My colleagues were surprised by this, but it was a strategic decision. For a start, I wanted to be able to excel at work, but with a one-and-a-half-hour daily commute, and kids that had never known me working full time before, I wanted to manage the adjustment in a way that worked best for myself and my family, and I felt that this was the way to do it. I was also able to showcase my capability in a way that opened doors for me to change functions, leave finance and move to customer development—something that I was thinking about doing when I left." This decision was followed by a series of promotions and other functional moves until, ten years after she returned to full-time work, Laurie was promoted to her current position.

"I don't have a fixed office any longer. It's another first in terms of how the role is imagined. But again, it's a strategic decision that helps on both the work and home front. It allows me to insert myself into the different business strands, and it allows me to work from anywhere. It can be difficult in the moment to appreciate that no career decision you make is permanent. What matters more is finding what works with your priorities at each stage of your life and being flexible about how you see your career. As long as you continue to build and add experiences to your 'portfolio,' you will position yourself to compete and win the roles you aspire to."

Consider:

› **Change who's at your table.** Or to frame it another way, who are you consciously or unconsciously benchmarking your career progress against and why? One frustration point for many working mothers is that even if they deliberately decide to take an alternative route towards their own career goals, they nevertheless continue to compare their careers to classmates or colleagues from a different stage in their lives. The result is frustration and anxiety or guilt. "I tell my kids constantly that they need to live their own journey, not compete with anyone else—but almost a decade after I left my old advertising agency to start my own design business, I still can't help tracking who is where and what accounts they have. I just can't seem to stop!" says Julie, a design consultant and mother of two in San Francisco.

> **Change the dialogue.** Rather than comparing yourself to others, redirect your thoughts by asking:
  • What are you doing today that you couldn't have done five years, three years, or even one year ago?
  • How have you stepped outside your comfort zone?
  • What experiences have you had or lessons have you learned that have given you a new direction or perspective?
  • How has your life improved? How have you improved?
  • What have you done that you thought you could never do?

Entrepreneurship

Female entrepreneurship is obviously not new—in fact, women have been engaged in home businesses and cottage industries for centuries. What's changed is the steady increase of women-owned businesses.

In the U.S. for instance, women are starting small businesses and stimulating new jobs at a rate that outdistances their male counterparts. The Bureau of Labor Statistics estimates that by 2018, female-owned small businesses, now just 16 percent of total U.S. employment, will be responsible for creating one-third of the 15.3 million anticipated new jobs.[69] The trend is also occurring in Canada, where female entrepreneurs hold a stake in 47 percent of small and medium-sized businesses and account for more than a third of all self-employed workers. According to RBC Group, female entrepreneurs are one of the fastest-growing groups, contributing more than $18 billion a year to the Canadian economy. About half of them are mothers.

Of course, both the scale and the success of these businesses vary widely. However, a new report published by American Express found that women-owned businesses have outperformed male-owned firms in number, size and revenue since 1997.[70] Despite the trends towards success, research by the Kauffman Foundation indicates that women still receive 80 percent less first-year capital than men (which consequently limits the scope of the enterprises they tend to launch).

Entrepreneur versus Mompreneur

Fifteen years after two mothers from Scarsdale, N.Y., coined and trademarked the term "mompreneur," it remains a divisive term among female entrepreneurs. The word is useful because it "very quickly crystallizes the idea that this is a person who has a business and a family," says Frances Wright, publisher of Calgary-based *MOMpreneur* magazine.[71] From my interviews, I found that opinions are divided between those who embrace it as a marketing and networking moniker, those who consider it demeaning (particularly when it's still an uphill battle for women to secure serious financing) and others who say it's only really suitable for women selling mom-and-baby-related goods and services.

Name: Katie Danzinger
Role: Founder, Nomie Baby
Children: Jake, 20; Jilly, 18; Josie, 7

"I have mixed feelings about the term 'mompreneur.' I am most proud of being a mommy, but I worry that the term 'mompreneur' can be seen as frivolous, or sends a message that what I'm doing is a small sideline hobby and is not a serious business," says Katie. Nomie Baby sells directly into the mom market. Her business began when she was looking for a way to keep her child's car seat clean.

"I 'accidentally' started my own business. I say 'accidentally' because Nomie Baby began when my littlest threw up in her car seat and I struggled to get the cover off to clean it—which involved a lot of time, mess and disassembling, only to read the care instructions, which said, 'do not machine wash.' I knew there had to be an easier way, so I searched for a solution. When my search came up empty, I knew an idea was born! I designed a cozy, removable, washable and waterproof cover for infant and toddler car seats that worked with the original design of the car seat, so no wrestling or struggling is required. The product was there but I had absolutely no idea what exactly starting a business would entail.

"Looking back, I'm glad I didn't know or I probably would have been too scared to go forward. There was designing the prototype, getting samples made, finding fabrics, talking with lawyers about filing for a patent, creating an LLC, web design, merchant accounts, EDI, QuickBooks, insurance, packaging design, shipping, storage, PR, marketing, sales . . . my mind was spinning. What I've learned over time is that many of these things come in sequence and don't all land on my desk at once. However, there are times when it does all seem overwhelming, especially since I am the only full-time Nomie Baby employee.

"Managing my work/mom/life balance is slightly easier because Nomie Baby is my own business; therefore, I can schedule meetings around school drop-off, sporting events and plays. It does mean, however, that there are days that I am answering e-mails in the middle of the night. Another way that I try to balance it all is to involve my family, so that they feel a part of my business life. My older two help with computer issues and have helped design marketing pieces, my littlest has helped sort the colors and sizes for shipments, and my husband's a regular source of advice and support."

Today the Nomie Baby line has expanded to include car seat covers for infants and toddlers, stroller blankets and stroller mittens. "Based on my experience of launching and building Nomie Baby over these years, I would advise women thinking about starting a business to be clear about whether they are focused on money or if it's more about a passion— and to remember that not everything needs to get done at the same time, so don't get overwhelmed; pace yourself."

A Need Creates a New Line

Virtually every guide to starting a business talks about finding a need that you can fill, starting with the suggestion of looking for something that you wish you could find or use. Parenting provides many opportunities for this—which is part of the mompreneur phenomenon. However, very few of the entrepreneurs I spoke to in the baby sector had intended to start their own businesses; they seemed to just evolve from their personal experiences as mothers.

Name: Jacqueline Lawrence
Role: President, TJL Enterprises, Inc., Creator of Colic
               Calm® and Tummy Calm®
Children: Kian, 10; Anders, 5

Jacqueline Lawrence loved her teaching career and wasn't looking to start a business. She just wanted to find a way to make her colicky baby feel better. "My plan was that after my maternity leave, I would go back to my teaching position in South Central. I was working at an inner city school with 14 to 18-year-old kids and it was hugely enjoyable for me."

At 35, when she got pregnant, Jacqueline left with an open understanding that as soon as she was ready, she would be back in the classroom.

"I never suspected that I wouldn't go back. But I had also never anticipated that our baby would have such severe colic—I didn't even know that colic like this was possible! For the first four and a half months of his life, our poor boy couldn't seem to sleep for more than twenty or thirty minutes at a time. He just looked like he was in constant pain.

"We tried every over-the-counter remedy, went from pediatrician to pediatrician, but all we were told was that by three months he would hopefully grow out of it and that the only alternative was to start him on acid reflux drugs." Although desperate for some sleep and semblance of routine, Jacqueline was unwilling to put such a young baby on such hard drugs.

"Just getting through each day became a challenge. I was barely functioning, and the idea of me working like we'd planned was just abandoned. Our entire focus became trying to find a solution to end our baby's suffering."

As her husband unexpectedly became the primary breadwinner, he was less available to help. Without Jacqueline's income, he was working longer hours (in addition to a three-hour commute). Neither had family anywhere near the Long Beach area that could help. Earlier in her career, while working in France, Jacqueline had her own gastrointestinal issues: "This was when I was first introduced to homeopathic medications since they were what had cured my problems."

She decided to look into them as an option for her son. "I started going to naturopaths and homeopathic doctors, as well as pediatric gastro-internists. I was also doing my own research, mixing up things in my kitchen in micro-doses."

She eventually came up with a combination of nine homeopathic remedies. "Of course I was paranoid about giving him anything that would harm him, and so I kept checking and then double-checking that the ingredient I was using would have no negative reactions." It took about two months of daily and constant research, mixing, checking and tinkering before she felt ready to try a few drops out on him.

"It was like a scene from a movie, my husband was anxiously holding him and I gave him a few drops. Then he drank it and started smiling and never went back to crying. It was the same thing on the second day and the third."

And so, that evening in 2003 Colic Calm was born.

"At first, I just thought of it as a hobby, something that I just wanted to share. But gradually I began to realize the benefits of helping others in need while working for myself from home. I'd never thought of myself as an entrepreneur before, but looking back, I realize I was always creating new teaching tools for my students, new materials to make the curriculum more interesting or relevant for them. Reframing how I saw myself made this venture seem like an extension of those experiences and so much less daunting."

Today Colic Calm is the only homeopathic gripe water that is regulated by the USFDA and Health Canada, and is the leading natural medicine for treating colic, gas and upset stomach in children.

In May 2012, Jacqueline launched a second product, homeopathic anti-gas drops intended for infants and older children.

"It took nine years to reach this point. There were FDA and Health Canada regulations and manufacturing standards to be met, but our company was profitable from the first quarter. I was comfortable with a very slow and steady start to it."

After the first year, Colic Calm grew steadily at 30 percent year in and year out. "In some ways it's a recession-proof business since people will always spend on health products for the kids—especially if they provide relief."

Five years after she started the business, she and her husband had a second son. "It was something that I thought would never happen after our last experience, so I like to say that Colic Calm made that possible as well." It wasn't just Jacqueline's self-image and career that was reinvented after the birth of her first son; it also changed the structure and fabric of their entire family. When her husband was laid off from his job, he started working for the homegrown company. Neither has to endure the California commute anymore. "I have an office I can walk to as well as a home office, so I can be around the kids while our nanny looks after them.

"It wasn't an overnight reinvention but a gradual chipping away towards a dream. I think so many moms have probably thought of something wonderful that the world needs, but haven't made the time for it or just let it go since they didn't see themselves as the kind of person that 'could do that.' And I would just want to remind them that you don't have to do it all yourself—as people see what you are doing and feel your passion and commitment, they will come to help support your endeavors."

Owning Your Time

The desire for flexibility and control are huge motivating factors for entrepreneurs. Almost all the entrepreneurs I spoke with acknowledged that they worked much more now than they had in their previous roles, but it was much better now because they had the ability to control how and when they worked. But the how was always secondary to the control that owning their time gave them.

Name: Allison O'Kelly
Role: Founder/CEO of Mom Corps
Kids: Nolan, 10; Ethan, 8; Declan, 2

Mom Corps is a national flexible professional staffing firm that Allison founded after she struggled to find flexible work that suited her growing family. Allison worked as a CPA at KPMG Peat Marwick prior to receiving an MBA from Harvard Business School. After graduating, she landed her dream job with Toys 'R' Us. "I was in the Toys 'R' Us management program, overseeing three stores—ready to move up to the next level—when I found out I was pregnant.

"At the time I hadn't necessarily considered what that was going to mean, but my managers were fantastic to me. I had planned on taking three months of maternity leave, and when that was up, I realized that I wasn't ready to go back, and they were OK for me to take another month. When I came back, they offered me a position three days a week from 8 to 4— hours that were literally unheard of in a retail environment. I'd been there for just over four years. I was in the Southeast Region then and we had no female district managers at the time. I was in line to be the next one and it was something the company didn't want to lose. And at the time I didn't want to lose out on that role either."

Allison made it through the end of the year, but then she quit. "The reason for me is that I realized it wasn't about part-time work or fewer hours, it was about the flexibility to control when I was working and how—and that was something that they just couldn't give me.

"The reality was that the traditional workplace just did not offer the balance between career and family that I was looking for. And while I felt personal pressure to leave a successful corporate career to focus on family, I also appreciated that Toys 'R' Us was also under pressure with the struggle to find and retain high-caliber employees.

"I hadn't previously thought it was the time to have my own business or be an entrepreneur, but when I left Toys 'R' Us, I started doing contract accounting work on my own. Small and mid-size businesses were very receptive, and soon I had more work than I could cope with, so I started looking for other people interested in flexible professional work."

This process led to the founding concept of Mom Corps in 2005. "The goal was to create meaningful opportunities for a large community of moms raising families and to fundamentally change the way companies fill their short and longer-term staffing needs.

"Mom Corps was launched when my second son was two months old. It was a crazy time but I also had all the flexibility I needed, which made a significant difference."

Mom Corps now has operations from coast to coast with a 100 percent freelance workforce and expects to reach more than $18 million in revenues in 2013. "I'm still working full time and then some—probably much harder now than I did at Toys 'R' Us, but the differentiating point is that I have significant control and flexibility. I have full-time child care (7:30–5:00) and a home office, but I have a twenty-four-hour clock.

"From what I see, employers are getting the message. It used to be that flexible work options were reserved for long-term or established employees, but now the business case for flexible work is getting out—that you can get high-quality candidates in a more cost-effective arrangement, and all they need to offer is some autonomy and flexibility."

Consider:
There are numerous excellent resources available for entrepreneurs (for a few of the websites and books I came across, please see Suggested Reading on page 263), but among the entrepreneurs I interviewed, there were a few common themes that kept coming up:

› **Prepare your family.** Even if you have always worked full time and although being an entrepreneur will most likely allow you some increased flexibility to your schedule, the erratic and often all-consuming pressures of having your own business mean that your partner and family will be called upon to step up or adapt in unexpected ways.

> **Prepare to be overwhelmed.** Literally every entrepreneur I spoke with mentioned being overwhelmed at some point, either by what they had taken on, the money they invested or the amount they had to do—or *something*. Practical to-do lists that broke down the large tasks and provided a sense of control over the situation were the most regularly referenced coping mechanism.

> **Invest in finding your community.** From local mompreneur groups to online industry communities, find the support group that fits your personality and style. Jana,* a mother of two who runs an education software start-up in Waterloo, had to try several before she found her fit. "I went to a couple mompreneur meet-ups and then a local small business group, but it didn't click for me—they were nice people, but I felt like our goals and styles weren't aligned. Being an entrepreneur can be lonely, so I really did want to find the right group for me—which I did, when I joined a group for women looking to raise start-up funding. It's an online forum but that works out even better for me since someone is there to message on those late nights when I'm working alone while my family sleeps."

Part-Time Work

Laura Vanderkam, a mother of three and author of the time management book *168 Hours: You Have More Time than You Think*, advises against part-time work from a financial, career and time-planning perspective. "In many organizations, saying you want to go part time is saying you don't want to move fast." Vanderkam also argues that the cost differential between part-time and full-time work is huge, whereas the time commitment is not.

"Women who work full time tend not to work THAT many hours—35 to 40, not 80. So it's not a huge difference between full time and part time. People who work full time often earn more than twice as much as part-time workers. They also move faster in their careers with things like getting raises and promotions. Working full time sends a signal you're serious and on track. It's hard to keep on track going part time. It's possible, but it's difficult. The economic cost of working part time is quite large compared to the amount of family time you're getting in return."[72]

Which raises the question, can you still have a "serious" career working part time? And how is "part-time" work different from consulting or freelancing? In Canada, the number of part-time workers has grown steadily in the past five years. While some of this is due to lack of available full-time work, according to Statistics Canada nearly half is by choice.

Among Canadian workers of both sexes aged 25 to 44, 26.5 percent work part time so they can have more time to care for their children and another 15.1 percent do so out of "personal preference."

Currently, 75 percent of women who work in the U.S. work full time. However, according to Pew Research, most working mothers (62 percent) say that they would prefer to work part time, and only 37 percent say they prefer full-time work.[73]

In the Netherlands, almost 75 percent of women are employed part time, and when asked whether they would like to increase their hours, just 4 percent said yes.[74] This engendered a discussion on the implications of part-time work—specifically, whether seeking part-time work is a signal that Dutch women are no longer striving towards equality in the workplace or if, instead, they just have an enlightened approach to work that values time and independence over career success.

In my interviews, the women I spoke with (from Canada, the U.S. and the U.K.) who had worked or were working part time told me that in addition to the stigma of not being viewed as serious about their careers, they also often worked far more hours than they were being paid. For women who had careers that allowed them to consult, this was much less of a problem. Terri,* a financial consultant in New Jersey and mother of three, told me, "If I actually calculated out my hours, most months I'm part time or even less than that, but since I now 'consult' rather than work at my old financial institution, no one other than my accountant really knows the truth. And yes, I do make it seem like I'm working full time to colleagues and clients, because perception and brand matter."

Practically, part-time work can be a better option than dropping out of the workforce completely. And while being "part time" in a corporate setting can be associated with negative career implications (in a way that being a "consultant" is not) a part-time schedule is an attractive option for those in the high-skilled service sector. I spoke with several pharmacists, dentists and optometrists who all had gone part time to navigate the years when they had little kids, and then returned to full time once they were older.

Name: Michelle Gallagher
Role: Pediatric Orthodontist
Children: Trevor, 21; Jenny, 18; Catherine,15; Tim,12; Ben, 8

"I took six months completely off after each of my children was born but other than that, I have worked continuously, although always part time," Michelle told me. "For most of it, I was part of a large dental practice, so I was on salary and would teach a class as well since I wanted another dimension to my career. My skills are in demand and being part time means I've kept up to date on industry changes rather than leaving fully, coming back but then needing to substantially update. As the kids get older I've thought of either going full time at the clinic or just teaching more. I've been very lucky to be in an industry where I get to have these kinds of choices, and it's something I encourage both my sons and my daughters to think about for themselves."

Part-time work also provides a managed source of the many other benefits that come with working, including fulfillment, commitment, autonomy and a belief in the importance of what we are doing.

———

Name: Nicky Poole
Role: Creative Director, 889 Yoga Studio
Kids: Two boys, 6 and 4

When Nicky was 21 she left New Zealand for India in what became a life-changing experience for her. "From there, I spent the next ten years working around Asia, studying yoga and meditation." In 2002, she moved to Vietnam with her job in the travel industry. But after two years, she left to open a yoga studio in Ho Chi Minh City. "There was nothing like it there at the time and I soon became very connected to the community that developed around the studio. It was a very personal mission for me. I was living upstairs from the studio and teaching about four classes each day."

In 2006, she unexpectedly became pregnant. "I was determined to teach as long as I could, but ended up closing the studio for the three months after my son was born to recover. I just wasn't sure how I was going to manage with a baby. But I was soon able to return to teaching, particularly since we were able to employ wonderful and relatively inexpensive help at home."

As well as working fifty hours a week at her business, Nicky began studying for what equates to a master's in yoga. It involved five hundred hours of advanced training, exams, essays and a great deal of travel. "I went to sessions with my teacher in four different continents in order to get the hours and specific training I needed. I left the baby with my partner and really used that time away to focus and learn. This was something I'd always wanted to do and could have done before, yet I didn't start it until I was a mother."

When her son was three, she and her husband moved to Canada, where he'd been accepted to business school. "Our eldest was three and I was seven months pregnant when we moved to Toronto. It was very hard. I didn't know anyone and was still incredibly upset to have had to leave a business I had so closely nurtured and built." She describes the period after her second son was born as one of the lowest in her life. "It was a rough winter. Looking back, I must have had pretty severe postpartum depression. I was feeling lonely, crazy and overwhelmed. Min [her husband] was studying all the time and full-time mothering just didn't suit me at all. Each day was just about trying to keep myself above water."

To get out, she started going to the occasional yoga class at her local studio. "At the time I couldn't even imagine how I would ever be able to get back to work, but they were looking for a new creative director and encouraged me to apply." In May, Nicky started working there part time. "From the start, there was an incredible relationship of trust and flexibility. I'm technically part time but it's actually a full-time role that I'm fitting or rather cramming into part-time hours. It makes it hectic and at times stressful—but it's what I want right now. There's a real misconception about part-time working mothers—that we aren't working as hard or aren't as dedi- cated or that our work and careers are not as important to us. It's very frustrating. Often, part-timers like me are not doing less, and we're certainly not taking it any less seriously, we're just being paid less, but that's a trade-off that we feel is worth more to us at that time. For me, it means I have the ability to still be the parent that I want." Since she started, Nicky has led the opening of an additional studio location, the renova- tion and relaunch of another one, and an expansion of the program on offer.

"For me, this arrangement is working perfectly, and with the kids soon in school full time, I can take the role full time and expand it even further."

The Portfolio Career

It used to be called "moonlighting"; now it's a portfolio career. This term applies to careers where instead of the convention of having one employer or job, people manage different identities and roles as a way to create a career that works for them.

I know from my own experience that a portfolio career has many advantages.

After the birth of my second son, I worked full time as a strategic communications consultant, but my schedule was split between three different organizations. For me, it was an ideal combination. I was never bored and was able to balance a more lucrative role with a more stable, established one. But it was also challenging—there were certainly times that I could tell that none of my three employers loved having to share me. I regularly felt pulled in many directions and I never seemed able to properly explain my work situation to friends or family.

The Sideline Career

What if your job is just a job to pay the bills, and your real dream is something else—a record, a clothing line, a book? Often the financial needs of starting a family mean that these dreams get shelved since juggling the bread-and-butter role with a family and other aspirations can seem like too much.

Emily Mills has a senior communications role at CBC; she is also mother of a four-month-old and the founder of the How She Hustles Network, a platform connecting thousands of women virtually and through a regular calendar of events. Unlike many leadership networks for women, How She Hustles is not just about a woman's day job; it also showcases the other gigs that women have, from passion projects or business ventures—the "side hustles" as Emily calls them.

"I'd define 'side hustles' as part-time businesses or profit-making projects. They are often based out of the home, can be income generators based on service delivery, can yield cash from online sales of various products, or make money based on a series of special events. For example, many popular side hustles include personal care services like mobile hairstylists or consultants who make extra wages by sharing knowledge on everything from grant writing to social media. Aside from bringing in extra funds to the home and fulfilling a personal dream to own a business, the side hustle appeals to many moms for additional reasons. This alternative career structure gives women an outlet to express their creativity in ways that their traditional jobs may not. It offers them a sense of autonomy—financially and in terms of decision-making. It allows them to redefine their personal and professional brand around their passions, not just focus on what they are formally trained or officially qualified to do."

As a way of integrating a side hustle or passion project into their day jobs, several women I spoke with have taken the approach of balancing a less demanding role with their true interests and family. "I'm deliberately working in a role that's below my abilities and credentials, but it pays well, it doesn't leave me exhausted and it allows me to both manage the family and still get one or two hours of painting in a day," said one mother, who has chosen not to leverage her advanced science degrees and instead works as a technical writer and recently had her first gallery showing a year after her second son was born. Similarly, another mom who is a hopeful entrepreneur said her current role in her city government is something "I can do with my eyes closed, and so I spend all my real time and energy working on this online business, hoping it will take off."

Is it cheating your main employer to do unrelated work at the office? Many feel that if you are doing the work you're supposed to, then you are keeping your end of the deal. And it's indisputable that most office workers inevitably waste some time during the day. According to a survey by Salary.com, the average office worker admits to wasting two hours of each eight-hour workday—and that's excluding lunch.[75]

When I was writing my first book, I was also working as a PR and communications consultant. All my contracts allowed me an hour for lunch—so I would be really focused all morning, leave at lunch and spend that hour at Starbucks writing. Another mother I knew used her commuting time and lunch breaks to study for her master's degree. Fitting something extra in during slow moments can be a way to incrementally move forward on other projects while maintaining your steady gig and not take time away from your family.

Consider:

> **Anchor yourself.** Floating between roles can be challenging—emotionally, professionally and financially. Instead, have at least one predictable (maybe part-time?) role and then build other gigs around it.

> **Set up permanent child care.** Even if your workdays keep changing, it's easier on you, your children and your child-care provider to keep their schedule constant.

Freelancing and Consulting

In 2013, *CNN Money* ran an article that dubbed the current economy "the age of the freelancer."[76] Daniel Pink, author of *Free Agent Nation*, attributes the recent rise in freelancers to several factors. For one, Pink says, the "dodgy economy has made employers loath to hire full-timers." Freelancers provide "the right talent for the right task at the right time," he says. Freelancing and consulting are common ways for women to both continue their career advancement and as well take more control over their schedule and ambitions. Instead of hoping for a promotion, you can bid for larger projects and higher day rates—without waiting for someone else's approval.

For Jane Allen, a partner and global group head in the renewable energy division and also chief diversity officer, Deloitte Canada, it was the freelance energy consulting projects that she did while her daughters were young that subsequently led to her lateral move to Deloitte. Similarly, in my own career, I was able to use freelancing and consulting to significantly raise my day rate and take on projects that I knew I was able to deliver on but that I would have had to wait a couple of years longer for if I had stayed in a corporate or agency setting.

But the freelance and consulting life is not a career strategy for everyone. Yes, you have more control over your schedule, minimize the dreary commute and, if you choose, you can frequently work in PJs or yoga pants—but there is also a great deal of uncertainty.

Learning to live with and plan for this uncertainty was one of the hardest adjustments for me—and I'm a strong supporter of freelance life. Credit is almost impossible to acquire as a freelancer, and when you are paid by the day, vacations and sick days can seem too difficult to justify. I remember a time when I was sick, my husband was away and my son was too sick for day care, but with the help of Gatorade and Redbull (for me) and a loop of cartoons and juice boxes (for him), I still put in a full day's work from my bed.

Claire Dederer's memoir *Poser: My Life in Twenty-Three Yoga Poses*, captures the stress of the freelance life, particularly as a new mother. Her household's income is low and unpredictable: they're not starving, but there are unsteady moments. When her children came along, her life changed into the divided and manic life of mother-worker, torn between the deadline and the playground. She has children who need her at inconvenient times, an extended family who think she should be "on tap" because she is not clocked into an office somewhere, and an occupation that can at times not feel like, or be recognized as, a real career. For women accustomed to a clearly defined role and professional path, the ambiguity inherent in freelancing is one of its biggest challenges.

As Julie, a freelancer and mother of three in London, U.K., who manages financial software on an ad hoc basis puts it, "Telling someone else what I do depends on how I see myself that day. Some days the clients I have make it seem impressive and I feel proud of how I'm managing my family and career. On other days, I feel like I'm wasting all this education and just fooling myself that I have a 'real' career."

Name: Rae Ann Fera
Role: Freelance Journalist and Content Curator
Children: Bronwyn, 6

I think of Rae Ann as the reluctant but strategic freelancer. She unexpectedly entered the freelance market and is currently using it as a way to prepare for her next career move and phase, while taking the opportunity to be flexible with her time and be more available for her young daughter. "The thing with freelancing is that it's inherently entrepreneurial, and I'm actually happiest as a collaborator and not as an entrepreneur, so I need to find a way to balance these two different push/pull forces."

After her daughter was born, Rae Ann had initially planned to move on from her job as the editor of *Boards*, a strategy, media and marketing publication for the advertising industry. "I loved that position, it had lots of travel, events, trips to Cannes, but after seven years working there, I thought that after I had a child I would be ready for a change and a bit of a break."

A few months into her maternity leave, Rae Ann was asked to return, since the magazine's publisher unexpectedly decided to leave. Since she'd waited to have children because of her love of her work, it was a tempting proposition but one that she ultimately turned down. But it did prompt her to return to the job after eleven months off. "It was actually a very good decision to go back because I knew the role so well. I wasn't too concerned about balancing the work side of things, but I was worried about all the events and late social nights that tended to go along with it. After my daughter was born, I did notice that I approached work differently; I did my job but I had to leave right at five, I wasn't able to put in the late hours, and I all but completely cut out the social side of things."

The return to work was going well until the economic downturn hit. "That, combined with the major change in digital advertising, hurt us badly." In May 2010, she found out that the magazine was folding. "It was devastating for all of us." After almost a decade at the magazine, Rae Ann had lots of options and offers in the industry

"But I didn't want to pigeonhole myself right away, and realized that I had to consciously fight against my desire to just take a role that I would be comfortable in." She also needed to figure out what it was she really wanted to do. After falling into the job in her mid-twenties, she'd never been forced to examine what other work she might be interested in. "I never realized how much of my whole identity I had invested in the role until I left."

When she and I talked, it had been two years since the magazine folded and she became a freelancer. "Right now, my mix of projects includes writing for Fast Company, programming an ongoing screening series for TIFF, occasionally teaching as a sessional instructor in the Faculty of Design at OCAD University and putting together the programming and content for industry and media events. What I'm looking to do is leverage the networks that I've built over the past ten years into all these different strands, and test a variety of roles and experiences to see what seems like the right next step. I'd still say that freelancing is an unnatural state for me. I'm very loyal when it comes to work, I like getting comfortable, and I miss the social side of being at an office . . . but I think of freelancing as being good for my personal and professional development. I knew I was the big fish in a small pond and now I'm learning to push myself outside of that comfort zone."

In addition to building her network, she's enjoying an unexpected degree of flexibility in terms of how and when she works. "I don't see it as a permanent career choice but as a strategic stopgap. Freelancing allows me to do something valuable that's moving me forward in my career without making a commitment to the all-consuming next senior role. I'm also enjoying the flexibility to be able to volunteer in Bronwyn's class or be there after school.

"The challenge is that I feel like I am always working—but the difference is that now I get to choose when I'm working, and what I've learned is that careers are not dependent on time and place but relationships and motivation."

Consider:

> **Why are you doing it?** If you are interested in consulting or freelancing, start by being clear on what you hope to achieve from the experience so that your strategic plan and approach can reflect these goals. Are your goals and motivation primarily financial? Do you see freelancing as a means to staying engaged in your sector or field?

> **Are you looking for a change?** Do you hope to ramp up your career by securing higher-profile or more challenging projects? Are you hoping to gain experience in a new area or field?

> **Respect the choice.** Treat freelancing with the same respect that you did your old office job—and make sure your partner, friends and family do the same.

> **Always be selling.** Be prepared to market yourself—constantly. If you hate job-hunting, the transition to freelance can be difficult, since you will always be looking or waiting for the next gig.

> **Have a financial plan.** Not only is freelance work irregular but there is generally a period of six weeks between submitting and receiving payment for your invoice—so be prepared.

Technology and How We Work

In 1994, the average workweek was 42 hours. For those on the so-called "fast track" or in more senior and competitive roles, the average workweek was 49 hours.[77] Since then, there has been a steady escalation in the number of hours worked—especially among professionals and knowledge workers. For those in extreme jobs (with unpredictable work flow, fast-paced and tight deadlines, work-related evening events and a great deal of travel) the average workweek can now easily be 70 to 80 hours.

Technology is what has enabled the blurring between work and life and further lengthening of the workday. A U.S. study found that as a result of answering e-mails on their smartphones, employees were putting in an average of almost one full day of extra work every week.[78] Ironically, as Harvard Business School professor Leslie Perlow's research found, constant connectivity doesn't actually enhance productivity. Professor Perlow and her team spent a year at the Boston Consulting Group (BCG) examining the work habits of employees. Not all that surprisingly, they found that when employees were able to take breaks from their digital devices, their health, happiness and productivity improved.[79]

"I Don't Know How Else I Could Work"

Even if it can feel like work is *always* there, virtually every working mother I spoke with mentioned how technology is what has enabled an entirely new set of career and work options, saying that without it, flexibility and balancing family would be impossible. From answering e-mails while at a soccer game, videoconferencing with clients and texting reminders to the kids, technology seems to provide an ever-growing arsenal of tools to manage home and office. "It's a double-edged sword," says Rachel Coker, mom of two young daughters and a full-time director at Binghamton University. "On some days, I'm on my cell phone navigating an issue at work while frosting cupcakes for a school event. In that sense, technology has made it possible to be present both at home and at work . . ."[80]

While technology has certainly made us all busier, has it helped working mothers achieve the elusive goal of work and family balance?

Eilees Trauth, professor of Information Sciences and Technology at Penn State, interviewed more than two hundred women, all working in the knowledge economy but living in several different countries. Her research found that since defining work and life balance is such an intensely personal (and ever-changing) matter, it's impossible to say whether technology is either positively or negatively impacting work and family. All that is certain is that a seismic shift is underway in *how* we work.[81]

In the course of my five hundred interviews, I came across only one woman who has deliberately taken the radical approach of curtailing technology as a means of succeeding on both her home and family front.

Name: Nancy Rector
Role: Partner, Enterprise Risk, Deloitte
Children: Two sons, 18 and 16

Unlike the majority of her colleagues, Nancy decided never to carry a smartphone, BlackBerry or any handheld device for work. It's a decision that she credits as having been essential to her success. "It means either I'm focused on work or I'm focused on family—but I'm never pulled between the two. I've never faced any resistance to setting personal limits," says Rector, who joined Deloitte as a chartered accounting student nineteen years ago after earning degrees in computer science and finance. "But it took a while to figure out how to make it work.

"In the summer, I start my workday at 7 a.m. so I can take Fridays off. I'm pretty meticulous about scheduling my time, and rather than trying to multi-task, I take a one-task-at-a-time approach. These very deliberate changes are the result of previously having had a schedule that really didn't work for me or my family, and realizing that this approach just wasn't going to be sustainable over the long haul."

Ten years ago, the Fredericton native routinely hopped on a plane most weeks, leaving her husband and two small children behind while she worked with organizations across Canada. "After my second son was born, the cross-country travel I was doing became really difficult. My eldest was only three and my youngest was six months and I'd be gone three or four days each week. The work was interesting but my family life was really suffering. I wasn't happy, and I needed a change. I constantly felt like I was missing too many family moments."

Rector wanted to stay with Deloitte, so she proposed a move to the Ottawa office, the home base for her many federal government clients, and a good employment market for her husband. There, she established a local enterprise risk practice, a group focused on internal audit, control assurance security, capital markets and regulatory consulting.

Her strategy and proposed plan worked, and Nancy was subsequently responsible for growing the practice group from six people to the forty-plus team it is today.

Three years after her second son was born, Nancy became a full partner. Within her own team, Rector is viewed as an advocate for flexible work arrangements, reduced workloads and leaves of absence. "As long as we're keeping commitments to clients and colleagues, it doesn't matter where or when the work gets done," says Nina Grimes, a senior manager who has worked alongside Rector for nine years and is herself a mother of two.

Grimes credits Rector for creating a "guilt-free" environment in which high expectations are balanced with schedules that respect people's individual commitments. "We make it work," says Grimes. "The reality is, if I didn't have the flexibility to balance family commitments, I wouldn't be here."

Career Planning for Family Balance

Part of the discussion following Professor Anne-Marie Slaughter's article, "Why Women Still Can't Have It All," was whether she was nudging younger women to lower their ambitions or rather make practical choices in the name of their future families. Others felt that finally women were being told the truth—that women can't have both because society simply doesn't sufficiently value people who choose to balance a family with a career.

One approach to navigating this issue is to deliberately choose a career that inherently lends itself with greater ease to the rhythms of family life. This isn't new of course. Traditionally, "female jobs" such as teaching and nursing were billed as being good family-friendly careers. Growing up, I remember my parents' friends actively encouraging their daughters to become pharmacists and dentists because these professions were considered to be among the best to combine with having kids. They were well paid, you could always find work (if your husband had to move for his job), and the work rarely came home with you.

Kathleen Gerson, a sociologist at New York University, interviewed young men and women about their perceptions of work-family issues before the real juggle began. She learned that both men and women were planning on equally sharing their work and home requirements. However, there was a persistent gender-based assumption among these young, still-childless men and women. Young men thought that if the equality ideal failed, their wives would be the ones to cut back on work. Young women agreed.[82]

So is part of the solution to encourage women to consider careers that are inherently more family-friendly? The term "family-friendly" usually refers to careers with some flexibility, or schedules that allow mothers to work around school hours, or work that can be done from home. Good maternity leave and other family-friendly benefits are also an asset. In Canada, the majority of employed women continue to work in occupations in which they have been traditionally concentrated. However, as the economic climate has shifted—with longer hours becoming the norm, commutes getting worse, job security disappearing and sole parenting on the rise—it's debatable whether these are still "family-friendly."

Career services website Monster.com compiled a list of "mom-friendly" jobs that includes roles like dental hygienist (the potential to pay well, part-time hours), market research analyst (work-from-home option), sonographer (since health care is an around-the-clock industry, mothers can work shifts around car pools and school schedules) and elementary schoolteacher.[83]

Among the working mothers I interviewed, most said they never considered whether their careers were good for families. Several women expressed regret that they hadn't given any thought to how they could adjust their careers to allow them to be successful while balancing work demands with those of their children. However, others were equally vehement that they wouldn't want to tell younger women to change and limit their ambition based on the needs of some future family. In the words of Dunniela Kaufman, a Washington lawyer and mother of two boys, "We can control the choices that we make but we cannot always control the framework within which we make those choices. For instance, whether or not we get married. And when. Or whether we will be able to have children. Or how our family might come together. Since those things are not always within our power, we can't and shouldn't try to build our lives around them. We can do what is in our power to make them happen, and make choices that make them more probable, but there are no guarantees.

"The best thing that a woman can do for herself is live her life to the fullest and educate herself so that she will have lots of options and always be able to support herself."

Name: Jessica Bayliss
Role: Nurse, Team Leader, Trauma & Orthopedic OP
Children: Meg, 11; James, 7

"Before having children, I'd been a qualified nurse for just two years, so I was a fairly junior member of the team. I hadn't gone into nursing with any idea of how it would be with children since the whole idea of family seemed very far away at that point. Most of the other members of the team who had kids worked part time, which I noticed when I had to cover any shortfall shifts if someone's child fell sick.

"Since becoming a mother, I have been promoted twice and am now fairly senior within my department. There have been sacrifices though, as I have definitely had to miss events going on in my children's lives. I also went back to school to further upgrade my skills when Meg was born. That said, my career is to some extents and purposes family friendly. Since I work shifts, I can swap slots with colleagues. On the other hand, the hours are long and then with the commute it's a twelve-hour day, so I often leave before the children are awake and frequently get home as they are going to bed or already asleep.

"Many of my colleagues who have children have ended up cutting hours at work to spend more time within the family. When I applied for my last promotion, I had just returned from my maternity leave. I was informed that promotion was only possible if I signed on to work full time, so I agreed. It was a crazy time. My husband had just embarked on a new career as a paramedic, so we had to juggle both of us working shifts with a five-year-old and a baby.

"But having children has made me a better person and a better nurse. I have more empathy and am a much kinder, more patient person. [My kids] have made me stronger and sparked the desire to want to achieve greater things so that I can provide a better life for them."

Beyond the 9 to 5
Much of the discussion and advice on career success and work life is still framed for and around a work schedule of five days a week (or

some extended variant of this) and a 9-to-5 or 8-to-6 day. However, about 40 percent of the American labor force now works some form of nonstandard hours, including evenings, nights, weekends and early mornings. With the projected expansion of jobs in industries like nursing, retail and food service, (all of which tend to require after-hours work), this share is expected to grow significantly.[84]

At the same time, working hours are also less predictable than they once were. "There's a greater variability and irregularity of schedules," said Lonnie Golden, a professor of economics and labor studies at Pennsylvania State University. "In surveys, more and more people are no longer able to specify a beginning or end of the workday." In response to the need, there are even day cares that have started offering twenty-four-hour care.

Although "night care" is still relatively new, an increasing number of child-care centers throughout the U.S. now provide evening and weekend service.

Across Canada, day cares are also beginning to offer extended hours with late programs that run from 6 p.m. to 11:45 p.m. to serve parents doing shift work.[85]

Name: Susan Quaiattini
Role: Staff Sergeant
Children: Perry, 18; Ben, 16; Noah, 14

Susan is going into her twenty-seventh year with the police force. During that time she's worked in everything from detective work to foot policing, in the office as well as training and education. She tells me that she always knew she wanted to be a police officer. "I didn't come from a policing family, which is something you still see quite a bit, but I was always very active and from a young age was just really drawn to the idea of a law enforcement career."

She went to university to study criminology and then tried out and was accepted for the force. Throughout her career, she's worked shift hours based on what's known as the standard force schedule. Practically, what that means is this:

> 7 day shifts of 10 hours (7:00–17:00), followed by 6 days off
> 7 evening shifts of 10 hours (17:00–03:00), followed by 5 days off
> 7 night shifts of 8 hours (23:00–07:00), followed by 3 days off

Although for those used to a more "predictable" or conventional workday, it probably sounds a bit overwhelming, Susan said it provided her family with numerous benefits. "When I speak at recruiting events, I find that many women are very concerned about how the shift work that policing requires would fit in with a family life of any kind—but I always found that it had many advantages. The benefit of shift work meant that I was also off on days that other parents weren't, so I could volunteer at the school, get stuff done around the house or take some time for myself to go to the gym during the day."

The rhythm of their family life adapted to her schedule. "If I had to work on birthdays or Christmas, we just celebrated a couple of days later or a week earlier. Many of my friends thought that this would be difficult, but it wasn't because that was what our kids were used to. I took six months [maternity leave] off with each boy and was able to fully disconnect from work, knowing that I was completely covered and that I wouldn't be missed since the size of the force is so large.

"With three children, working shifts and having a personal life can be challenging, and so my husband and I decided to hire Rosie, who was our live-in caregiver for over nine years. Policing can be demanding and very unpredictable. If I received a call that would take me into overtime, I couldn't just leave. By having a live-in caregiver, I didn't have to worry about getting home on time to take the children to school, etc. I knew my children were being looked after, so I could concentrate on my work.

"Another advantage that policing has for working moms is that the opportunity for promotion is up to you. You apply for it when you're ready. Unlike in many companies, it doesn't depend on someone "sponsoring" you. You just have to meet the requirements to enter into the process. I only got promoted once I had kids. I told my husband that if you want me to succeed then I need at least three or four hours outside of work where I can study.

"From a police constable position, I have been promoted two times, from PC to Sergeant and then from Sergeant to Staff Sergeant. Police and shift work may sound challenging for working mothers, but it's been a good career and work life for our family."

———————

Name: Sabrina Smith
Role: Patient Services Technical Leader, BC Biomedical
          Laboratories
Children: Jordan, 15; Sarah, 10

Unusual hours can help when it comes to managing child care, although it can be hard on both the parents and the relationship. It can also make it difficult to have two equally demanding careers. Sabrina's role involves overseeing 350-plus technical lab assistants and fourteen supervisors. She's responsible for making sure the teams follow all regulatory requirements and that they are compliant with all documentation, including spot checks, performance reviews, technical training and development.

Sabrina started at BC Bio in 1994 as a microbiology technologist and has worked her way up to this position in 2010. "Staying home was never an option for me, not financially or personally. I don't think I would have been a good mother if I stayed home and I never wanted to be in a position where I couldn't support my family. I started as a lab technologist, then I was promoted to supervising fifty to sixty people and my role just continued to grow from there." She also continually took additional courses from technical seminars to management courses.

"We never had to pay for any type of child care. My husband would work night shifts at SuperStore, so he would come home between 6:30 and 7 most mornings and be able to walk the kids to school and give them breakfast. I would work from 8 to 4 and so be able to cover the afternoons and evenings. He would sleep during the day while the kids and I were out. He would have Sundays and Mondays off and most of that time he would be sleeping, which made it hard to find time to be together. But we make sure that once a year we take a week together—we leave the kids with my dad—and that's something we both look forward to.

"Child care is the biggest issue for our staff (which is 90 percent women). We have a lot of shifts that start at 6:30 a.m. and it's incredibly difficult to fill them because getting day care or child care at those times is still so difficult.

"Shift work is hard, though. I used to work Saturdays and Sundays, but then I had to stop because I felt like I had zero time to connect with the kids—and especially as the kids got older, I wanted to be there for them more. Parenting older kids is so much harder and I wanted to be around as much as I could when they were facing the big decisions.

"Our schedules mean that Kelvin [her husband] has had to take a very secondary role in terms of his career. We've been together for over twenty-two years and married for nineteen. We never planned an arrangement like this—it just sort of happened—but we both accept the way it's worked out that I have a career and he has a job."

SIX

Change on the Home Front

Office and work issues used to be viewed and discussed in isolation from issues related to home and family—as though what was happening in one didn't actually impact the other. In large part this was made possible by the traditional model of the stay-at-home wife and mother, who was fully responsible for what was happening with the kids, their schooling and all other domestic issues.

Today, although the ideal of the nuclear family with Dad as the primary earner and where Mom stays home remains a driving and powerful cultural template, according to the U.S. Bureau of Labor Statistics, it's a family model that applies to just 16 percent of households.[86] Instead, over the past thirty-five years, there has been a steady surge in the number of women who have become the primary earners in their families, going from 11 percent in 1976 to approximately a third of all families in Canada, the U.S. and the U.K., with an ongoing steady increase anticipated. About 40 percent of women now earn more than their husbands, and according to books such as *The Richer Sex: How the New Majority of Female Breadwinners Is Transforming Sex, Love, and Family*, this is only the beginning of a seismic shift that will reshape the issues of work/life balance, career success after children, female ambition and family life.

For a start, the prevalence of mothers in the workforce has forced the realization and appreciation that what happens on the home front is profoundly connected to the challenges and successes at work.

A Note on Guilt

I don't think I ever *really* felt guilty for anything much—until I had kids and began to regularly experience the horrible feeling that I could have done more or done better, been nicer or more patient when it came to something to do with my kids. It turns out guilt is the great equalizer among women: 94 percent of moms, regardless of whether they work outside the home or not, report regularly feeling guilty.

The good news is that working is no longer a primary motivator for this guilt. A recent survey found that eight out of ten mothers enjoy being a working parent and 64 percent say work does not interfere with their ability to be a good parent, and over half say that they feel having a job makes them a good role model for their children.

(From: "Are We Finally Starting to Banish Working-Mom Guilt?" *Today Moms* February 27, 2012, http://moms.today.com/_news/2012/02/27/10499447-are-we-finally-starting-to-banish-working-mom-guilt?lite)

The Domestic Trap

Almost twenty-two years since Arlie Hochschild first chronicled the toll that "The Second Shift" is having on women's careers, health and families, the gendered expectations around housework still have not changed substantially. Men's participation in the domestic sphere continues to be largely discussed as optional while for women it's assumed.

In her TED talk "Why We Have So Few Women Leaders," Facebook COO Sheryl Sandberg commented that the greatest challenge for working mothers is on the home front, saying, ". . . if a woman and man both work full time and have a child, the woman essentially has three jobs, since she's doing twice the housework the man does and three times the amount of child care." The long-term result? "Not surprisingly, it's the woman who ends feeling like day-to-day life is getting out of control and that to cope, *she* should ramp down, take a break from it or just step away altogether."

The Pew Research Center estimates that women (even those with full-time jobs) spend about six hours more in household work than their male partners and an additional three hours more in child care.[87] The good news is that Millennials (those born between 1981 and 2000) have a much greater tendency than any other generation to be defined by their emphasis on equality in their relationships. In one study, the Families & Work Institute found that 75 percent of this generation believes they will create equal life partnerships that don't follow traditional gender norms. Even if they don't quite succeed, they will still help move this issue forward and towards a better place.

"One of my biggest observations about Millennials is their desire to customize their careers and lives to their own preferences," says Lindsey Pollak, best-selling author of *Getting from College to Career* and an expert on Gen Y in the workplace. "As a Gen Xer, I remember so clearly believing there was an age at which I had to be married, have a child, be successful in my career. Millennials seem much more willing to create their own paths and timelines. Also, many Millennials are the children of working moms, so they have their eyes wide open about the challenges and opportunities of integrating a career and parenthood. I'm often surprised how many college freshmen are already asking me questions about how they can eventually balance work and family—even the young men."

Parenting

It's impossible to separate parenting trends and expectations from the impact they have on the success or the struggles of working mothers. "We have changed the standards of what constitutes good mothering," is the conclusion of Suzanne Bianchi, a University of Maryland sociologist who has conducted extensive studies to compare how American mothers, from the 1920s to the present, have made use of their time.

Bianchi found that mothers today—*whether or not they work*—spend more time per child than did mothers in the "family-oriented 1960s" because they shift time away from housework and other non-child-centered tasks, to instead focus on their children.[88] In *Perfect Madness: Motherhood in the Age of Anxiety*, Judith Warner also examines the impact of what she calls the "soul draining" perfectionism that's turned parenting from "conception to college into a competitive sport." Warner contends that the gains of feminism have become no match for the frenzied perfectionism of modern parenting. She defines this cultural construct as the "mommy mystique," which tells women that they have the knowledge and know-how to make "informed decisions" that will guarantee the successful course of their children's lives. As a result, every decision seems to be incredibly important, creating an exhausting premise that results in women feeling depleted and without the sense that they can manage more than one thing.

More recently, in *The Conflict: How Modern Motherhood Undermines the Status of Women,* French feminist philosopher Elisabeth Badinter has argued that the over-parenting tactics of the new generation of young mothers, the "coddling, co-sleeping, obsessing about organic diapers, breast-feeding into the toddler years and in the process tethering themselves in a way not seen since the 1950s is what is holding women back." Among the women I interviewed, the desire for flexible work was predominantly driven by a desire to adapt schedules in order to parent in a certain way, a way that seemed incompatible with either their own previous work schedule or a partner's more hectic and less forgiving one.

Cultural norms also heavily shape parenting or more specifically, mothering expectations. Anjum Choudhry Nayyar is the founder of Masalamommas.com, the first online magazine for mothers and moms-to-be with a South Asian connection; she is also mother to six-year-old Annika and three-year-old Liam. "Many moms [in our community] feel judged not only by our 'peers' or fellow moms but also by extended family, many of whom have cultural biases when it comes to women working outside the home and on what being a 'good mother' involves. These pressures frequently shape the career choices and decisions they subsequently make."

The women I interviewed for this book had all found ways to work flexibly (starting a business, working from home, working a compressed week) and had professionally continued to succeed while doing so. However, many did explicitly say that even if they hadn't taken those paths, they would have considered the career sacrifice of stepping down or back more than worth it for the sake of their children.

The Extended Family
From a "Western" perspective, family usually refers to some variant of the immediate nuclear family. However, in other countries and

Is All-Day School Part of the Answer?

It's an idea that regularly does the rounds on websites and blogs: Why can't or why haven't we made the school schedule match the work schedule? Admittedly, it would be expensive and it would take time to implement, but it would also be one of the most helpful changes that society could make in support of all working families.

Currently, the system reflects the needs of an agrarian society where stay-at-home moms dominated. The day ends at 3:30, which requires finding after-school care or programs. The year ends in June, which means finding summer care or paying for expensive camps. After-school programs are filled to capacity, which means parents are often desperately constructing patchwork solutions of nannies, nanny shares, structured programs, activities and the support of family or friends. If one part of the child-care house of cards collapses, the whole structure is threatened. "From three till four each day I'm technically at work, but until I get the call that the kids have been walked home and are safely in my neighbor's house, I'm just on edge," said Emily,* a lab technician and single mother of twin third-graders in Morristown. "A longer school day would eliminate that daily anxiety for so many working moms."

There is hope that the school system might catch up to work-place realities. U.S. President Barack Obama endorses the idea. In Britain, Prime Minister David Cameron launched a commission that will, in part, explore the idea of extending school hours. However, even this may not be enough. "The reality is that many parents do not work the traditional 9 to 5, and no matter the hours of school, arranging child care is a challenge," said Kelly Ann Heaney, an Ontario teacher and the mother of four boys.[89]

Establishing school hours that fully sync with the modern workforce might be impossible, but even some small adjustments could hugely help support working parents.

cultures (as well as immigrant communities), it includes aunts, uncles, grandparents and cousins, as well as nieces and nephews, all of whom might be involved in the upbringing of a child—an arrangement that provides these working mothers with a distinct advantage. For instance, professional women in BRIC countries (Brazil, Russia, China and India) don't expect their careers to be sidelined or even slowed by children. Instead, the entrenched role of the extended family in daily life and the low cost and prevalence of domestic help alleviate some of the pressure of balancing a career and family.[90]

In India, for instance, 42 percent of graduates are female, and 80 percent of working women describe themselves as very ambitious, and that ambition doesn't diminish as they get older. In America, by contrast, there's a real drop in ambition among women by the time they reach 40—coinciding with the pressures of family and child care.

Name: Nancy Gupta*
Role: Senior Vice President, Investment Fund Company
Children: Amit, 4

"It was a wonderful delight to find out that I was pregnant at 42. My 30s had been spent building my career and traveling the world (I graduated from university at 24, but then after a few years of work, I went back to school to complete my MBA at age 30). I worked hard and my career progression followed a successful upward trajectory. I remember saying to myself, 'If I don't have a baby by the time I'm 35, I'll do it alone.' Somehow I never got around to taking the step of being a single mom.

"In 2000, while living in Chicago, I began working with a new investment fund and with the demands and excitement of that position and the opportunity to build a business, getting into a relationship and motherhood again took a back seat. The priorities were on building the fund and investing the capital. Then, in April 2006, I visited India and had a series of meetings that left me feeling that *this* was where the action was happening. It was then that I decided to pack my bags and by August 2006, I was living and working in the thriving city of Mumbai, India.

"While I was there, I met my now husband. He was in the country on a work assignment. In May 2008, I was pregnant and at that time I was the managing director of a U.S.-based fund with global offices. It was a role that represented the culmination of ten-plus years in venture capital and international business. We were in the midst of building out the business in India; so the option of taking significant time off for the baby, i.e., an actual maternity leave, was completely out of the question.

"Realizing that I would soon be a working mom with a baby and BlackBerry in hand, I began to surround myself with support: I got a live-in nanny lined up, full-time driver, and hired a full-time housekeeper. Fortunately, I also had the flexibility to work from home, and when I was traveling for business it was my son, the nanny and myself sharing the hotel room! I never really thought about not working after the baby. I always felt it would make me a better mother, which it has. I envisioned being able to do it all, mostly because I had no other choice.

"I also thought that I would take a delayed maternity leave, when the baby was a toddler or even four or five years old. At the time, I was willing to jump back into work so as to not lose any career momentum. It may not have been the perfect work/life balance, but it was the cards I was dealt with. Plus I simply wasn't in a financial position to stay at home. I wanted to be closer to my family as the baby's due date came closer, so I returned to Chicago when I was seven months pregnant. During the few weeks leading up to my due date, I had a major work deliverable. I joked that my son knew this and that's why he was a helpful ten days late—so I could finish up my assignment.

"I started checking work e-mails the day after my son was born. Unfortunately I also had to be back in India for a work commitment in April, which meant less time in the U.S. than I'd hoped. When Amit was about six weeks old, we flew back to Mumbai. My mom accompanied me and was planning to stay for a few months to help me adjust and my husband was awaiting our return. Unfortunately my mother suffered a minor stroke almost immediately after we landed and was admitted to hospital for four weeks for the recovery. Life just doesn't go as planned sometimes.

"During that time I still had to fulfill my work commitments, adjust to being back in India and to being a mom. Even though my husband was incredibly supportive and was able to spend significant time with Amit whenever I had to be at the office, I felt very alone in the city of millions. To be honest, it felt like I'd been hit by a truck—it was one of the most difficult times of my life. In the weeks that I returned to India, I felt overwhelmed by it all. I was fortunate to have very capable staff attending to all the household concerns: cooking, cleaning, errands, etc. That freed up my time to focus on the most important tasks: nursing Amit and doing my work. I basically worked as much as I could and would only leave my home office to attend to meetings around his feeding times. I got my strength from Amit—looking at his face and realizing that this little soul depended on me.

"I do feel that I was extremely fortunate to have been able to affordably 'outsource' so many elements of being a working mother (the housework and cooking, for instance). Instead, I was able to focus on having quality time with my child and also resume my career. There is no doubt in my mind that I would not have been able to 'jump back into the saddle' so quickly after having a baby if I was in the U.S." When her son was two, Nancy and her son returned to Chicago, to be closer to her family.

"I miss the help I had in India—now it seems that I'm constantly behind on laundry and cleaning. I realize that it will always be a challenge to find that perfect work/life/family balance, but I'm OK with not finding the perfect solution. I try my best to live in the moment. I can settle for what works' for the upcoming week."

Getting Help

"I remember my mother getting up each weekday at 5 a.m. to make sure the house was clean and dinner was made, before getting us and herself ready and then going to her full-time job as a secretary in an insurance company. She did this for over thirty years. We never ate

The Male Perspective

What happens on the home front also impacts dads. Although they were not the focus of the book, during the course of my research, several fathers e-mailed me with their perspective on the issue (having heard about the project from colleagues or from a blog or article I'd written). Specifically, many mentioned how their wives' unexpected decision to stay home with their children affected their own careers and choices.

In 2011, for the first time since the downturn in 2008, the number of stay-at-home mothers rose slightly. The biggest increase was among young mothers between 25 and 35 years.[91] I had always assumed that women who made this choice did so with the support of their partners. But it turns out that 55 percent of men (husbands and partners) say they are either envious or angry when their wives or partners decide to scale back.[92]

For many this resentment is the result of the extra wage-earning responsibility that has been shifted onto their shoulders, and their concern about their ability to make up the shortfall in income, particularly if they felt it wasn't part of the original relationship arrangement. This was certainly the perspective of the fathers that contacted me—all unprompted—to share their frustrations about their wives' or partners' post-baby decisions.

"I never wanted a so-called traditional marriage, but when Barb* decided not to go back to work, I didn't feel like I could force her to and so here we are. I feel like I've morphed into my dad," wrote John,* a financial editor and father of two (his wife was formerly a CA).

"I resent the tight financial situation that her decision has put us in. I always thought we would be a dual earning couple. It's a lot of stress and not what I had planned on when we got together," wrote Andrew,* a litigator and father of two (his wife was formerly an HR manager).

> "After our third daughter was born, my wife said she needed to scale back and after a year of being part-time, she left work altogether. I'm not sure that having her home helps the kids enough to justify all the financial cutbacks we've had to make as a family."
>
> —Brian,* an engineer, father of three (his wife was formerly also an engineer).

out and she never had any help," says Kara Martin, a single mother of two boys, eight and ten years old, and a Chicago OR nurse. "I often wonder how she got the energy, especially when I'm getting drive-through for the kids and then opening a bag of pre-cut carrots to try and balance it out."

In the over five hundred interviews that I did, the most common response to the question of what would you advise other women was to "Get as much [household] help as you can afford."

In her most recent book, *The Outsourced Self: Intimate Life in Market Times*, sociologist Arlie Russell Hochschild follows on from her early identification of the second shift that working women face to the growing trend of outsourcing even the most intimate types of work (dating, planning a wedding, raising our children and cooking for our families) as the time demands in our professional life continue to increase. As Linda Duxbury, a professor of business and organizational health at Carleton University in Ottawa, frames it, "You can pretty much pay for anything now and those people that can afford it, are doing just that."

Whether it's convenience foods or live-in child care, families in all income brackets are looking for help creating more time for themselves away from work and in order to find ways to make the time they can spend together with their partner or children more enjoyable.

"Many people are working fifty hours a week, and their partner is working fifty hours a week. When you've got that and you're squabbling about who is going to do this and who is going to do that, it's much better for the couple to spend the money on help than put stress on the relationship by arguing over things that really don't or shouldn't matter that much," continues Duxbury. "When people say it seems stupid to pay someone, I always say, 'It's cheaper than a divorce.'"93

How Are You Using Your 168 Hours?

I was introduced to this approach to work/life balance by a surgeon married to another surgeon with four kids under seven. She very successfully and happily manages her professional and home life based on the book *You Have More Time than You Think* by Laura Vanderkam, which advocates being more aware and deliberate with our time, and focusing on our core competencies, in order to more productively use our time. Based on this, the woman I interviewed has outsourced virtually everything in her life but what she loves doing: her work and family time. This involves a personal shopper and trainer (who both come to her house), grocery delivery, a housekeeper to make the meals, a nanny to do the backend for the kids, a night nanny and a cleaning service.

It sounds (and is) expensive but there is a real logic to it.

Vanderkam argues that if you worked 50 hours a week and slept 8 hours a night, you would still have 62 extra hours each week—and so the problem is not just that we are too busy but that we aren't making the best use of those extra hours.

Her suggestions on changing this include:

> ›   Start by figuring out where your time actually goes—for a spreadsheet to track it, see www.my168hours.com.
> ›   Focus on your core competencies—what can only you do and what can someone else easily do for you?
> ›   Do work that makes you happy.
> ›   Spend less time reacting and more time focusing on work or experiences that actually matter to you.

Our Relationships

In *Lean In,* Sheryl Sandberg discusses at length the importance of having the right partner in order to achieve professional success. "I truly believe that the single most important career decision that a woman makes is whether she will have a life partner and who that partner is. I don't know of a single woman in a leadership position whose life partner is not fully—and I mean fully—supportive of her career. No exceptions," she writes. "And contrary to the popular notion that only unmarried women can make it to the top, the majority of the most successful female business leaders have partners."[94]

Who we do or don't marry and form families with has always had a significant impact on our career and life choices, but until recently there was a tendency to separate them out and discuss each in a silo. My last book, *First Comes Marriage: Modern Relationship Advice from the Wisdom of Arranged Marriages* was based on more than three hundred interviews with women who decided to have an arranged marriage— with the goal of seeing what lessons might transfer over to the dating lives and relationships of women who would never consider the arranged marriage option. One of the key lessons was that for most of us, whom we marry is one of the biggest decisions we will ever make, since it shapes where we live, our careers, how we identify and define ourselves and what our day-to-day experiences are like. Viewing and discussing marriage in those practical terms offends all of our cultural notions about romantic love and how it is supposed to work. Most women put more research, thought and analysis into choosing a college or career than they do into whom they date or eventually marry. And yet that decision directly and profoundly impacts all their career and family plans, ambitions and goals. But increasingly, there has been a wider call for and discussion around whether we need to encourage girls and women to think more carefully about how their spouse impacts their career.

For instance, the U.K. media focused heavily on a speech made by Helen Fraser, the chief executive of the Girls Day School Trust (a leading girls' school association), in which she asked whether "what too many women face nowadays isn't a 'glass ceiling' because of their sex but a 'nappy wall' if they choose to have a child as well as a career." She added that "it's not just about finding a husband who does the hoovering and makes the dinner. It's about finding one who really understands that it is important for you to thrive and do well in whatever *you* chose to do."[95]

The challenge of course is how do you know if the person you are dating really will be the partner you are looking for? Sheryl Sandberg shares the story of a woman who "tested" out potential suitors by deliberately canceling plans for work reasons and noting the reaction.

But for many of us, it can be difficult to know just how careers, like relationships, will evolve over time.

Name: Jodi Butts
Role: Senior Vice President of Corporate Affairs and
            Operations, Mount Sinai Hospital
Children: Aidan,7; Ava, 5

Do couples that get together when they are still in school have a greater sense of equality in the relationship? Jodi and Gerry met when they were both in graduate school. She was studying Canadian history at the MA level, then later attended law school at the University of Toronto, and he was pursuing a PhD.

At the time of our interview, she was a senior leader at one of North America's top research and teaching hospitals and Gerry was the President and CEO of the World Wildlife Fund (WWF) Canada. "When Gerry and I were just friends and before we started dating, I confessed to him my fear was becoming Murphy Brown. I always knew I wanted a family but was concerned that I would get focused on career and let my personal life slide. When we first started dating and even up to our wedding, Gerry had always discussed having a writing career, and so on the day we got married, I thought I would be the main breadwinner with my law degree and that he would be focused on the tough slog of a professional writing career.

"When we returned from our honeymoon, Gerry left his position at a polling firm and instead started working for an opposition politician and then things just took off for him in that sphere. He had been working at a political and corporate commercial polling firm during our engagement and I knew him when he worked for a senator, so politics was already in our life, but even on our wedding day, I would not have predicted his career path. So in short, it evolved into something that I had no foresight of."

Jodi had started her legal career at a boutique litigation firm, which she hated: "Every case was Asshole A v Asshole B, the battle of the balance sheets." She decided to leave and, in partnership with a former mentor, started her own full service firm. "I really liked it; I learned a lot about the practice of law and customer service and was earning very decent money compared with my Bay Street colleagues.

"But then I had a miscarriage and that was followed by difficulties conceiving. It was around that time that Gerry's career was stabilizing and so I went on a hunt to find something that required less management on my part. I thought being an employee would be easier for a while than being a business owner. After many lunches, I learned of a low-level opportunity at Mount Sinai Hospital as a privacy officer. I took a salary hit to switch sectors, but I loved the mission and being a part of an organization that was full of smart professionals but not all lawyers." A year in, she was promoted to the legal counsel position.

A year later she had her first child. "I took a year off and then came back already three months pregnant." Again, she took a full year off. Gerry, whom Jodi describes as an "awesome and committed dad," was away a lot during this time. "Political jobs and high-profile leadership roles mean a lot of travel and evenings out, which I understood but it didn't make it easier. I was sitting at home with the babies, feeling lonely and spinning my wheels, and so when I returned to work after my second maternity leave, I really dove into work. I actively worked to convince the board and senior management that I wasn't going anywhere—plus, during the months at home, I had really missed the positive feelings work provided: accomplishment, a sense of drive, and ambition fulfilled.

"Two years after returning from my second maternity leave, I was promoted to VP heading up purchasing, security, ethics while serving as general counsel and privacy officer. Within a year of that, my boss left and I took on the acting role, and then was awarded my current position. I've now been in this role for sixteen months.

"Sustaining balance with two busy careers is hard on the home front. Yes, there are day cares, nannies, schools, activities, etc., but it's up to the two of you to engage in 'project delivery' of family life, and it's a daily struggle, not because you don't want to be with your kids or help your spouse, but because it's exhausting, can be a titch boring, demands an extraordinary amount of patience and there's a finite number of hours in the day.

"Our relationship has been essential to my success. I often say that I wish I could put my spouse selection on my CV as one of my achievements!"

(Update: Approximately a year after I interviewed Jodi, both she and Gerry left these roles. Gerry has taken on a senior strategic political role with the Liberal Party of Canada, and Jodi is now Executive Director of Rise Asset Development (a micro-finance and financial initiative that provides loans and mentorship to entrepreneurs with mental health and addiction challenges). She also joined the Board of the Wellesley Institute, a think tank on urban health.)

A Marriage, but Not a Partnership

Of course having a supportive partner, both personally and professionally, is the ideal. When it works, it means help at home and with the kids as well as someone vested in your success to discuss both micro and macro career issues with (from how to best handle a political situation at the office to when it's time to move on to a new and more challenging role).

I personally feel very lucky that my relationship with Rana gives me both of those, but am also very aware that the idea of a real partnership in a marriage where both are pursuing their independent goals is a very recent one. Most of the women I saw growing up did not have relationships where the men were encouraging of their wives' career ambitions. Add in the stresses of cultural differences and immigration, and it becomes clear that this generation of women often succeeded in spite of the hurdles that their partners presented.

Name: Anu Singh*
Role: Senior Vice President, IT Systems and
          Engineering
Children: A daughter, 31; two sons, 27 and 23

"When I was 24 years old and in the middle of doing my Ph.D. in human genetics, my parents were granted immigration from

India to the U.K. I was keen to go with them and have the opportunity to study overseas—the catch was that, to be able to join them, my father insisted that I first get married.

"I agreed and they arranged a match for me with a friend's son who was also doing his Ph.D. in engineering and was already in the U.K. He came back to India for our wedding, but we didn't meet in person until after the ceremony, when we were already married. After a year in the U.K., my new husband and I moved to the U.S. By this time, my Ph.D. had been abandoned, but my career ambitions hadn't. As soon as I got to the U.S., I started looking for what I could do that would lead to a career. I went to job agencies but they suggested I become a secretary, which was not what I wanted. Instead, I went to the local community college to see if I could take some courses that might help make me more employable since my credentials from India were now fairly meaningless.

"I signed up for accounting and programming, even though I wasn't sure what the latter involved. A helpful woman at the college helped me apply for a loan to pay for the courses. It was hard since it was completely different from what I'd done before and I remember being the only woman in my programming classes—but I graduated and since demand was high for programmers, I got my first real U.S. job.

"I can't say my husband was at all supportive. He's a good man, but his view on my career was that if I was going to do this, it was something that I was doing on my own; he wasn't going to be involved or offer any help. The way he saw it was by this time he had a good engineering job and financially we could make it work, so I didn't *have* to do this but was *choosing* to. And so, he didn't see having to support my career or ambitions as being part of his role. I told him I didn't need his help and that became true. I began progressing rapidly at work and loved my job, and so even when we started to have kids, I always knew it was going to be all on me to manage work and family, but I was determined never to slow down or stop.

"I only had six weeks' maternity leave with each child and then they went to day care. Those years were not easy—I would be up at five getting all three ready, then driving in the snow to drop them off, going to work, then coming home, making dinner, doing baths and as much other housework as I could. Looking back, I should have hired help but I just never did. I remember once when my daughter was sick, I had to take her in to work with me on the weekend since I didn't want to ask my husband for help—maybe it was a pride thing or that both of us were so stubborn in those early years. She had a fever and I was holding her on my lap while I tried to finish a program I had been writing. Just as I was almost done, she hit a key and erased hours of work. I just burst out crying.

"The example that my mother had set for me is what kept me going. In India she had a hard life, money was always tight and my father was a difficult man to live with. But when she moved to the U.K., at the age of 60, she went to the community college and became a design engineer. She got a job at the global engineering firm of Hawkes & Siddley. She worked there for the next fifteen years. Having her own income and education changed her—she was the happiest I had ever seen her.

"In some ways it was easier for me because I never doubted what I wanted to do. Even the nights that I had no sleep or the kids were crying and sick, I knew that by working at a job I loved and was good at, I was taking care of myself and my family, and that as hard as some of those moments were, they would pass. Of course for my daughter I want something different, something easier, but often I think she is paralyzed by choices and seems stuck about what to do with her degrees and her relationships. My path was simpler in many ways."

Dad as the Primary Caregiver

According to the National At-Home Dad Network, there are currently about 7 million fathers in the U.S. who are at home with their children. The exact number seems to vary depending on factors such as whether they are working freelance, running home businesses or not doing paid work, but regardless, there is a definite rise in and trend towards stay-at-home dads. According to U.S. Census data, the number of stay-at-home dads has doubled in the last decade.[96] As

The New York Times observes, "The identity of the at-home dad is evolving, on the playground and in the culture at large. To this new cohort, the decision to stay home with the children is seen not as a failure of their responsibilities as men, but as a lifestyle choice—one that makes sense in an era in which women's surging salaries have thrown the old family hierarchy into flux; and men have embraced more fluid interpretations of careers that place a premium on fulfillment, not money and status."[97]

The recent economic upheavals are part of this rise in stay-at-home fathers. U.S. federal statistics show that men lost two and a half times as many jobs as women did in the recession. A number of the women whose stories are either discussed elsewhere in the book or on the website have partners who either have dramatically scaled back their own careers or are now fully at home with the children. Interestingly, very few had deliberately planned this arrangement. Instead, most said it just evolved as the logical decision based on the best interests of the family.

All the women I spoke with respected their husbands' choices and felt grateful that as a result, they were able to focus on their careers—guilt free. "I know he loves our kids and nurtures them. It makes my job way easier, knowing that I don't have to worry about what's happening on the home front," said Sarah, a PR executive at Hill+Knowlton and mother of two.

Taking Turns: A New (and Better?) Model

Hanna Rosin, author of *The End of Men: And the Rise of Women*, suggests that the future of professional couples will be free-flowing partnerships, or "seesaw couples," in which each spouse continually adjusts his or her role in response to changing family circumstances, with neither person's career or ambition taking primary dominance. "A husband can work to support his wife through school and then she can take over and be the hotshot lawyer," Ms. Rosin writes. "Anyone can play the role of breadwinner for any period," she adds.

With the timeline of careers being extended and a fluctuating economy, this sounds like an ideal arrangement to allow both people to engage in family and professional life in a new way—provided, of course, that both partners actually do get their turn.

Name: Jessica Hicks
Role: Grade three teacher and Grade Level Coordinator
Children: Heather, 3

"When I was living in Miami, I taught children with autism at a private school, spent four years teaching second grade at a private school and then two years teaching third grade. After Heather was born, I stayed home for almost two years. This wasn't part of my plan though. The economic downturn meant my husband was laid off from his job and when he was offered another one, we moved to Greensboro, NC. I started looking for teaching jobs, but there was a hiring freeze on in Greensboro and I couldn't find anything. I'd wanted to be back at work so this was fairly frustrating.

"Even when I was a teenager I knew that I wanted to work and not stay at home when I had kids. I love working and feeling valued and being a part of something. My mom worked full time and raised my sister and me. My stepmother worked full time and raised her daughter, so I grew up surrounded by working mothers. Not working for those two years was very uncomfortable. I felt like something was missing from my life."

In Greensboro, while Jessica was at home with their daughter, her husband was working as a restaurant manager with twelve-hour days and changing shifts. "We were both unhappy with our situation—there wasn't much time to be a family.

"One day my husband and I were watching a show called *House Hunters International.* The episode showed a teacher looking for an apartment in Abu Dhabi. The episode discussed all the benefits of working in the U.A.E., such as a tax-free salary, free health care, free accommodation, yearly flights home, and a one-month salary bonus for every year teaching." Drawn by the opportunity for a better life, Jessica did some research and applied for a job. In August 2010, after a phone and then an in-person interview, Jessica and her family moved to Abu Dhabi.

"Professionally I knew that this opportunity would help me become a better teacher and open up doors for me in the future. But before I took the job, I made it clear to my husband that now *he* would be at home and *he* would have to take on the primary responsibility of taking care of Heather. I was very worried about this change and debated if I should take the job since he was not used to having that level of responsibility with her. But he assured me that he would be fine taking care of her and that I should take the job.

"We had never talked about taking turns before. It just happened. At first Miguel had a very hard time. He wasn't used to taking care of Heather that much and had to adjust to not working. He had to make decisions that he normally wouldn't have had to make. For instance, he had to call a list of nursery schools, visit them and decide which one would be best for our daughter. I think he felt stressed to meet my expectations.

"Overall, the benefits far outweigh the challenges though. After my husband began to adjust to having to take care of Heather, he was able to go from being a simple figure in her life to being very important and involved. He adores Heather and looks forward to taking her to nursery school, being a part of the 'mom group' at the school. He is a great father and so playful.

"Right now, Miguel is working on his master's degree in elementary education. When he's finished, he plans to also teach at a private school in Abu Dhabi. The opportunity for teachers here is outstanding. Today, in addition to teaching the core subjects of English, math and science, I'm also the grade level coordinator. This means extra responsibilities including creating a weekly plan to send home to parents, leading grade level planning meetings and ensuring teachers know about upcoming events and meetings. My next goal is to teach at the college level. I am thinking about taking a certification class to teach adults English as a second language.

"Before we moved to Abu Dhabi, I was solely responsible for Heather's upbringing. I stayed home with her and made all the decisions for her. Now, she has both of us raising her. Her dad and I share the responsibilities and both care for her. She sees two people working together for her well-being— which is a better role model for her own life."

Consider:

Co-parenting. Looking to cultivate more hands-on parenting from your partner? These were some of the tips I heard in my interviews:

> **Start small.** A bike ride, a solo park date—encourage easy ways for your partner and the children to spend some regular time alone.

> **Don't micromanage.** It can be so tempting to correct "mistakes," or lay out everything in advance—resist. Instead, let your partner parent *their* way.

> **Ask your partner to take on specific tasks.** Delegate specific tasks from dentist appointments to swimming lessons and then trust they will get done. No typed pages of instructions or reminders.

Commuting

When I was growing up, my family moved every four years for my dad's job. Each new house decision was based on the quality of the schools and minimizing my father's commute. In a decision that I increasingly understand and respect, my father refused to drive more then ten or fifteen minutes for work, claiming it was a waste of his time and life. He was lucky enough to make this work his entire career—today he lives across the street from his office. So does my brother, who is an accountant in Vancouver. And I primarily work from home.

In cities across North America, the average commute time is steadily increasing and so is the number of people who regularly have an "extreme commute" (defined as ninety minutes or more).[98]

Commuting adds a series of complications, both big and small, to a parent's life. The distance factor reduces time spent at home with the family, and it leaves little room for error when arrangements on the home front break down. I remember once sprinting from Soho in Central London to Hampstead in North London in under fifteen minutes since I was so anxious about getting to my son's day care on time on a day when the Tube was down and the traffic was completely jammed, and none of my appointed backups were answering their phones. (For those who aren't familiar with London's geography, Google Maps tells me this distance on foot should have taken me fifty-three minutes.)

Commutes are getting longer because of traffic congestion but also because greater distances are becoming more common for a number of reasons—among them, household economics. This recession has seen the number of couples living apart for financial reasons rise.[99] Joanna,* a high-tech sales executive, was relocated from her job in Houston to Dallas. The mother of three girls in grades seven, nine and twelve, she didn't want to disrupt their lives but also couldn't refuse the transfer. "They were laying people off in our company and our family couldn't make it on one income. So I decided that I would go and they would stay. I'm hoping to find something back where they are, but I've had this arrangement now for over sixteen months. The girls are pretty busy and my in-laws live close by so they can help out a bit, but it's certainly not what I would have planned or wanted."

Name: Arsheya Devitre
Role: Senior Manager, (at a Fortune 200 U.S. environ-
          mental waste company)
Children: Leyla and Jai, 5

Three years ago, Arsheya managed her company's entry to China and was sent there to work in the new entity. After business school, Arsheya was working in a junior role for Nestlé in London. At the time, she had followed her husband Alok out to the U.K., and then on to Egypt, where she worked at Citibank as the head of Quality & Customer Service. "I was career focused before we had children, but at the time, Alok's career was more advanced than mine, and since he was in the oil industry, he had the opportunity to work in all these interesting places. So while I looked for the best jobs I could, it was dictated by the location and timing of Alok's job. I was also junior enough to be more flexible in finding a job in each location we went to. Eventually, his work took us to Houston, Texas.

"I always hoped that I would have both a well-adjusted family and a successful career, but before you actually have kids, it can be difficult to imagine how it will really play out. I think that belief was the result of how I was raised. My parents always encouraged me to pursue a career, and my mother, who had sacrificed her own career for my father's, had often told me how she wished she had remained involved in something of her own.

"Once we had kids, I was almost better able to focus on my career since I could actually plan around the reality of a family versus imagining how it might work. I did know that I found it very difficult to be at home full time—it requires a level of patience that I don't have in large measure. After the kids were born, I started to look for a job. I wanted to spend the first year or so with them and the timing worked out well in that I started working again after they turned one. The catch was that the job was in New Hampshire and we lived in Texas. But it was an interesting industry and opportunity, so I accepted the role and spent Monday to Friday in New Hampshire and the weekends at home with Alok and the kids.

After about eight months of commuting to NH, I started traveling to China every two weeks. Truthfully, for me it was harder to stay at home—I think I would not have thrived personally or as a mother if I had continued not working. I think I was able to manage it with some sacrifice and a lot of luck. Luckily, we could afford a nanny and it helped that the kids were only one when I started commuting. Since they were so young, I convinced myself that they weren't old enough to care when I left!

"Also, Alok was a fantastic, hands-on father and made sure that for the most part, he was able to come home at a reasonable hour to relieve the nanny every evening. If we were both traveling, either his parents or mine would fly in to be at home with the kids. So I had a lot going for me to make it work. Nevertheless, I had friends and neighbors who thought I was not making the best decision as a wife or mother by taking on a commuter job, but I believed if I had the right support system in place, it would work out. The plan was also that the commuting arrangement would not be long term.

"Of all the things I just mentioned, I'd say that Alok was the biggest enabler, as he was very supportive of me (except when I was too tired on weekends to do anything social and he was dying to go out) and rarely made me feel guilty for the way we were choosing to live. It's not always easy but I've learned to compartmentalize the different parts of my life. I also know that people have invested in me, emotionally and financially, and that they are counting on me, which gives me the motivation to move through any rough patches."

After about two years of this arrangement, the family moved to China. Alok left his finance executive job with the plan to pursue some entrepreneurial ventures and Arsheya became the primary breadwinner. "The move was probably a bigger switch for Alok than me because for the first time, we were moving for my job and not his. There were many times when we'd meet new people and they'd automatically look to Alok and ask what brought us to China and what his job was. He'd take it in good stride and was proud to say that my work had brought us over.

"I think it's a great model for our children to see that there are no gender or geographic limits in pursuing life and career choices."

Consider:

> **Moving.** If you are moving for a company, don't be shy about letting your employer know what you are giving up. When Arsheya was considering moving to China, she let her employer know that if she took the role it had to have financial compensation that made up for her husband leaving his job.

> **Be confident about career gaps.** Don't be scared of having career gaps to explain to prospective employers. "Every time we moved, there was a period of six months to a year until I found a job, but that was OK and people understood the breaks in my career as I had a reasonable explanation (moving, babies, work permit issues)," notes Arsheya.

The Family Business

In 2011, my husband ran for federal office. The election opportunity was both slightly unexpected and undertaken on very short notice. From building a website to finding an office, bringing a staff together, raising money and of course, getting the campaign started, we had never worked such long hours on anything together. I put my client work on hold and dedicated myself full time to the efforts.

The rest of our family got involved as well. My mom came to stay with us during the week to keep the kids on a semblance of a schedule. My sister-in-law was at the campaign office most evenings, usually with dinner in hand. My dad was there every afternoon, putting up signs, fund-raising and knocking on doors.

It was the closest experience I'd ever had to working in or with a family business, and it seemed incredibly appealing: the ability to create the work or office environment you want and (in theory) have more control over both your family and career life. Of course, nothing involving either family or business is entirely easy or straightforward. The challenge of work/life balance is inevitably more difficult when it's your own company and your colleagues are your family.

A survey of family business owners found that 56 percent are constantly trying to improve their work/life balance, 39 percent said a family business meant you can never take a day off and 44 percent said it led to more stress.[100] "Business always comes home, to the table, on vacation and even into bed with us. No matter what we try and do, our conversation or moods circle back to what's happening at the studio," said Tara,* who is part of a husband-and-wife interior design team in New York and mother of two. "I tell my kids, make your life easy, don't work with your husband, work for someone else and let them have the headaches." Despite the lack of balance, over 60 percent say their discussions of work at home rarely or never cause problems, while 75 percent say discussing home issues at work presents no difficulties.

For working mothers, a family business has several distinct advantages. First, either you're the boss or you're related to the boss, so you most likely have more flexibility on when and how work gets done and hopefully face less of a career penalty for traditional career obstacles like time off for maternity leave. The flip side of course is that depending on the size, scale and nature of your family business, maternity leave may not be an option. Similarly, the financial vulnerability of less established or cyclical businesses may add an additional element of stress to family life.

The Rise of Women in the Family Business

From Jeanie Buss of the Los Angeles Lakers to Christie Hefner of Playboy to Marilyn Carlson Nelson, who took over from her father at Carlson Cos., the giant travel, lodging and restaurant company, there is now no shortage of father-daughter success stories.

A convergence of several trends has led to the increase of women leading family businesses: the increasing number of women graduating from business schools, the rise in women learning the management trade with major companies, and just the growing number of female CEOs generally. All of these foreshadow a further rise of family-owned businesses headed by women.[101] Female leadership is going to affect a wide swath of the economy. According to a Citigroup report, families own or control 90 percent of U.S. businesses. They also employ half of all workers.

However, there are unique challenges to being the boss's daughter.

Name: Sarah Aboody
Role: Ever-changing, T-Zone Health Inc.
Children: Mimi, 3; Annika, 1

"I don't even have a real title. I don't have proper business cards. If I need to give one, I guess it would be online marketing? But it really depends on what part of the business I'm focused on at the time."

It's a common dilemma for entrepreneurs, but if you're not the founder or owner of the company, the professional ambiguity takes on a different dimension. T-Zone Vibration is Sarah's family business. It imports fitness and other equipment from China and has done this for the past forty years. They have thirty full-time employees, as well as additional salespeople, seasonal staff and freelance consultants.

Sarah is the primary earner in her family (her partner, Eric, is an artist and gifted photographer) and she's never really worked anywhere else. Sarah says the business is not simply part of her life but a central aspect of it. She's also very used to a lack of work/life division.

"Growing up, our living room was the office and that continues to this day, although we have an office space for our employees now. I probably speak to my father twice a day, but it's always just about work."

That blurring of boundaries is something that she's used to and just accepts but admits is harder for her partner to understand. "If something needs to be done, there's never any question that I will put off everything else until it's done. That might mean I'm driving back from the cottage to come into the city to help my dad with something that is urgent, but it would never occur to me to say no. I've also seen the business lows my parents went through and understand why they work the way they do."

Sarah had never specifically planned to go into the family business—it just happened. "I graduated with a degree in English and cinema studies, then took a PR course. While I was thinking about what to do next, my dad suggested I come help him for a two-week stint. I never left."

The flexibility and leeway of a family business sounds alluring, especially for working mothers trapped by the confines or the demands of an office schedule. And there's another bonus: her bosses are extremely invested in the health and well-being of their only grandchildren. But there are challenges.

"There's no feedback or evaluations, and for the longest time it was something I was just doing because I felt I had to. It was only after Mimi was born that I actually began to find my job fulfilling and enjoyable. Maybe becoming a mother gave me a different perspective on what work means for my family? I'm not sure actually. But I do know that before I had always been a kind of floater, just doing whatever needed to be done and working out of a sense of duty. I think I've done every job in the company over the years, and while I was invested in our shared livelihood, there wasn't any sense of personal satisfaction."

After Mimi came along, Sarah began to proactively carve out a more definitive role for herself so she could have a real sense of ownership over parts of it.

"Even though Eric has a flexible schedule, having a more structured role seemed like a way to better manage work after Mimi—that way I wouldn't just get pulled in all these different directions. So, I ended up taking on the online and marketing work, which no one was doing at the time. We rebuilt the website, launched our social media campaign and started a blog. I also took charge of most of the graphic and print material.It was the first time that I was able to definitively show what my contribution was and have a real sense of the impact that I was having on the business, and I loved it."

Consider:

> **Claim a niche.** Whether it's a family business, a small business or a start-up, look for ownership over discrete projects or tasks that can lead to measurable deliverables. It's essential to personal and professional success.

How We Make Our Families

Although the concept of the "traditional" nuclear family continues to define the norms and expectations of family life, it's a model that is actually in the minority.[102] With the rise of same-sex unions, the increase in lone parents, common-law arrangements, stepfamilies, IVF, surrogacy and adoption, the paths and structures of families have never been more varied or diverse.

It also made me wonder, how does the way we construct our families impact our careers?

Name: Punam Mathur
Role: HR VP NV Energy
Children: Richard, 22; Joseph, 14; Tai,12

Punam's career highlights include having been the SVP of the Las Vegas Chamber of Commerce and leading the MGM Mirage Diversity Initiative (under her watch MGM, a company of over seventy thousand, was named for the first time as one of the "50 Best Companies for Minorities").

All of this happened alongside her decision, at 36, to begin fostering children (with no partner support), three of whom she subsequently adopted. "At 36, I did a life review. I was proud of what I'd accomplished professionally, but children were missing and having a family was non-negotiable for me. At the time, I was the SVP of the Las Vegas Chamber of Commerce, a very public and all-consuming role. I was on a weekly television show, a weekly radio show and out at events six or seven nights per week."

"It was after I did my midlife evaluation that I realized that I needed to follow this desire to be a mother and that it wasn't going to happen as long as I was in a role that required this 24/7 commitment. And so I gave my three months' notice." During those three months she got a call from an icon in the gaming industry who was looking to recruit her. "I had a series of conversations during which we talked about the sort of role that they wanted to create for me. I hadn't come to this personal realization to risk losing it and so I told them directly that ultimately I just wanted to be a mom and that, although I wasn't one yet, I wasn't willing to jeopardize that calling, no matter how tempting the new role and offer was.

"They responded instantly and said that hearing that just made me more desirable to them. Looking back, I always say that was the moment that I received 'permission' to really embrace my authentic self and pursue both motherhood and my work equally." She accepted the role in 1996, ". . . and subsequently, it was my boss who regularly held me accountable for my parenting goal, regularly checking in to see what was I doing to make my motherhood goal into a reality?" By 1998, she had completed all the paperwork and checks required to become a foster parent and soon began the adoption process.

"I met Richard when he was nine. He came from a difficult background colored by abuse and neglect. Literally, the day after Richard arrived, two-and-a-half-week-old Joseph came into our lives. A year and a half later, my two boys were followed by Tai, who at five months was just coming out of the drug addiction she had been born with.

"The first year," she recalls, "was really a bit of a blur. My kids instantly, literally overnight, shifted the rotation of everything, yet it felt like the most natural thing for me.

Despite how quickly it seemed to happen, it didn't feel desta-bilizing; it made me feel grounded. I fostered my children because, while I didn't have a biological clock ticking, I did have a yearning to be a mother. For me, fostering and adopt-ing was not my last option—it was my first. And I think that makes me different from a lot of people.

"Becoming a mother changed how I managed and approached work. I'd always been very type A, a real control freak—now I delegated more and better, really letting people do their jobs. It was the same on the home front. I'd always taken pride in doing everything myself, but I realized that was no longer possible or the best way to spend my time and so I essentially farmed out everything that wasn't related to work or my kids. I also learned to ask for help for the first time, at work and at home. It was both humbling and empowering."

Two years after starting her family, Punam rose up in the gaming industry to become an SVP.

"I decorated my office walls with tons of the kids' art and vacation pictures and if I happened to find a binky in my pocket or briefcase when I was with people, I would just pull it out and laugh.

"It's not that there wasn't some eye rolling," she acknowl-edges. "I just didn't have time to notice or care about it."

When MGM was acquired, the CEO approached her about developing the diversity initiative for the organization. "As a woman of South Asian descent, with three children who don't match—this was a dream job for me. My real success came when I found a way to be the mother I wanted to be as well as with the career I was capable of—and in a way that reflected my own values rather than expected norms. And so, it was a privilege to be able to create a work environment and organi-zation where people, the biggest line item in a business, were able to feel valued as their authentic selves."

Single Parents—by Choice

Like Punam, many emotionally and financially empowered women do not want to wait hopefully for someone to come along in time for them to have a family.

"Most of the women I've talked to simply are used to taking matters into their own hands and don't want to miss the awesome experience that is parenting." says Mikki Morrissette, founder of ChoiceMoms.org and former editor and writer at *The New York Times*. Mikki uses the term "choice moms" to refer to women like herself who proactively and conscientiously decide to become single mothers. "My count is that today roughly fifty thousand women choose single motherhood each year. The census takers don't collect this data, but I based this number on the fact that a recent U.S. Census report indicated that more than 100,000 unmarried women above the age of 30 gave birth during the previous year. An estimated half of those are cohabiting women who simply are not married, which gives us fifty thousand who do not have a partner and are old enough to know how birth control works. Even if that number seems generous, consider that current industry trends indicate that at least one-quarter of the 125,000 adoptions each year involve single women, which is not included in this data.

"Because of data about teenage single moms and those unexpectedly suffering from divorce, the image is that most single mothers are impoverished, overwhelmed and emotionally tapped out. But the typical 'choice mom' is in her thirties or forties when she becomes a mother. Most of those I surveyed reported making at least $40,000 a year and have a postgraduate degree. We tend to have strong family values, or we wouldn't have made the decision to go ahead and have a family on our own."

Name: Mikki Morrissette
Role: Freelance Journalist and Editor; Founder, Choice Moms
Children: Sophia,14; Dylan, 9

"I got divorced in my early thirties. I had a high-paying career, owned my home and didn't want to rush into another relationship in order to build a family. In between the time I left my marriage in 1993 and had my daughter in 1999, I did fall in love with someone who already had children and didn't want any more. It broke my heart that he ended our relationship the day after my 35th birthday. But in hindsight, of course, it never would have worked for me to *not* have my two children, or for him to pretend he wanted more. So things worked out beautifully, as it turns out. Before I became pregnant, I had lived in New York City for almost eighteen years. All but one of my friends were single and childless. Essentially, I had been married to my career, working fifty-hour workweeks on a regular basis.

"Both of my children have the same biological donor, but we don't use the term 'father.' We refer to him as bio-dad. He was a friend of mine in New York City. When I was talking to him one night about my intention to have a child on my own, he volunteered to be the donor. At the time I was considering asking two other longer-term friends—preferring that method to motherhood than an anonymous donor or adoption (my brother was adopted and had issues with not knowing his biological roots). But after about six months of getting to understand his motivations for wanting to be a donor to a child he would not raise, I knew he was the right candidate for this process.

"When I had my daughter, I assumed that for me to have a high-paying job was what she and I needed. But what I discovered organically in time is that we wanted flexible time, a bigger family, more time for the outdoors and creativity, proximity to grandparents. I never thought I would be inclined to leave NYC, but within two years of becoming a mother, a life in corporate publishing no longer appealed to me. It was time for another big change. I relocated to my home state of Minnesota. I wanted to raise my daughter close to family and a non-work community. I published *Choosing Single Motherhood* and started my own multimedia business.

"After I moved, and had more space and time, I realized I wanted to have a second child. Dylan was born just shy of my 42nd birthday. What I learned is that life changes dramatically after you become a mother. It's not simply because you are up late at night and spend a few years changing diapers. It's because children open up your heart and your mind to a much wider experience than we had before they arrived.

"So . . . be prepared and be flexible to change. You can't plan everything. And even if you think you have, it will change anyway. And always find new ways to build your village, because no one—married or not—can parent well in a vacuum."

Name: Jennifer Meehan
Role: Managing Director, Sonic Boom Creative Media
Children: Sophie, 3

"As a woman in the business world, one of my strengths has always been the ability to directly have the tough conversations. But I also don't shy away from those conversations with myself. Sometimes those are often the most difficult.

"I started working when I was 23 in marketing and I was good at it. I was committed to a career but I had also always wanted to get married and have a family. Family is incredibly important to me, and a future without one seemed impossible. Certainly I wanted the two-parent dream, but I started waking up in the middle of the night thinking, 'Holy shit, I am 39 years old! I have the rest of my life to meet someone, but I don't have forever to have a child.'

"I knew my life would not be complete without having a child. It was one of those moments where you realize you've spent too much time focusing on your career and not enough time focusing on yourself. Instead of being sad, I decided to do it by myself. I would move forward, pursue my dream and worry about the details later.

"My parents were always very supportive of me having a child on my own, so when I had this major epiphany (Easter weekend of 2009 to be exact) I was not nervous sharing it with them. They were over the moon, as were my friends and extended family. Of course, I had just been promoted to practice lead months before at Edelman (my previous employer) and so I felt a little worried about how a pregnancy would fit into my new role. Was I letting them down?

"I went to a clinic, chose a donor and amazingly, the process worked on my second try! I was nervous about sharing the news at work, but my boss at the time (Lisa Kimmel) was fantastic about it. She said, 'This is the rest of your life, don't be ridiculous.'

"I took an eleven-month maternity leave; I wanted to be able to fully immerse myself in motherhood. It was messy to unplug completely like that—particularly in a client-based industry, but for me, it was worth it. Coming back, I had to change my work style. I learned to draw the line with clients and colleagues instead of always being available like I had been in the past. Whenever I speak to my younger colleagues, I tell them that even though you're single you still need to prioritize having a life outside of work.

"But since becoming a mother, I've also found that I connect with my clients on another level now as well.

"I couldn't do this without the support of my parents, who luckily live minutes away from us. Their involvement helps with the guilt that is definitely there and gives me a break now and then for some much-needed me time."

———

Name: Sharon* White
Role: Social Worker
Children: A son, 3

"I found myself in my late thirties, single, having a successful career but recognizing that I really did want a child. I had dated men but for various reasons these relationships didn't lead to anything further. I'd traveled to India and China, looked into adopting a child and was told that since I was a single woman, adoption would not be an option for me. I remember feeling sadness when friends would tell me they were pregnant for the third time and I couldn't muster anything in me to fake being happy for them . . .

"I did eventually meet someone online and we began a 'relationship' . . . It was very intense very soon and in hindsight perhaps that was a red flag. We were dating for about six months and had seen each other about five or six times for two-week periods as he lived in another city.

"I went to my ob-gyn to ask about fertility issues. I had some health concerns and I wanted to discuss the process of getting pregnant, only to find out that day that I already was pregnant! My 'partner' at the time was excited but our contact and communication decreased thereafter. In the end the relationship with this man did not work out and I knew deep down I was left with the issue of being a single parent in my forties.

"Although, I knew I wanted to be a mother, I began to feel a huge sense of guilt for my son, as I was sad for him to not have his father in his life. I remember thinking my parents would likely 'disown' me, but my family has been amazingly supportive. I don't think my extended family has been as open, but that hasn't impacted me. My father and brother adore my son and he loves them. My sister and mom are also completely in love. He is the only grandchild at this time and I really think that makes a difference.

"I remember the day I told my parents that I was pregnant. I told them separately. My mom I took out to lunch and she was excited and just felt things were going to work out with his dad. My dad was in shock and did the 'I raised you differently' speech.

"My son had a very difficult introduction to the world . . . I was told he might have heart complications and didn't actually tell anyone I was pregnant until after I was told he was OK at five months. I was in a high-risk pregnancy clinic for a variety of health issues, and when he was born it was an emergency C-section delivery because he was in distress and they were unsure he would live.

"My introduction to motherhood was not what I anticipated. I was dealing with feelings of the relationship with his dad ending and with my extended family having lots of questions, and being there for this little being. He had a very difficult time with breast-feeding and I remember thinking, 'This is the hardest thing in the world.' My postpartum period was brutal. Whatever I had envisioned motherhood to be, it didn't work out quite that way. I had to adjust to him and his temperament.

"Returning to work was worse than my experience of breast-feeding, which I had to stop at six months due to low milk supply, and I struggled with the sense that I was a failure. I think I was likely depressed for the first few weeks returning to work after a year of maternity leave. I remember dropping my son off to day care and crying in my office. My son had a difficult time with his transition and revolted by not eating all day while at day care. Two months after going back to work, I had to have heart surgery and was away from my son while in hospital, which was incredibly difficult. I think I believed my career was 'over' and it would remain flat. I've had to put my private practice on hold, as I don't have child-care coverage outside of my day care and frankly do not want to be away from him for so long.

"I remember doing my first trauma assessment with a client after returning to work as a mother and just crying during the session. I never had done that before and thought this was a sign again I needed to change my job. But what I've actually found after being back a year is yes, I do get emotionally upset easier and at times I'm disturbed to my core. The best way I can describe my journey to becoming a mother and a better therapist, I think, is 'being broken open.' I feel as though whoever I thought I was, or wanted to be, I just had to put it aside and make room for a new paradigm.

"But motherhood has brought an aspect to my being that was never there. The well is deeper, more powerful and forgiving. I have had to be open to the process of motherhood instead of me defining what it was going to be for me. I had to radically accept that motherhood was happening to me. Clients who I worked with prior to being a mother commented on a change in me and a more 'calm' person. My colleagues have said a similar thing. I am much more transparent in who I am and what my limitations are. Of course I have my difficult days but what gets me through it all is the fact that I am truly blessed to be a mom and I do have a belief that he chose me to be his mother for a reason and I will do it to the best of my ability.

"My parents still struggle with what others will think about me being a single mother. But I can't fix it or control it for them. Perhaps it's my selfishness. I think motherhood has allowed me to be kinder, softer and more patient with myself."

– SEVEN –

Dollars and Cents

S ix months after my first son was born, I began looking into child-care options. I didn't know what my next career move was going to be, but I wanted to go back to work and knew I needed to sort out a child-care arrangement immediately (we were living in North London at the time, so I knew it was going to be both expensive and quite probably difficult to find day-care or nursery spots).

I started by calling the local chapter of a national U.K. nonprofit that provides advice to parents and connects new mothers by their neighborhood. I asked the "Mommy Volunteer" who answered my call if she had any child-care resources she could share with me, since I was looking at the choices I had for my son.

"No," she told me flat out. "A mother should be home with her child for at least the first two years."

Then she hung up.

I was stunned.

"But what if she can't afford to?" I asked the dial tone.

It was my first real introduction to how money (admittedly always an awkward topic) is so often neatly removed from the discussion surrounding working mothers.

The Money Divide
My theory is that since the issues and stories of fairly privileged women (usually with successful husbands) are still what dominate the

"having it all" working-mom discussion, financial realities are often easily glossed over.

Instead, when discussing motherhood and work, words like "choice," "options," "priorities," "work/life balance," come up frequently. But at the end of the day, one reality is unforgettable: most women, like men, are working for money to pay the bills, put food on the table and support their family.

A Pew Research Center study released in March 2013 reported a spike for the first time in the share of working mothers who said they would prefer to work full time; 37 percent said that this was their ideal, up from 21 percent in 2007. However, the shift towards full-time work has less to do with career ambitions or a desire to "lean in" and more to do with financial realities. Life is more expensive, and financial uncertainty is everywhere.

"Women aren't necessarily evolving toward some belief or comfort level with work," says study co-author Kim Parker, an associate director at the center. "They are also reacting to outside forces and in this case, it's the economy."[103] Among women who said their financial situations aren't sufficient to meet basic expenses, about half said working full time was best for them. Of the women who said they live comfortably, only 31 percent said full time was their best situation.

Money and Your Identity

Today, according to recent research by the National Partnership For Women and Families, mothers are the primary or co-breadwinner in six out of ten U.S. families and it's a trend on the upswing. Most of the women interviewed for this book referenced how the ability to support themselves and their families is an essential part of their personal and professional identity. Approximately 60 percent of the women I spoke with were the primary or dominant earner in their family unit—and yet, barring some of the exceptions featured in the book or site, few were willing to be identified by this label.

Name: Eva* Gallagher
Role: Senior Manager, Financial Investment Firm
Children: Chloe, 9

"For me, my post-baby success story really started when I realized that for Chloe to have the life I wanted to be able to give her, we needed to earn more as a family. My 'aha' moment came shortly after, when I consciously gave myself permission to go ahead and out-earn my husband. This wasn't easy for either of us but especially since somewhere along the line, I had internalized that if I earned more than my partner it would somehow negatively impact our relationship.

"Once I changed my thinking on that, I was able to actively find the opportunities that led to the high-profile work that resulted in getting two promotions in the years after Chloe was born and making almost $40,000 more than my husband."

Nevertheless, Eva preferred not to use either her name or her company name because, "I think that would be just pushing it. I will add though, that I regularly tell Chloe that it's OK to earn more than the man you marry, so hopefully these hang-ups don't carry on to her generation."

How We Value Work

Part of the challenge in discussing how money fits into our post-baby identities and careers is the confusion about how we value work. For instance, how we do (or actually don't) value the work that stay-at-home moms do regularly underpins our broader political, cultural and media discussions on work and motherhood.

Consider the controversies that surrounded Anne Romney in the 2012 U.S. presidential election. She became a lightning rod for commentators, columnists and bloggers around whether the work that stay-at-home moms do is the same as having a job (for the record I would say it absolutely is). But does it change if you are incredibly wealthy like she is? Is it still a job? And what does this discussion indicate about our cultural relationship with motherhood and money?

We know that the work stay-at-home moms do is incredibly valuable. For the moment, set aside the often quoted sentiment that "you can't put a price on raising your children" and consider that according to Salary.com (which does an annual survey of what it would cost to hire someone else to do the approximately twenty jobs that being a "mom" involves), in 2012 the median salary for a stay-at-home mom should be $112,962.[104] Blogger Penelope Trunk describes how when she had her first child, she was earning a solid six-figure salary at her job, which she then left to be with her son. For money, she wrote columns from her kitchen counter. She describes how she felt like a stay-at-home mom (since that was the important thing to her at that time), but she was still the primary breadwinner for her family.

She contrasts her experience with that of a friend who has three kids under the age of six and quit her teaching job to be a stay-at-home mom. She also worked sporadically writing book reviews, which earned as much as each of Penelope's columns. But since the family did not depend on her money, she and her husband call her a stay-at-home mom.

"The difference was not the amount of hours we worked, or the amount of time we were with our kids but the portion of the family's income that each of us earned."[105]

I noticed a similar trend with the few women I spoke with who were very wealthy—largely due to their partners. Although they were all contributing to the broader world in a way that added real value, they tended to downplay their contributions since their families weren't depending on their salary—which I found interesting since the working-mom debate has always been dominated by women whose work lives are clearly no longer about paying the bills.

Name:	Sonia* Sanderson
Role:	Founder, Financial Nonprofit with national presence
Kids:	Three daughters, 13, 8, and 6; one son, 11

"I know I'm not a role model for your book; I probably once was though," Sonia tells me when we first meet. "But I'm interested in hearing more about the project." Sonia began her career as a corporate litigator on Wall Street. She had her first child, went back after two months and kept going. Two years later she did it again with her second. And then, shortly after her son turned two, her husband sold his start-up company for an incredible $50 million.

To me, it sounds like the dream. Sonia left her law job to spend more time with the kids. They had another daughter and Sonia decided that she needed to do something more, and so she launched her nonprofit.

"I only know how to work one way, so I essentially kept the schedule that I had always worked on—which meant a lot of travel, a lot of late nights." They had another child and Sonia's organization continued to grow. "We added fifteen cities to our reach since my youngest daughter was born."

When I point out that this certainly sounds like post-baby success, Sonia dismisses it. Work is so closely tied with money that it seems it can become difficult to value our own worth when it's not about a financial bottom line. "I know that I'm in this incredibly lucky position. Although I will say that no one in my family, especially my mother or sisters, understands why I work so hard building this venture, and I do worry that my kids will resent the time away from them, especially since I didn't have to do this; I'm choosing to."

Cost of Stepping Away

For a middle-income family today the average cost of raising a child till 17 is approximately $235,000[106]—a stress-inducing number for most families, particularly when children are still associated with lost earnings for most women. Among the group of women that I interviewed, over 80 percent reported that even if they had experienced an initial earnings dip, they subsequently went on to earn more than they had prior to their pregnancies.

While this sounds promising (and is), it also doesn't reflect what their male counterparts are earning or what they *might* have earned if they either didn't have children or if our economic world still didn't penalize the majority of women for having children.

Jane Waldfogel, a Columbia economist, has analyzed the pattern of female earnings over their life span. What she found was that when women enter the workforce in their early and mid-twenties, they earn nearly as much as men. For a few years, they continue to almost keep pace with men in terms of wages. At ages 25 to 29, women earn

87 percent of a male wage. However, when women hit their prime child-raising years (ages 30 to 40) many off-ramp for a short period of time—with disastrous consequences on the financial front. Largely as a result of these career interruptions, by the time they reach the 40-to-44 age group, women earn a mere 71 percent of the male wage.[107]

This discrepancy happens even though most women step away from work for surprisingly short periods of time (on average a total of 2.2 years). MIT economist Lester Thurow sums up the situation as, "The thirties are the prime years for establishing a successful career. These are the years when hard work has the maximum payoff. Women who leave the job market during those years may find that they never catch up."

Equal Pay

Despite growing data and discussions on the increase in women out-earning their partners, working women *still* earn on average $10,000 less annually than men—which, as the National Partnership for Women and Families notes is the equivalent of ninety-two weeks of groceries or thirteen months of rent. The wage gap costs a U.S. woman and her family more than $430,000 in lost income over a lifetime (or almost the cost of raising two kids). The issue of equal pay was an underlying theme in numerous interviews—especially for women working in large corporate organizations. A few did manage to address the issue head on, but even among an interview pool as successful as this, most acknowledged that it is so systemic and difficult to accurately prove on an individual basis that even if they suspected or knew they were being discriminated against in this way, they let it go. As one woman at a large global accounting firm told me, "They can always find *some* reason for the difference, maybe that he traveled a bit more than me, that I took six months after each of our two children. But even though it burns me that my husband and I are at the same level in the same firm and he earns more, I have just learned to let it go."

Study after study has found that, contrary to the common misconception, the wage gap is not about personal choice. "Even when all relevant education, career and family attributes are taken into account, there is still a significant, unexplained gap between the wages paid to women and men in the United States," the National Partnership for Women and Families says.[108]

Consider:

> **The wage gap exists in traditionally male professions.** Even when women choose "non-traditional," higher-paid majors, a wage gap exists. Women in science, technology, engineering and math are paid 86 percent of what their male counterparts are paid.

> **One year after graduation,** women working full time are paid only 80 percent as much as their male colleagues, even when controlling for field of study and age.

> **Women's wages.** Among all workers 25 years and older with some high school education, women's median weekly wages total $388 compared to a total of $486 for men.

> **The wage gap exists across a wide spectrum of occupations.** Women in the service industry are paid only about 75 percent of the mean weekly wages paid to men in equivalent positions. In 2008, the average starting salary of a new female physician was $16,819 less than her male counterpart after controlling for observable characteristics such as specialty type and hours worked. A newly minted female MBA graduate is paid, on average, $4,600 less at her first job than a new male MBA graduate.

> **Even when women make the same career choices as men, they are paid less.** A 2003 GAO study concluded that even after accounting for "choices" such as work patterns and education, women are paid an average of 80 cents for every dollar paid to men.

> **Women without children are paid less.** Even when childless women and men are compared, full-time working women are paid only 82 percent as much as full-time working men.

> **Women with children are paid less.** Mothers are penalized for caregiving while men are not; the 2003 GAO study found that women with children are paid about 2.5 percent less than

women without children, while men with children enjoy an earnings boost of 2.1 percent, compared with men without children. In other words, working mothers pay a penalty while working fathers receive a bonus.

Child Care

The cost of child care is one of the primary pulls that takes women out of the workforce (basic day care costs now range from $600 a month per child to as much as $2,000 in urban areas). When families do the accounting of the income in versus the post-tax cost of child care, the numbers often prompt the decision to have one parent stay home for a few years and, "Even though many women now earn more than men, typically it is the woman who considers dropping out," says University of Toronto economics professor Michael Krashinsky.

Child-care choices are fundamentally very personal decisions and the right option depends on numerous factors, including career development, goals, income, family size, culture, family support, cost, availability and government programs or subsidies.

Certainly the raw costs are daunting. Rick Robertson, an associate professor of finance and accounting at the University of Western Ontario, offers this example: A family paying $600 a month for day care needs to cover an annual bill of $7,200, before taxes. The arrival of a second child doubles that to more than $14,000, while a third would boost it to almost $22,000, all on a pre-tax basis. Costs vary greatly depending on where you live, but parents in big cities are likely grappling with monthly bills that are significantly higher.[109]

Nevertheless, during my interviews (with the exception of a few women who managed primarily with family support), I consistently heard about the role that child care, whether a nanny or day care, had in their professional success, since the challenge is that the child-bearing and caring years directly coincide with the traditional career growth years of the twenties or thirties.

Overcoming the initial reaction to the numbers requires a real shift to long-term thinking—that the costs will be worth it in the long run.

Name: Dr. Janice Stein
Role: Director, Munk School of Global Affairs,
University of Toronto
Children: Isaac, 31; Gabriel, 27

"For the first four years after my boys were born, the monthly costs of their child care was pretty much the equivalent of my monthly salary. I was happy to use my salary this way. Their care was excellent and I had the peace of mind necessary to continue to do research and write. We need to see and respect our children's caregivers as partners."

Her ability to continue to do research made a significant difference. Today, Dr. Janice Stein is the director of the Munk School of Global Affairs at the University of Toronto. She is a specialist in Middle East studies and the psychology of decision making. Her list of accomplishments and honors is extensive: She is a fellow of the Royal Society of Canada, and an Honorary Foreign Member of the American Academy of Arts and Sciences. She has been awarded numerous academic awards and honorary degrees by universities and global institutions as well as the Order of Canada. She is the author of *Afghanistan: The Unexpected War* and *The Cult of Efficiency* as well as over more than eighty other books, chapters and articles on intelligence, international security, negotiation processes, peace-making and public policy. She's also a regular media commentator on national and international media outlets and is a frequent speaker.

"The body of work that I am still most recognized for and that is most often cited is the research and writing that I did in the period after my two boys were born. Not only was it a really creative time for me but I was also able to focus in a way that I never had before. I made the most of the time I had at work because I so much wanted to spend time with my boys at home, and I made the most of the time I had with them because I wanted time to do research. I could not have done any of this without the unstinting support and encouragement that I received from my husband. That support continues today, more than forty-eight years after we were married."

Janice had a strong role model in her mother. "She was one of the first women to go to law school in Quebec, but it was in the 1930s, when women were not admitted to the bar [to write the licensing exams that allow you to actually practice]. She went to law school out of interest and for the challenge—she came in second in her class and my father was third. It was eight years after she graduated before women were allowed to be called to the bar and by then she had moved on to a phenomenal career in public service.

"I received tenure before I had my first son, but that wasn't by plan or design—it was just that I had problems getting pregnant, and so my first son wasn't born until I was 38. There was no conflict about work—I was overjoyed to be a mother." She had three months' maternity leave, and at the time, she was teaching in both Toronto and Montreal. "It wasn't the best time for women in the academic or professional environment. There were actually very few women on faculty (only four in a department of one hundred) and there were serious issues of equal pay and a lot of comments about women professors, mat leave and their contributions. I pretended I didn't hear it. That generation has largely gone and we now have wonderful male colleagues who ask me regularly to reschedule meetings so that they can be at their children's birthday parties. I'm delighted to do that."

EIGHT

Where To from Here?

When I began researching and writing *The MomShift*, I kept returning to the questions:

1. What is success in the context of this discussion?
2. Why are we still here talking about this issue?
3. Where will this discussion go from here?

From a practical perspective, I initially felt that I had to clearly define some parameters around success in order to sort through what stories should qualify to be part of the project. Success is ultimately an individual framework and so titles, salary or platform didn't seem to be appropriate. Instead, I thought I would focus on women who were more successful in the five to seven years after starting their families, since those seemed to me like the most difficult and challenging years.

But I soon realized that this was a flawed approach on many fronts. For a start, I realized that older children present a greater challenge than little ones—making my cut-off point arbitrary and irrelevant. I also came to appreciate that post-baby career success is ultimately such a personal and constantly changing journey that no one standard should be applied to it. As tech entrepreneur and best-selling author Lauren Bacon put it, "Too often our definitions of success are lazy, they just refer to what we associate with the picture on the cover of the business magazine—and as a result, we focus primarily on the external aspects of what we think success should look (money, title, number of employees or people you're seen with in photo ops) rather than the stuff we actually might want or crave most."

An Ongoing Journey

Over the past five years, I would regularly receive e-mails from women whom I'd already interviewed but who were now contacting me to tell me that I had to remove their story since they had left their job, switched roles, been downsized, taken a step back or sideways or were launching something different and they no longer felt "successful," and that I perhaps should reconsider including them in the project. They were scared, anxious and often frustrated that the post-baby success that they thought they had achieved now felt like it was disappearing.

Very often, they didn't know what was next for them and were hoping I had some ideas. I tried to be helpful, but most of all I wanted to share the overarching lesson from all the five-hundred-plus stories I've heard: that navigating family and career success in a way that fulfills you on both fronts really is an ongoing and constantly changing journey.

Staying in the game and continuing the search often against difficult work and family odds itself constitutes success.

When I was looking for interviews I also noticed that virtually all of the women I approached, even those that regularly receive external recognition, felt uncomfortable in the first instance with identifying themselves as "successful."

While part of this had to do with modesty, it was also the result of their expectations, their ambitions and often the peer group that they were judging themselves against. Among new moms, there was often the question of whether they would be able to live up to their potential. Many had always believed that they would first reach a certain level of professional establishment before they became parents, and worried if circumstances had proved different and they were now trying to reconcile their own often artificial sense of how things *should be* with how they were—even if it was a positive story.

Name: Fatima Damji
Role: Financial Officer and Project Manager, University
          of British Columbia
Children: Omar, 6; Kaseem, 3

"Before I had kids, I thought life ended when kids came, so I always thought that I had to be in my 'final' position job, where I was 'successful' before I had kids. Now I realize that it's all doable, just in a different way," says Fatima. By any measure, Fatima is more successful in her career than she was before children. However, like many working mothers, she occasionally struggles with the idea that maybe she should be doing more, faster.

Today she's an upper middle manager at the University of British Columbia (UBC) and she's one step (out of five) away from her "top wage" category. In the past year and a half that she's been at UBC, she's had a 50 percent performance-based salary increase.

Before her son was born, she was working as an independent project consultant to nonprofits and thinking about going back to school. "I was trying to find a full-time role, since my client work was sporadic and often clients just wouldn't pay me. And to be honest, before the kids, I don't think I had the confidence to go after them."

To supplement her income, she would pick up shifts at the pharmacy that she had worked at when she was a student. "After my son was born, I wanted to have greater financial stability, to feel 'safe.'" She took a temp office role on campus when her son was one, and by the end of her first day there, they realized she had far more skills than they had expected. "At the end of my first day, I'd gone from organizing data for the grant proposal that they were working on to being given responsibility for writing half of it."

Despite the definite career successes she's had since having her children, she's not yet where she wants to be. Of course, no one considers that even without kids, they might still not have achieved particular career goals by a set time. "In a weird way I didn't grow up till I had kids. I think it helped me to become ambitious, and more organized and more confident. I really feel like I can do anything. I wouldn't be afraid to have kids, because I don't think it's going to ruin everything (which I thought before)."

Fatima captured these issues in our discussion when I asked her via e-mail whether she feels successful now. Her reply: "I guess it depends on what you consider success to be. Is this the job I'm going to do for the rest of all time? No. Is it the job I wanted more than anything? No. Is it better than any of the jobs I've had before? Yes. Is it a good job? Yes. Does it offer me flexibility? Yes. Can I use it to move to other positions? Yes. Does it interest me? Yes.

"Ultimately, I consider success to be doing well in the situation I'm in. As in—am I the most successful I have ever been? Yes. Am I the most successful I will ever be? No. Could I be more successful at this moment in time? Yes.

"Am I willing to do what it takes to get there? Yes—but only in my own time. I know I could be much more successful if I finished my upgrading faster and I worked longer hours and weekends, etc., but I have no desire to do that with two young kids. I'd rather take my time and have these precious years with my kids too. I'm not wasting my time though—I regularly do courses and other things that are pushing me ahead at a steady pace.

"Ironically, before I had kids I always thought I needed to have all my schooling done, but I've actually done more post-university training after the boys than before. The truth is that before kids, I was lazy career-wise and was content to coast. I was ambitious but I always thought I would start seriously pursuing my goals in the future, when my life calmed down. I guess I felt like I just had a lot of time. Post kids, I realized that life is never going to be any calmer and that I just need to start doing it now.

"In addition to courses on sustainability and a certificate in project management, I also invested in career counseling and exploration while I was on maternity leave—to help figure out what things I was really good at, what I enjoyed and where I should strategically focus my energies and efforts. Post kids, even though I am more busy, I am more efficient—and in many ways, my life hasn't changed much. I just changed the way I do things. In some ways I felt like it prepared me for the rest of my life. I say, bring it on!"

(Update: Fatima is now entering the last year of an executive Certified Management Accountant (CMA) program.)

Fatima's responses reminded me of a quote that Rebecca Woolf, mother of four and founder of the Girls Gone Child multimedia platform, sent me, "Motivation, thy name is parenthood." Fatima is also like most of the women I spoke with who said that they haven't yet reached the place where they feel "successful," but many felt happy that they were on a path that works for them and is headed towards that place. As Janice Stein told me, "I continue to hugely enjoy my career, but I don't think you ever know if you are successful, in part because the idea of success is often so abstract; you know when you fail but I'm not sure that you know when it works—it's an internal standard that you're competing against."

So Where To from Here?

As I was working on this book, *New York* magazine ran a cover story that generated lots of hype both on- and offline. The story was on "The Retro Wife," and it discussed how "Young, educated, married mothers find themselves not uninterested in the metaconversation about 'having it all' but untouched by it."[110]

Ten years ago, Lisa Belkin ran almost exactly the same story when she wrote "The Opt-Out Revolution" for *The New York Times Magazine*. What's worse, essentially the same percentage of working mothers leave the workforce today as did then and for virtually the same reason (31 percent with the decision to leave most often being precipitated by the birth of their second child).

So is this discussion now just going in circles?

In a response piece, Lisa Belkin argued that while the rate of exit and even the reasons for leaving might be the same, the context is different. Today women decide to leave or stay in the workforce with far more information than they had in 2003.[111] And this is where I hope this book and these stories fit in, sharing the variety of positive options that women *do* have and the variety of ways we can create our own version of success. The stories shared in this book are just a sample of the full and growing collection of MomShift profiles.

While each one is unique, there are overarching patterns of success and larger lessons that we can apply to our own thinking and decisions. One very important thought to take away is that career choices and patterns are far more fluid and wide-ranging than they used to be, more than many of us realize, and that there is no single perfect job or path to career success.

A successful and fulfilling career after children is not the result of one lucky break, but rather the outcome of a consistent series of opportunities, actions and performances over time, done in a way that works for each woman's ambitions, goals, families and circumstances. Equally important is that life happiness and contentment are the result of having the confidence to make the choices that feel right for us as individuals—ideally without being overwhelmed by the choices and decisions that other mothers are making.

While they might have phrased it differently, all the women I spoke with referenced either directly or through their comments that they were not trying to "have it all" but finding day-to-day solutions to manage the ever changing challenges and success points.

It's also what the next generation of women are looking for: a nuanced middle-ground approach to what has until now been discussed and defined by extreme stories at either end of the spectrum.

Anusha Deshpande is a first-year student at Harvard Business School, and she's part of the generation that is already acutely aware of this debate. "Family and career are still presented as such a dichotomy, and we never hear that there's obviously a middle ground." Still, she said, "For me, when I think about having it all, I think it means a lack of life-defining sacrifices in the realm of either family or career. Not having a superstar career doesn't mean you've somehow failed."

Not one woman of the over five hundred I spoke with felt that they had solved the work/life balance issue or really identified with the idea that they "had it all."

Nor did they expect to.

Most were no longer even interested in continuing to view their lives in this way and instead are just working towards trying to continue to create a satisfying balance of having both a full, loving family life and a rewarding (and often demanding) professional life.

This, to me, seems like progress.

Join Us

I plan to continue to build the roster and database of stories, and regularly update the stories of the women featured in order to follow them on their journeys and as they navigate new challenges and opportunities.

I would also like to invite you to please share your experiences, feedback and stories for the website. What advice would you like to share with other women based on your own story and observations? What do you wish you had known about motherhood and careers? And what have you learned since then? What are you concerned about now for yourself, for your daughters or for your sons? What do you see as your next chapter on this journey?

You can find out more about the online project as well as access more practical lessons, tips and ideas based on the interviews or join the ongoing discussion at www.themomshift.com.

You can also contact me directly on Twitter: @RevaSeth.

I genuinely hope to hear from you.

Best,
Reva

DISCUSSION GUIDE

Introduction: Welcome to the MomShift
› Why do you think we are still here having this discussion?
› Did you think motherhood would impact your career? How?
› What factors, influences or role models have most led to your beliefs and assumptions about the working world?
› Have you noticed a distinct difference in how generations view this issue?

Chapter One: Is There a Right Time or a Best Time to Have a Baby?
› Would you say there is a "right" time to have a baby? Do you think having a child at a different age or stage would have helped or hurt your career or family life? What shapes these views?
› Do you think we need more discussion on the realities of biology and the difficulties that are often associated with IVF?
› What would you or do you advise your daughters on this issue? What about your sons?

Chapter Two: Maternity Leave: The Big Jump
› From an employer perspective, what would help make maternity leave more successful?
› How can we help small businesses better manage the practical challenges of maternity leave?
› What do you think of the focus on the career and family decisions of high-powered female CEOs and celebrities?
› Do you think we need to hear more about working dads and the challenges and decisions they face as well?
› Do you think that "paternity leaves" and other government mandated programs to involve fathers are the way to move this issue forward?
› How have you seen romantic relationships be an asset, a detriment or completely irrelevant to career success? Does this view change

for men and their partners? Why or why not? Do you think women should be encouraged to consider this issue when they are thinking about marriage and relationships?

Chapter Three: Reinvention

› How did becoming a mother impact your identity both at work and at home? Did you feel prepared for the shift?
› Based on your experiences, what would be your advice to other new mothers on this issue?
› How did motherhood impact your confidence? What would help improve women's post-baby career confidence? Who should help facilitate these measures?

Chapter Four: Staying on the Ladder

› Working mothers are not a new issue—but what do you think is holding corporate culture from changing faster to reflect the needs of their female employees? Or do you think we are almost getting there?
› Why have new industries like technology or venture capital already developed such a male-centric culture?
› Do you think that younger women should or shouldn't be encouraged to consider how future children and motherhood will impact them? What about raising this issue with our boys?
› Do you think ambition and motherhood are presented as being incompatible? If yes, what do you think leads to this impression?
› When men enter female-dominated professions, they tend to quickly rise up through the ranks (also known as the glass escalator syndrome)—this isn't the case with women in male-dominated industries. Why do you think that is?
› Discuss the idea of separating how you earn a living versus what you do with your life. Is this a good model for working mothers to aspire to?
› How has the concept of a career changed? And how is it continuing to change? What do you think of when you think of how a "career" should look or operate?
› Do we need more career advice based on alternative career models? What have your experiences with alternative career models been?

Chapter Five: How We Work

› Why do you think remote working and flexible schedules are still so difficult to implement?
› What cultural shifts are needed to change the ongoing requirement for corporate face-time?
› Discuss the cultural perceptions around freelance and part-time workers—could a focus on changing these stereotypes be one way to support working mothers?
› Should more women be encouraged to pursue entrepreneurial ventures? Why or why not?
› Most businesses owned by moms are small businesses—should they be pushed to grow or is it a flaw in our perspective that we always think bigger is better?

Chapter Six: Change on the Home Front

› How can we solve the fifty-fifty home front issue? Do you think the issue will be very different for our sons and daughters?
› How do ethnic cultures or religion shape the way motherhood and careers are viewed? Should this be addressed more in the career advice that we give or the programs and policies implemented?
› How can we address the myth and anxieties of the perfect motherhood? Why is our generation struggling with this?
› How do the different ways we create our families shape our careers?

Chapter Seven: Dollars and Cents

› How do money and finance play into your views on work and family? Consider and discuss how the broader framework of working mothers incorporates financial realities.
› Discuss inequality and pay—from your experience, what are the factors that result in this continuing? How and can women address this inequity when they find it applies to them?
› Do you think the rise of the female breadwinner can and will substantially change the nature of working families, work/life balance and corporate (work) life?

Chapter Eight: Where To from Here?

› Consider who you are tracking either consciously or unconsciously when it comes to how you feel about your career. How would changing that also shift the framework of how you see your own successes?

› How does thinking of post-baby career success as an ongoing journey change your views, pressures and the expectations that you have for yourself?

› How have your children positively shaped your career? Or how do you hope that they will?

SUGGESTED READING

From academic literature to witty blogs, research for this book was both hugely enjoyable and slightly overwhelming. These are just a few of the books, blogs and articles that particularly provoked, shaped or inspired me.

Books

For a deeper look at the changing nature of careers:
> *The Shift: The Future of Work Is Already Here,* by Lynda Gratton
> *Rework,* by Jason Fried and David Heinemeier Hansson
> *Blind Spots: The 10 Business Myths You Can't Afford to Believe on Your New Path to Success,* by Alexandra Levit
> *The 4-Hour Workweek,* by Timothy Ferriss
> *The Anti 9 to 5 Guide,* by Michelle Goodman
> *One Person/Multiple Careers,* by Marci Alboher
> *What Should I Do with My Life,* by Po Bronson
> *CEO of Me: Creating a Life That Works in the Flexible Job Age,* by Ellen Ernst Kossek and Brenda A. Lautsch

For more practical tips:
> *Nice Girls Don't Get the Corner Office: 101 Unconscious Mistakes Women Make That Sabotage Their Careers,* by Lois P. Frankel
> *Being an Entrepreneur: Escape from Cubicle Nation,* by Pamela Slim
> *The Boss of You: Everything a Woman Needs to Start, Run and Maintain Her Own Business,* by Emira Mears and Lauren Bacon
> *Spark and Hustle: Launch and Grow Your Small Business Now,* by Tory Johnson
> *Your Million Dollar Dream,* by Tamara Monosoff
> *On Women and Their Careers: Lean In,* by Sheryl Sandberg
> *Mrs. Moneypenn's Career Advice for Ambitious Women,* by Mrs. Moneypenny (an FT columnist) and Heather McGregor
> *Womenomics,* by Claire Shipman and Katty Kay

> *The XX Factor: How Working Women Are Creating a New Society,* by
> Alison Wolf
> *The Athena Doctrine: How Women (and the Men Who Think Like Them)
> Will Rule the Future,* by John Gerzema and Michael D'Antonio
> *Off-Ramps and On-Ramps: Keeping Talented Women on the Road to
> Success,* by Sylvia Ann Hewlett

On the home front:
> *Getting to 50/50,* by Sharon Meers and Joanna Strober
> *The Second Shift,* by Arlie Russell Hochschild with Anne Machung

For a look at how parenting norms impact careers:
> *The Conflict: How Modern Motherhood Undermines the Status of Women,*
> by Elisabeth Badinter
> *Perfect Madness in the Age of Anxiety,* by Judith Warner
> *Bringing Up Bébé,* by Pamela Druckerman

Some Favorites Online

> *ForbesWomen*
> *WSJ The Juggle*
> *Femme-o-nomics*
> *The New York Times Motherlode*
> *Working Mother*
> Lisa Belkin (*The Huffington Post*)
> *Jezebel*

ACKNOWLEDGEMENTS

I began the MomShift in early 2009 and over the years, I have become gratefully indebted to so many without whom this project and book never would have happened.

First a thank you to all the women whose stories I share in the book: you answered my many questions, my follow-up questions and introduced me to other women. I learned so much from each of you and was inspired by every conversation we had.

I also want to thank all the women whose names are not listed but whose views, ideas and experiences shaped the focus of this project.

Michelle Wolfson and Lindsey Pollock, thank you for all your work and early feedback on the initial proposal. A huge thank you to my agent, Robert Mackwood, for making my plans for the MomShift a reality.

I am grateful to Deloitte, Edelman, Fraser Milner Casgrain, KPMG, MarketStart, Ryerson University, Scotiabank and Unilever for their support of the project and for the introductions that they made possible. I would especially like to thank early champions of the project, including Jane Allen, Lisa Kimmel, Tuula Jalasjaa, Kate Broer, Michael Bach, Alison Leung and Ken Jones.

To my very patient and gifted editor Pamela Murray: thank you so much for understanding what I was trying to do and for all your suggestions, ideas and time. It has been an absolute pleasure working with you. I also want to thank the rest of the Random House Canada team: Marion Garner, Deirdre Molina and Ashley Dunn, and freelance editors Doris Cowan and Stacey Cameron for all their time and dedication on this project.

On the home front, I'm proof that it really does take a village. I'm very lucky to have parents who regularly come down to help us out; Rakhi Henderson, my wonderful sister-in-law (who is one in a shrinking group of people who can handle all three boys solo); my friendly neighbors who regularly entertain our kids; and especially Mary Jane Fuertes, who is an incredible nanny to our boys.

Finally, to Rana: When we met I got so much more than just a husband; I got a true partner. I'm grateful for all your ideas (including inventing the name The MomShift!), for making me laugh each day, for understanding the angst of WIAF and for never being cranky due to child-related sleep deprivation. I couldn't imagine doing this whole real grown-up life/work/family thing with anyone but you.

NOTES

[1] See U.S. State Department, *Independent States in the World*, Fact Sheet (January 2012), http://www.state.gov/s/ins/rls/4250.htm#note3.

[2] Judith Warner, *Perfect Madness: Motherhood in the Age of Anxiety*, (New York: Riverhead Trade, 2006) 261.

[3] Joel Kotkin and Harry Siegel, "Why the Choice to Be Childless Is Bad for America," *Newsweek*, February 19, 2013, http://mag.newsweek.com/2013/02/18/why-the-choice-to-be-childless-is-bad-for-america.html.

[4] Judith Warner, *Perfect Madness: Motherhood in the Age of Anxiety*, (New York: Riverhead Trade, 2006) 261.

[5] Gretchen Livingston and D'Vera Cohn, "The New Demography of American Motherhood," (May 6, 2010), http://pewresearch.org/pubs/1586/changing-demographic-characteristics-american-mothers.

[6] Anne Milan, "Fertility: An Overview 2008," *Statistics Canada*, http://www.statcan.gc.ca/pub/91-209-x/2011001/article/11513-eng.htm.

[7] Joanna Barsch and Lareina Yee, Special Report, *Unlocking the Full Potential of Women In the US Economy*, McKinsey & Company (April 2011): 6.

[8] Judith Timson, "Baby before Salary? That Might Not Be a Bad Idea," *The Globe and Mail*, June 22, 2012, http://www.theglobeandmail.com/life/parenting/baby-before-salary-that-might-not-be-a-bad-idea/article4361939/.

[9] Michelle Stacey, "Are You Playing Baby Roulette?" *Glamour*, http://www.glamour.com/health-fitness/2011/09/are-you-playing-baby-roulette.

[10] Ibid.

[11] Aimee Groth, "Sheryl Sandberg: The Most Important Career Choice You'll Make Is Who You Marry," *Business Insider*, December 1, 2011, http://articles.businessinsider.com/2011-12-01/strategy/30462131_1_powerful-women-sheryl-sandberg-facebook-coo#ixzz259SFgFpG.

[12] Sheryl Sandberg, *Lean In*, (New York: Knopf, 2013) 115.

[13] Penelope Trunk, "Get Pregnant at 25 if You Want a High-Powered Career," June 25, 2012, http://blog.penelopetrunk.com/2012/06/25/get-pregnant-at-25-if-you-want-a-high-powered-career/.

14 Anne-Marie Slaughter, "Why Women Still Can't Have It All," *The Atlantic*, June 13, 2012, http://www.theatlantic.com/magazine/archive/2012/07/why-women-still-cant-have-it-all/309020/.

15 Cathy Gulli, "Suddenly Teen Pregnancy Is Cool?" *Maclean's*, January 17, 2008, http://www.macleans.ca/culture/lifestyle/article.jsp?content=20080117_99497_99497.

16 Jenna Goudreau, "Big Families Are Back in Style," *Forbes*, July 29, 2010, http://www.forbes.com/2010/07/28/work-life-balance-college-tuition-kate-gosselin-forbes-woman-leadership-cost-of-raising-kids.html.

17 Belinda Luscombe, "Should Women Get Paid Maternity Leave if They Weren't Pregnant?" *TIME*, September 8, 2011, http://healthland.time.com/2011/09/08/should-new-moms-get-paid-maternity-leave-if-they-werent-pregnant/.

18 Jasmine Budak, "The Dark Side of Maternity Leave," *Canadian Business*, September 8, 2011, http://www.canadianbusiness.com/business-strategy/the-dark-side-of-maternity-leave/.

19 Karen E. Klein, "When Moms Who Run Businesses Take Maternity Leave," *Bloomberg Businessweek*, September 20, 2012, http://www.businessweek.com/articles/2012-09-20/when-moms-who-run-businesses-take-maternity-leave.

20 Canadian Press, "Most Mothers Take Maternity Leave," *Metro News*, July 30, 2012, http://metronews.ca/news/canada/316408/most-mothers-take-maternity-leave-statscan/.

21 Katie Hellmuth Martin, "Keep Calm and Ignore Them: Maternity Leave #2," March 10, 2012, http://www.tinshingle.com/blog/keep-calm-and-ignore-them-maternity-leave-2.

22 Rachel Mendleson, "Canada Maternity Leave: Women Quitting Jobs after Childbirth a Wake-up Call for Businesses," *The Huffington Post*, June 19, 2012, http://www.huffingtonpost.ca/2012/06/19/canada-maternity-leave-women-quitting-jobs_n_1600955.html.

23 Robyn Doolittle, "Female equality in the workforce remains elusive, even in Toronto," *Toronto Star*, Friday, July 27, 2012, http://www.thestar.com/news/city_hall/2012/07/27/female_equality_in_the_workforce_remains_elusive_even_in_toronto.html.

24 Sheryl Sandberg, *Lean In*, (New York: Knopf, 2013) 151.

25 "No Mother's Day Celebration for Women Returning from Maternity Leave," Press Release, Slater & Gordon, March 10, 2013.

26 Taffy Brodesser-Akner, "The Breastfeeding Conspiracy," Babble.com, January 18, 2010, http://www.babble.com/baby/breastfeeding-problems-low-breast-milk-supply-lactation-consultant/.

27 Sylvia Ann Hewlett, *Off-Ramps and On-Ramps: Keeping Talented Women on the Road to Success*, (Boston: Harvard Business Press, 2007) 30.

28 Khadeeja Safdar, "More than Half of American Woman Are Breadwinners, Study Finds," *The Huffington Post,* June 12, 2012, http://www.huffington-post.com/2012/07/12/more-than-half-american-women-breadwinners_n_1668140.html.

29 Katherine May, "More Younger Canadians, Including Men, Facing Child and Elder Care Responsibilities," *Ottawa Citizen,* March 27, 2013, http://www.childcarecanada.org/documents/child-care-news/13/03/more-younger-canadians-including-men-facing-child-and-elder-care-res.

30 "No Mother's Day Celebration for Women Returning from Maternity Leave," Press Release, Slater & Gordon, March 10, 2013.

31 Louise Peacock, "Just One in Ten Fathers to Take Full Paternity Leave," *The Telegraph,* July 18, 2011, http://www.telegraph.co.uk/finance/jobs/8643557/Just-one-in-ten-fathers-to-take-full-paternity-leave.html.

32 Jenay Cassidy, "Is There Paternity Leave in Baseball?" The Work & Family Researchers Network, July 18, 2011, https://workfamily.sas.upenn.edu/content/there-paternity-leave-baseball.

33 "Having a New Mum Identity Crisis?" BabyExpert, http://www.babyexpert.com/baby/new-mum/having-a-new-mum-identity-crisis/1919.html.

34 Sylvia Ann Hewlett, *Off-Ramps and On-Ramps: Keeping Talented Women on the Road to Success*, (Boston: Harvard Business Press, 2007) 36.

35 Sue Shellenbarger, "Getting from At-Home to On-the-Job, Even Now," *The Wall Street Journal,* July 29, 2009, http://online.wsj.com/article/SB10001424052970204563304574316540263060898.html.

36 Monica Appelbe, "For Better or for Worse: Husband and Wife Businesses," Intuit Blog, February 14, 2011, http://blog.intuit.com/money/for-better-or-for-worse-husband-and-wife-businesses/.

37 Lindsey Donner, "5 Questions to Ask before Starting a Business with Your Spouse," The Young Entrepreneurs Council, August 2, 2011, http://theyec.org/5-questions-to-ask-before-starting-a-business-with-your-spouse/.

38 Richard Florida, *The Rise of the Creative Class*, (New York: Harper Business, 2005).

39 Elisa Garcia, "College Students with Children Need Campuses with Childcare," *Institute for Women's Policy Research,* May 3, 2011, http://www.

iwpr.org/blog/2011/05/03/college-students-with-children-need-campuses-with-child-care/.

40 Libby Copeland, "Boomer Moms Find Themselves in a New Phase of Life—and Work," *Chicago Business*, May 7, 2012, http://www.chicagobusiness.com/article/20120505/ISSUE03/305059985/boomer-moms-find-themselves-in-a-new-phase-of-life-and-work.

41 Joe Friesen, "Why Canada Needs a Flood of Immigrants," *The Globe and Mail*, Thursday, January 10, 2013, http://m.theglobeandmail.com/news/national/time-to-lead/why-canada-needs-a-flood-of-immigrants/article4105032/?service=mobile.

42 Jan C. Ting, "Downsides of High Immigration—Room for Debate," *The New York Times*, October 16, 2011, http://www.nytimes.com/roomfordebate/2011/10/16/fewer-babies-for-better-or-worse/downsides-of-high-immigration.

43 Sheryl Sandberg, *Lean In*, (New York: Knopf, 2013) 115.

44 Roy Adler, "Women in the Executive Suite Correlates to High Profits," European Project on Equal Pay, www.equalpay.nu/docs/en/adler_web.pdf.

45 "The Bottom Line: Connecting Corporate Performance and Gender Diversity," Catalyst, January 2004, http://www.catalyst.org/knowledge/bottom-line-connecting-corporate-performance-and-gender-diversity.

46 "Engaging and Retaining Talent," The Human Capital Institute, http://www.humancaptialinsitute.org/hci/tracks_engaging_retianing_talent_.guid.

47 "Plateauing: Redefining Success at Work," Knowledge @ Emory, November 8, 2006, http://knowledge.emory.edu/article.cfm?articleid=1009.

48 Bureau of Labor Statistics, *Number of Jobs Held, Labor Market Activity, and Earnings Growth among the Youngest Baby Boomers: Results from a Longitudinal Study*, July 2012, http: //www.bls.gov/news.release/pdf/nsloy.pdf.

49 Jeanne Meister, "Job Hopping Is the 'New Normal' for Millennials: Three Ways to Prevent a Human Resource Nightmare," *Forbes*, August 14, 2012, http://www.forbes.com/sites/jeannemeister/2012/08/14/job-hopping-is-the-new-normal-for-millennials-three-ways-to-prevent-a-human-resource-nightmare/.

50 Herminia Ibarra, Nancy M. Carter, and Christine Silva, "Why Men Still Get More Promotions than Women," *Harvard Business Review* 88, no. 9 (2010): 80-85.

51 Curt Rice, "Why Women Leave Academia and Why Universities Should Be Worried," *The Guardian*, May 24, 2012, http://www.theguardian.com/higher-education-network/blog/2012/may/24/why-women-leave-academia.

[52] Ibid.

[53] Mary Sheppard, "Women Are Changing the Face of Medicine: But Are Underrepresented in High-Level Positions," CBC News, March 7, 2011, http://www.cbc.ca/news/health/story/2011/03/07/f-women-medicine-iwf.html.

[54] Nancy Groves, "From Past to Present: The Changing Demographics of Women in Medicine," *Ophthalmology Times*, February 2008, http://www.aao.org/yo/newsletter/200806/article04.cfm.

[55] R. Jagsi, K. A. Griffith, A. Stewart, D. Sambuco, R. DeCastro, P. A. Ubel, "Gender Differences in the Salaries of Physician Researchers," *JAMA*, 2012; 307(22): 2410-2417, doi:10.1001/jama.2012.6183.

[56] Timothy L. O'Brian, "Why Do So Few Women Reach the Top of Big Law Firms?" *The New York Times*, March 19, 2006, http://www.nytimes.com/2006/03/19/business/yourmoney/19law.html?pagewanted=all&_r=1&.

[57] Leah Eichler, "Maternity Buddies: Staying Linked to the Workplace," *The Globe and Mail*, November 18, 2011, http://www.theglobeandmail.com/report-on-business/careers/career-advice/maternity-buddies-staying-linked-to-the-workplace/article4200796/.

[58] Perry Hewitt, "It's Time to Find the Women in Tech," *Forbes*, November 9, 2012, http://www.forbes.com/sites/techonomy/2012/11/09/its-time-to-find-the-women-in-tech/.

[59] Sheryl Sandberg, *Lean In*, (New York: Knopf, 2013) 16.

[60] Ibid.

[61] Penelope Trunk, "Beware of the Girl Ghetto," *Penelope Trunk*, March 31, 2011, http://blog.penelopetrunk.com/2011/03/31/bnet-column-beware-of-the-girl-ghetto/.

[62] Jenna Goudreau, "A New Obstacle for Professional Women: The Glass Elevator," *Forbes*, May 21, 2012, http://www.forbes.com/sites/jennagoudreau/2012/05/21/a-new-obstacle-for-professional-women-the-glass-escalator/.

[63] "Edelman's GWEN Program: Helping Women Lead and Succeed," April 23, 2012, http://edelman.ca/2012/04/23/edelmans-gwen-program-helping-women-lead-and-succeed/.

[64] Sylvia Ann Hewlett, *Off-Ramps and On-Ramps: Keeping Talented Women on the Road to Success*, (Boston: Harvard Business Press, 2007) 54.

[65] Ibid.

66 Sheryl Smolkin, "Telecommuting, Other Flexible Work Options Alive and Well," *Toronto Star,* March 17, 2013, http://www.thestar.com/business/personal_finance/2013/03/17/telecommuting_other_flexible_work_options_alive_and_well.html.

67 Jon Stewart, "Moms at Tech Start-Ups Say They Can Have It All," *USA Today,* August 16, 2012, http://usatoday30.usatoday.com/tech/news/story/2012-07-25/tech-moms-work-family-balance/57076260/1.

68 Deborah L. Jacobs, "Why a Career Jungle Gym Is Better than a Career Ladder," *Forbes,* March 14, 2013, http://www.forbes.com/sites/deborahljacobs/2013/03/14/why-a-career-jungle-gym-is-better-than-a-career-ladder/.

69 Mark D. Wolf, "Women-Owned Businesses: America's New Job Creation Engine," *Forbes,* December 1, 2010, http://www.forbes.com/2010/01/12/small-business-job-market-forbes-woman-entrepreneurs-economic-growth.html.

70 "Report Shows Women-Owned Businesses Growing at Above Average Rate," BuildMyBiz, April 15, 2013.

71 Andrea Gordon, "Mompreneurs: Powerful Business Network or Pink-Collar Ghetto?" *Toronto Star,* Thursday, October 20, 2011, http://www.thestar.com/life/parent/2011/10/20/mompreneurs_powerful_business_network_or_pinkcollar_ghetto.html.

72 Ruth Graham, "Laura Vanderkam: Serious Career Women Don't Work Part-Time, Even With Kids," *The Grindstone,* Wednesday, March 14, 2013.

73 "Women, Work, and Motherhood," Pew Research Center, April 13, 2013, http://www.pewresearch.org/2012/04/13/women-work-and-motherhood/.

74 Claire Ward, "How Dutch Women Got to Be the Happiest in the World," *Maclean's,* Friday, August 19, 2011, http://www2.macleans.ca/2011/08/19/the-feminismhappiness-axis/.

75 Michelle Goodman, *The Anti 9-to-5 Guide: Practical Career Advice for Women Who Think Outside the Cube,* (Emeryville: Seal Press, 2007).

76 Gary M. Stern, "Welcome to the Age of the Freelancer," *CNN Money,* November 27, 2012, http://management.fortune.cnn.com/2012/11/27/freelance-jobs/.

77 Dale Archibald, "Our Ever-Expanding Work Week," Brave New Work World, 2007, http://www.newwork.com/Pages/Opinion/Archibald/Work%20Week.html.

78 "Smartphone Use Can Mean a Never-Ending Workday," CBC News, July 30, 2012, http://www.cbc.ca/news/business/smartphone-use-can-mean-a-never-ending-workday-1.1264581.

79 "Remaking the Workplace, One Night Off at a Time," Knowledge@Wharton, July 3, 2012, http://knowledge.wharton.upenn.edu/article/remaking-the-workplace-one-night-off-at-a-time/.

80 Melissa Beattie Moss, "Probing Question: Has Technology Made Life Easier for Working Moms?" Penn State News, May 18, 2011, http://news.psu.edu/story/141829/2011/05/18/research/probing-question-has-technology-made-life-easier-working-moms.

81 Ibid.

82 Orit Avishai, "Young Women Are Ambitious, but Worried," CNN Opinion, Saturday, March 23, 2013, http://www.cnn.com/2013/03/23/opinion/avishai-young-women/.

83 Charyn Pfeuffer, "Best Jobs for Working Mothers," Monster.com, http://career-advice.monster.com/job-search/company-industry-research/best-jobs-working-mothers/article.aspx.

84 Sabrina Tavernise, "Day Care Centers Adapt to Round-the-Clock Demand," The New York Times, January 15, 2012, http://www.nytimes.com/2012/01/16/us/day-care-centers-adapt-to-round-the-clock-demands.html?pagewanted=all&_r=1&.

85 Adriana Barton, "Hush, Little Baby: Daycares Begin to Offer Night Care," The Globe and Mail, January 16, 2012, http://www.theglobeandmail.com/life/the-hot-button/hush-little-baby-daycares-begin-to-offer-night-care/article621200/.

86 Alex Williams, "Just Wait until Your Mother Gets Home," The New York Times, August 10, 2012, http://www.nytimes.com/2012/08/12/fashion/dads-are-taking-over-as-full-time-parents.html?adxnnl=1&pagewanted=all&adxnnlx=1381931813-pyMYmKo+U8dIBFW+3uSILg.

87 Frank Pompa, "Men vs. Women: How Much Time Spent on Kids, Job, Chores?" USA Today, March 14, 2013, http://www.usatoday.com/story/news/nation/2013/03/14/men-women-work-time/1983271/.

88 Judith Warner, Perfect Madness: Motherhood in the Age of Anxiety, (New York: Penguin, 2006) 72.

89 Leah Eichler, "School Daze: Carving Out a Career on the Kids' Schedule," The Globe and Mail, June 29, 2012, http://www.theglobeandmail.com/report-on-business/careers/school-daze-carving-out-a-career-on-the-kids-schedule/article4381141/.

90 September 2011 Economist Human Potential Conference, Sylvia Ann Hewlett from the Center for Work-Life Policy.

91 Lisa Miller, "The Retro Wife," *New York,* March 17, 2012, http://nymag. com/news/features/retro-wife-2013-3/.

92 Sylvia Ann Hewlett, *Off-Ramps and On-Ramps: Keeping Talented Women on the Road to Success,* (Boston: Harvard Business Press, 2007) 39.

93 Cathy Gulli, "Life with Help: How Did We Get So Useless?" *Maclean's,* May 15, 2012, http://www2.macleans.ca/2012/05/15/life-with-help-how-did-we-get-so-useless/.

94 Sheryl Sandberg, *Lean In,* (New York: Knopf, 2013) 110.

95 Daniel Miller, "Girls Should Be Ambitious in Their Relationships and Find a Cheerleader Husband," *Daily Mail,* June 14, 2012, http://www.dailymail. co.uk/news/article-2159091/Girls-told-ambitious-relationships-cheerleader-husband.html.

96 Lois M. Collins, "Number of Dads Staying Home with Kids Doubled," *The Desert News,* June 18, 2012, http://www.desertnews.com/article/ 865557644/Number-of-dads-staying-home-with-the-kids-doubled. html?pg=all.

97 Alex Williams, "Just Wait until Your Mother Gets Home," *The New York Times,* August 10, 2012, http://www.nytimes.com/2012/08/12/fashion/ dads-are-taking-over-as-full-time-parents.html?adxnnl=1&pagewanted=all &adxnnlx=1381931813-pyMYmKo+U8dIBFW+3uSILg.

98 Penelope Trunk, "How to Decide if Your Commute Is Too Long," *Brazen Careerist,* December 20, 2007, http://blog.penelopetrunk. com/2007/12/20/how-to-decide-if-your-commute-is-too-long/.

99 "Long-Distance Moms," *Forbes,* Thursday, February 18, 2012, http://www. forbes.com/2010/02/17/working-mother-commute-career-forbes-woman-leadership-family.html.

100 Massachusets Mutual Life Insurance Company, *The MassMutual FamilyPreneurship Study: What Every Entrepreneur Wants to Know About Being in Business with a Family Member,* 2012.

101 Peggy Drexler, "Tricky Currents Greet the Women of Business," *The Huffington Post,* August 2, 2007, http://www.huffingtonpost.com/peggy-drexler/tricky-currents-greet-the_b_62194.html.

102 Virginia Galt, "The Changing Face of the Canadian Family," *University Affairs,* December 5, 2012, http://www.universityaffairs.ca/the-changing-face-of-the-canadian-family.aspx.

[103] Jennifer C. Kerr, "More Working Moms Want Full-time Jobs," *The Associated Press*, March 14, 2013, http://globalnews.ca/news/409167/poll-more-working-moms-say-full-time-work-ideal-for-them-economy-at-play/.

[104] Benjamin Bridgman, Andew Dugan, Mikhael Lal, Matthew Osborne and Shaunda Villiones, *Accounting for Household Production in the National Accounts, 1965–2010*, May 2012, http://www.academia.edu/2755856/Accounting_for_Household_Production_in_the_National_Accounts_1965-2010.

[105] Penelope Trunk, "Maybe No Moms Are Working Moms," *Penelope Trunk*, December 13, 2010, http://blog.penelopetrunk.com/2010/12/13/maybe-no-moms-are-working-moms/.

[106] Sam Hananel, "Cost of Raising a Child Climbs to $235,000 for Middle-Income Families," *The Huffington Post*, June 14, 2012, http://www.huffingtonpost.com/2012/06/14/cost-of-raising-a-child-c_n_1597729.html.

[107] Sylvia Ann Hewlett, *Off-Ramps and On-Ramps: Keeping Talented Women on the Road to Success*, (Boston: Harvard Business Press, 2007) 46.

[108] "Fact Sheet: The Wage Gap Is Harming Women and Families," The National Partnership For Women & Families, May 2012.

[109] Roma Luciu, "Should You Stay at Home or Pay for Child Care?" *The Globe and Mail*, Tuesday, August 7, 2012, http://www.theglobeandmail.com/globe-investor/personal-finance/household-finances/should-you-stay-at-home-or-pay-for-child-care/article4465673/.

[110] Lisa Miller, "The Retro Wife," *New York*, March 17, 2012, http://nymag.com/news/features/retro-wife-2013-3/index1.html.

[111] Lisa Belkin, "The Retro Wife Opts Out: What Has Changed, and What Still Needs To," *The Huffington Post*, March 19, 2013, http://www.huffingtonpost.com/lisa-belkin/retro-wife-opt-out_b_2902315.html.

INDEX

Investment Fund Company, 210
Iran, 116
Irving Oil, 106
isolation, 52, 154, 185, 188, 212
IT jobs. *See* tech sector
IVF (in vitro fertilization), 18–20, 232
iVillage (websites), 105–6

Jagsi, Reshma, 134
Jalasjaa, Tuula, 122–24
job engagement, 36, 66, 90, 149, 150,
    223
job hopping, 120–21
job satisfaction 11, 26, 36, 43, 51, 58,
    69, 80, 81, 84, 94, 96, 107, 109, 131,
    133, 135, 140, 144, 148, 149, 154,
    193, 206, 215, 218, 220, 231
jobs
    childless candidates, 6
    extreme, 195
    fathers with children, 6
    for new immigrants, 113–16
    looking for on mat leave, 52–54, 55
    loss of, 46, 57, 59, 63, 121, 163
    online postings, 149
    over- or under-qualified for, 63–64
    quitting, 63
    security, 199
    sharing, 168
    (*See also* "female jobs"; female talent
        retention; full-time work;
        part-time work)
JOHNSON'S Baby (products), 106
joint academic degrees, 110
Journal of Human Reproduction, 18
*Journal of the American Medical
    Association*, 134
joy, 11, 102
"jungle gym" metaphor, 121, 174–82
junior positions, accepting, 97

Kaplan (co), 103, 106
Karakoram Mountain (Pakistan),
    108
Katz, Lawrence, 7
Kauffman Foundation, 178
Kaufman, Dunniela, 199
Kaye, Kelleen, 18, 19
Keohane, Nannerl, 23
Khanna, Ayesha, 98–100
Khanna, Parag, 98–100
kidney cancer, 90
Kids & Company, 31
Kimmel, Lisa, 160–61, 237–38
Klinger, Sonia, 98–99
knowledge workers, 71, 99, 120, 195
    (*See also* tech sector)
Kogod School of Business (American
    University), 158
KPMG, 9–10, 54, 183
Krashinsky, Michael, 248
Krill, Kara, 38–39
Kuwait, 163

Lang, Amanda, 12
Las Vegas Chamber of Commerce,
    232, 233
lateral moves, 66, 192 (*See also* "jungle
    gym" metaphor)
laughter, 203
law associates, 137
law careers, gender gap, 136–41
law firm partners, 137
law school deans, 137
Law Society of Upper Canada, 137
law, jobs in, 84, 136–40
Lawrence, Carolyn, 47–48
Lawrence, Jacqueline, 180–82
lead generation, 60
leadership gap, 151, 159 (*See also*
    gender disparities; stereotypes)
leadership training, 119, 124, 149–50

organizational skills, 146–47, 149
Other Side of Silence, The (Hewitt, Farida Azhar), 108
Outsourced Self, The (Hochschild), 214
outsourcing help, 31, 214–16
  cost of, 244
over-parenting, 208
ownership mentality, 139
ownership, sense of, 86, 101, 231, 232
oxygen-mask parenting, 144

Pakistan, 108
panic attacks, 92–93
Papua New Guinea, maternity leave, 39, 41
parental engagement, 88
parental leave
  adoption, 35
  and commitment to career, 72–73
  cost of, 73
  legal entitlement, 72
  same-sex couples, 38
  split, 71–72
  sustainable model, 73
  (*See also* maternity leave; paternity leave)
parenting blogs, 28
parents
  internalizing roles, 143–44
  supportive, 141, 237, 238, 239, 245
  unsupportive, 240
  working with, 230–32
  (*See also* elder care; family business)
Parker, Kim, 242
partner, making, 127–28, 138, 168, 198
part-time work, 7, 43, 60, 107, 168, 185–89, 214
passion, 49, 84, 179, 182, 190
passivity, 146
paternal role model, 22, 159–60, 228, 224, 230

paternity benefits, 72
paternity leave, 38, 39, 41
  cultural block, 72–73
  paid, 72
  self-employed, 44
  shared, 72
  statistics, 71n, 72
  sustainable model, 73
  unpaid, 72
patience, 101, 150, 164, 200, 219, 227, 240
patriarchy, 118–19
Peace Dividend Trust, 87
Pecaut, David, 111–12
pediatrics, 132
Penn State University, 201
pensions, 121, 167
People & Computers magazine, 58
Pepperdine University, 129
Perfect Madness: Motherhood in the Age of Anxiety (Warner), 5, 207–8
perfectionism, 117, 207–8
performance reviews, 127
Perlow, Leslie, 196
personal care products, ingredients, 93
personal networking, 82, 103
personal shoppers, 215
personal time, 101, 149, 150, 157, 161, 202, 203, 204
pharmacists, 187, 198
physical distance, and working together, 101
physician-researchers, meritocracy, 134
Pichardo, Carolina, 28
Pink, Daniel, 191
pitching, 147
Piurko, Tara L., 137
planning ahead, 26, 36, 44, 48–52, 68–69, 82, 136, 146–47, 149, 150, 157, 237 (*See also* reinvention)

REVA SETH is an author and entrepreneur who regularly speaks on issues related to working mothers. She began her career as a corporate lawyer and then moved into strategic and corporate communications. Seth has written for *The Atlantic, The Globe and Mail, Canadian Business, The Huffington Post* and has been featured on numerous radio and television shows including *20/20, Canada AM,* and *Steven and Chris*. She lives in Toronto with her husband and three boys.